Resist Everything Except Temptation

Resist Everything Except Temptation

The Anarchist Philosophy of Oscar Wilde

Kristian Williams
Foreword by Alan Moore

Resist Everything Except Temptation: The Anarchist Philosophy of Oscar Wilde

© 2020 Kristian Williams
Foreword © 2020 Alan Moore
This edition © 2020 AK Press (Chico, Edinburgh)

ISBN: 978-1-84935-320-5
E-ISBN: 978-1-84935-321-2
Library of Congress Control Number: 2019947413

AK Press	AK Press
370 Ryan Ave. #100	33 Tower St.
Chico, CA 95973	Edinburgh EH6 7BN
United States	Scotland
www.akpress.org	www.akuk.com
akpress@akpress.org	ak@akedin.demon.co.uk

The above addresses would be delighted to provide you with the latest AK Press
distribution catalog, which features books, pamphlets, zines, and stylish apparel published
and/or distributed by AK Press. Alternatively, visit our websites for the complete catalog,
latest news, and secure ordering.

Part of the section "Declarations and Evasions" is adapted from Kristian Williams, "The
Soul of Man Under . . . Anarchism?" *New Politics*, Winter 2011.

A longer version of "Refuse to be Broken by Force: Prison Writing and Anti-Prison
Writing" was published by the Institute for Anarchist Studies as "'A Criminal with a
Noble Face': Oscar Wilde's Encounters with the Victorian Gaol" (2009).

Cover illustration by Agustín Comotto (www.agustincomotto.com).
Cover design by John Yates (www.stealworks.com).

Printed in the USA on acid-free paper.

For Emily-Jane,
with gratitude and love

❧

—for those whom the gods have given a friend,
they have given *two* worlds—

CONTENTS

Green Carnation; Black Flag

Here is cognitive dissonance, with the faintest redolence of absinthe: Oscar Wilde and anarchy. How are we to reconcile the privileged aesthete—who reputedly turned everything into an epigram and for whom seriousness was apparently anathema—with the mutable, demanding, and entirely straight-faced doctrines of Bakunin, Proudhon, Godwin, or Kropotkin? Where can we forge a connection between the ideal of each human being as their own sole leader, and the decadent icon whose experience was far removed from that of the working-class youngsters that he favoured, although patently not far enough? Surely, other than in some unlikely parlour-game, there is no reason why the champion of artificiality should share even a sentence with the planet's oldest and perhaps most castigated form of politics.

Except that this is far too limited a reading, of both Wilde and anarchy. It denies Wilde the radicalism and furious opposition to authority that is there in everything he ever wrote, and it denies anarchy the largely unacknowledged fierce romanticism that is arguably at its heart. It ignores the passionate manifesto of Wilde's "The Soul of Man under Socialism" and the shocking acid-attacks on Victorian mores that were his comedies, and it refuses to consider modern anarchy's emergence, via William Godwin, from an eighteenth-century clique of revolutionary artists, proto-feminists, and writers that included the sublime Romantic visionary William Blake. Such a restrictive view, of serious politics versus frivolous art, leaves anarchy as a purely utilitarian creed with no commitment to the beautiful, while it leaves poetry as no more than a lyrical phantasm without anger, animating fire, or purpose.

That Wilde was born into an aristocracy, through no fault of his own, is greatly mitigated by the fact that he continually strived to bite the hand that fed him. His entitlements were many, his insider status guaranteed, yet he constructed himself as unapologetically, extravagantly other. As Irishman, as social critic, as gay man, and ultimately as convicted criminal and exile,

Wilde positioned himself at the edges of his world and times. Deliberately self-marginalised, he sought the outlands of experience, and in this at least is much like Blake, born middle class on Golden Square but following his art and conscience into poverty, and anarchy, and Lambeth. It may be that the Romantic of conviction must be always situated out beyond the regulated limits of civilisation's discourse; must seek that abundant wilderness of ideas which encroaches past the thinkable, that she might better see the thing that is her subject, lest the romance be no more than a confection without any purchase on the real. If this unkempt Arcadia outside society is the committed poet's natural environment, then anarchy is surely only the implicit ethos of that fertile, teeming, revelatory territory.

It should also be said that Wilde's predilection for the lower orders was significantly more than a mere sexual peccadillo, than a humdrum fetishizing of the other, than the fondness for a bit of rough. One cannot without difficulty bring to mind any compelling reason why, after its vicious cruelties and betrayals, Oscar Wilde should feel the least affinity for the entitled class that was his heritage. Conversely, one cannot escape the earnest camaraderie and sympathy he found amongst the other abject souls in Reading Gaol, nor that in his disgrace—when even former kindred spirits such as Aubrey Beardsley feared the taint of their association—it was Leonard Smithers, the reviled lowlife pornographer, who rushed to Wilde's assistance with the publication of the author's work in Smithers's admirable *The Savoy*, a welcome haven after ripples from Wilde's trial had grown to the vituperative waves that sank *The Yellow Book*. It might be that when cast into the depths, into the penitentiary gutters of existence, Wilde discovered them to be already full with stars.

In our present era, in this maelstrom left by the collapse of even a pretended order, with the concept of society unburdened by self-serving, psychopathic leaders looking ever more attractive, the ideas that anarchy provides would seem more useful and more necessary than they've ever been, but in these austere times we should not let those vital principles take on the colourations of austerity: let anarchy be rich in its imaginings and unashamed of loveliness. If it addresses that which is most ugly in our current cyber-feudalism, in our social structures and their absence of humanity, then let it have an ethical aesthetic that reflects its blazing aura and alluring ideologies. Now that the bowling-ball black bombs with sputtering fuses haven't worked, can we admit that it has always been the music, writing, art, and wit of anarchy that were its most efficient tools, its sharpest weapons? And if that should be the case, can anarchy afford to spurn the missile-battery of rhetoric and splendour that is Oscar Wilde? Much better, one would think, that he be in its tent and eloquently pissing out. Much better, for both anarchy and art, that their two pyrotechnic spirits should put by their differences.

In *Resist Everything Except Temptation*, Kristian Williams argues for that reconciliation with a voice informed by years of patient scholarship yet steeped in absolute compassion. Impeccably reasoned and without a surmise that is unsupported, Williams's powerful hypothesis searches beneath the perfume and the powder of Wilde's massively distracting public image—the elaborate persona he himself constructed, under its obscuring overlay of subsequent opinion—to reveal a convinced dissident and radical humanitarian; an anarchist dispensing bullet words from his impressive bandolier vocabulary, whose carefully prepared explosive charges were the verse, the sentence.

This illuminating work rewards Wilde's critics and enthusiasts alike, presenting as it does a burning thirst for justice at the core of his extravagant performance and providing serious motive for those never-serious observations, that feigned moral languor. Simultaneously, it invites the modern anarchist to enter into an embrace—possibly awkward at the outset—with a sensual and electrifying soul of poetry that could do more to shift this planet on its listing axis than a thousand upraised fists.

Whether a fop or firebrand, you should make this masterful book your priority.

Alan Moore,
Northampton,
June 16, 2019

The Soul of Man under ... Anarchism?

To the Depths

Wilde the Philosopher

Oscar Wilde is remembered today chiefly as a wit and a dandy, as a gay martyr, and as a brilliant writer, but his philosophical depth and political radicalism are often forgotten. His plays are still performed, his fiction and poetry still read, his aphorisms often quoted. Yet most people, I think, would be surprised and perhaps a little perplexed to hear him described as a political philosopher.

What we remember of his plays is the humorous dialogue; what we forget is the element of social satire that gives the comedy its bite. Of Wilde's character we recall his hedonism; we forget his generous spirit and his abiding sense of kindness. In short, we hold to the surface and neglect the depth (a fitting memorial, it may be said, to a man who always privileged the image over the reality—or who seemed to). Wilde preferred a delightful inversion to a careful syllogism, a clever phrase to a sober sermon, and temptations to commandments. His mode of thought was often paradoxical; his mode of expression, ironical; and like Kierkegaard he preferred to indicate his views by an indirect method. None of this should be taken to imply, however, that there is no substance behind the shimmer, no truth within the paradox. It only requires that we should read as Wilde wrote—flamboyantly, courageously, with the same ironic detachment, and with the deepest human sympathy. Beneath the ostentatious declarations, the clever lines, and the deliberate absurdities—or perhaps *not* beneath them, but *through* them—Wilde was working out a social theory and a system of values at once ethical, political, and aesthetic.

Oscar Wilde stood as a living challenge to Victorian society. He symbolically embodied an inversion of English respectability. He made a philosophy of his individuality, crowned beauty as higher than morals, named style and appearance as among the deepest values, claimed life as one of the fine arts, and declared pleasure "nature's test, her sign of approval."[1] He would, as his friend Stuart Merrill put it, "profess himself an anarchist"—"between two glasses of champagne."[2]

Resist Everything Except Temptation locates Wilde in the tradition of left-wing anarchism and argues that only when we take his politics seriously can we begin to understand the man, his work, and his life.[3] The argument is partly biographical, partly critical, partly historical, and partly philosophical. I have, therefore, drawn from a wide array of sources, including Wilde's writing, that of his peers and predecessors, the work of critics and biographers, the writings of socialists and anarchists, and various related histories. (In doing so, I have maintained British spellings in quotations, with all the extra *m*'s and *u*'s, where they occur, but to minimize visual distraction I have silently altered punctuation in keeping with American usage.) I try, of course, to connect Wilde's political ideas to his life and his work; I also try to situate those ideas historically, to show how they relate to the affairs of his time and how they extended the critical and imaginative scope of anarchism. But most of all I try to take seriously the questions that Wilde posed to himself and the answers he suggested. These include questions about the relationship between culture and politics, between utopian aspirations and practical programs, and between individualism, group identity, and class struggle. All of these uncertainties are still very much with us, though sometimes in different form.

A Biographical Sketch

One of the challenges of writing about Wilde is the need to sort through the legends, myths, and apocrypha that have accumulated around him, some of them propagated by Wilde himself. When the actress Lille Langtry claimed that Oscar Wilde brought her a single flower every day, he reflected with satisfaction, "To have done it was nothing, but to make people think one had done it was a triumph."[4] As he said to Yeats, "I think a man should invent his own myth."[5]

"Truth," Wilde declared on another occasion, "is independent of facts always, inventing or selecting them at pleasure."[6] Nevertheless, the main facts of Wilde's life are fairly well known.[7]

Oscar Fingal O'Flahertie Wills Wilde was born in 1854 in Dublin, Ireland, to a prominent if unconventional Anglo-Irish family. He was educated at Trinity College and at Oxford University, where he excelled in classics and became affiliated with the Aesthetic movement. After graduating, he wrote a play and a slender volume of poetry, neither of which were well received, then spent a year touring North America and lecturing on the role of art in society.[8] Returning to the UK, he settled in London, where he edited a magazine, the *Woman's World*, and married Constance Lloyd. They had two sons.

It is not clear when Wilde discovered that he enjoyed having sex with men, but in 1886 he met a young man named Robbie Ross, who was to become one of his dearest friends. Their relationship began with an act of seduction (initiated by Ross, then just seventeen) and continued until the end of Wilde's life, after which Ross served devotedly as his literary executor. The decade after their meeting saw Wilde reach the height of both his productivity and his popularity, creating nearly all of the work for which he is now remembered: *The Happy Prince*, "The Critic as Artist," *The Picture of Dorian Gray*, *Salomé*, and, most famously, his four society plays.

In 1891 Wilde met Lord Alfred Douglas, with whom he had a passionate if tumultuous affair. Their romance drew Wilde into a feud with Douglas's father, the Marquess of Queensberry, whose abusive personality had already permanently alienated his own family. Queensberry's grudge and Wilde's arrogance combined bitterly, the result being Wilde's imprisonment for "gross indecency," the legal term for homosexual acts other than sodomy. He served two years, then lived the remainder of his life in exile, virtually penniless. He wrote little after his release and died in 1900.

Freedom: Anarchism

To show Wilde among the anarchists, or to find the anarchism in Wilde, it is necessary to have an idea as to what anarchism *is*. The question is a vexing one, which no one can answer definitely. Anarchists are a quarrelsome lot, adverse to formal doctrine yet somehow still prone to sectarian schism.

Among their number we can find many different, sometimes incompatible theories and programs, and just outside their circle there are always a larger number of near-anarchists, whose actual views and practices may resemble those of the anarchists proper, though perhaps their justifications and pedigrees are somewhat different.[9] The precise boundaries are difficult to locate and frequently shifting.[10]

For our purposes, what is important is to understand how anarchism was understood in Wilde's day. In the 1880s and 1890s anarchism, as a distinct tendency emerging from the socialist movement, was quite new, especially in England where it was also largely a movement of immigrants.[11] A fairly authoritative summary of its program can be found in the first issue of the long-running journal *Freedom*. There, in 1886, the editors outlined their agenda:

> We are Socialists, disbelievers in Property, advocates of the equal claims of each man or woman to work for the community as seems good to him, or her—calling no man master—and of the equal claim of each to satisfy, as seems good to him, his natural needs from the stock of social wealth. . . .
>
> We are Anarchists, disbelievers in the government of man by man in any shape and under any pretext. . . . We dream of the positive freedom which is essentially one with social feeling; of free scope for the social impulses, now distorted and compressed by Property, and its guardian the Law; of free scope for that individual sense of responsibility, of respect for self and others, which is vitiated by every form of collective interference, from the enforcing of contracts to the hanging of criminals; of free scope for the spontaneity and individuality of each human being, such as is impossible when one hard-and fast line is fitted to all conduct. . . .
>
> We deprecate as wrong to human nature, individually, and therefore collectively, all use of force for the purpose of coercing others; but we assert the social duty of each to defend by force if need be, his dignity as a free human being, and the like dignity in others, from every form of insult and oppression.[12]

Declarations and Evasions

Oscar Wilde's Socialism

In his most famous political tract, "The Soul of Man under Socialism," Oscar Wilde advocates for an anti-authoritarian socialism, which would serve the cause of individualism and bring about a cultural rebirth.

The society Wilde imagines is one in which the arts, the sciences, and the whole of intellectual life prospers; a society without property, prisons, or crime—in which no one is hungry and machines do all the dirty, distasteful, tedious work. It is a society in which everyone is free to choose his own path and flourish in her own way, to prosper not in petty financial terms but in terms of character and personality. "The true perfection of man lies not in what man has, but in what man is," Wilde wrote. This socialism, which will produce "true, beautiful, healthy Individualism," will free us, not only from the dangers of poverty but from the demands of wealth as well: "Nobody will waste his life in accumulating things, and the symbols for things. One will live."[13] In this essay Oscar Wilde makes many striking pronouncements, among them: "the form of government that is most suitable to the artist is no government at all"; "there is no necessity to separate the monarch from the mob; all authority is equally bad"; and "all modes of government are failures."[14]

Wilde's is a socialism in the service of individualism. It is a socialism based more in aesthetic ideals than in economic theories. It takes as its model the artist rather than the proletarian and is as much concerned to free the repressed bourgeois as the oppressed worker. Its tastes are aristocratic; its ethics, bohemian. It is at once deeply spiritual and thoroughly heretical, ethical and antinomian, rebellious and harmonious, egoistic and universally compassionate, urgent and utopian. It is, in a word, anarchism. Yet the word does not appear anywhere in Wilde's essay. Instead Wilde expressed indifference, almost disdain, for ideological labels. ("Socialism, communism, or whatever one chooses to call it," he begins one paragraph.)[15] Does Wilde deliberately avoid the word *anarchism* because of its sectarian connotations? Or is he issuing a subtle snub, siding with William Morris against David

Nicoll in the dispute that had recently divided the Socialist League?[16] Or is it perhaps something greater—that no label is needed or that none will suffice?

The Kiss of Anarchy

So far as I have discovered, Oscar Wilde referred to himself as an anarchist on two occasions.

The first occurred in 1893, two years after publication of "The Soul of Man." Wilde wrote to a French periodical, responding to a list of questions: "Autrefois, j'etais poete et tyran. Maintenant je suis artiste et anarchiste." ("In the past I was a poet and a tyrant. Now I am an artist and an anarchist.")[17]

This statement indicates the direction of Wilde's political development and connects it decisively with his development as an artist. It stands as a direct repudiation of remarks he made earlier in his career. In the poem "Libertatis Sacra Fames," published in 1880, Wilde had written:

> Better the rule of One, whom all obey,
> Than to let clamourous demagogues betray
> Our freedom with the kiss of anarchy.[18]

He is somewhat more ambivalent in his "Sonnet to Liberty," which appeared (along with "Libertatis") in his 1881 collection, *Poems*. There he begins by distancing himself from the oppressed masses, "whose dull eyes / See nothing save their own unlovely woe." And he claims not to care about political conflict or the issues at stake:

> all kings
> By bloody knout or treacherous cannonades
> Rob nations of their rights inviolate
> And I remain unmoved.

"And yet," he begins the final lines of the poem:

and yet,
These Christs that die upon the barricades,
God knows it I am with them, in some things.

With *which* things is he with them? The poem ends without specifying, but
Wilde does hint at it earlier in the verse:

the roar of thy Democracies,
Thy reigns of Terror, thy great Anarchies,
Mirror my wildest passions like the sea
And give my rage a brother—! Liberty!
For this sake only do thy dissonant cries
Delight my discreet soul.[19]

It is not the "children" of liberty that move him, not their "unlovely woe,"
nor the treachery of kings, nor the "rights" of nations; it is the "roar" and
violence of the upheavals that "mirror" his "passions" and his "rage." It is the
spirit of revolt that they share. Rebellion makes them brothers and allows
the poet to see those who "die upon the barricades" as "Christs."

We can detect here, in a less developed form, something of the sentiment that was later to inspire "The Soul of Man under Socialism." Each
composition celebrates liberty, of course. But, more than that, they also share
the notion that oppression makes people insensitive and dull. Both refuse
to treat the poor as objects of pity and instead praise them when they resist.
Both engage in the aestheticizing of rebellion and promote the idea that
social conflict reflects individual feeling. And both the poem and the essay
identify their rebels with Christ.

Still, while touring America in 1882, Wilde felt that the more conservative poem best expressed his views. "Does the 'Sonnet to Liberty' voice
your political creed?" a reporter from the *San Francisco Examiner* asked. "No,"
Wilde replied, "that is not my political creed. I wrote that when I was younger.
. . . Perhaps something of the fire of youth prompted it. . . . If you would like
to know my political creed . . . read the sonnet 'Libertatis Sacra Fames.'"[20]

Yet there is hardly a line in "Libertatis" that is not contradicted somewhere in "The Soul of Man under Socialism." In 1880 Wilde declared himself "nurtured in democracy" and "liking best that state republican." In 1891,

he wrote: "Democracy means simply the bludgeoning of the people by the people for the people."[21] In the poem he is down on "clamourous demagogues" who "betray Our freedom with the kiss of anarchy"—while in the essay he is fond of "agitators," who "sow the seeds of discontent," because "[w]ithout them ... there would be no advance towards civilization."[22] In the poem he is quite clear: "I love them not whose hands profane / Plant the red flag upon the piled-up street"; whereas later he expressed a preference for the "paving-stone" over "the pen."[23] In his poem he worries that, "beneath the ignorant reign" of the rabble, "Arts, Culture, Reverence, Honour, all things fade." And in "The Soul of Man" he remarked that "popular authority and the recognition of popular authority are fatal" to the arts—yet it is in large part because of its promise for the arts and for learning that he advocates socialism: "The community ... will supply the useful things, and ... the beautiful things will be made by the individual.... [I]t is the only possible way by which we can get either the one or the other."[24]

Perhaps the only portion of the "Libertatis" that would be at home in the later essay is Wilde's hope for a world "where every man is Kinglike and no man / Is crowned above his fellows." This is the only radical sentiment to be found in the poem—and, with its paradoxical form, it is also the most Wildean. It is at once egalitarian and aristocratic, but clearly Wilde was still "a poet and a tyrant," not yet "an artist and an anarchist." He had not yet found that the secret of individualism lay in socialism—and vice versa.

Rather More Than a Socialist

Wilde's second profession of anarchism came in 1894, a year after the first. He told a journalist from the *Theatre*, "We are all of us more or less Socialists now-a-days.... Our system of government is largely socialistic.... What is the House of Commons but a socialistic assembly? ... I think I am rather more than a Socialist. . . . I am something of an Anarchist, I believe."[25] Wilde here positions anarchism as a type of socialism—but a type that, paradoxically, goes further. Anarchism *is* a socialism, but anarchism is *more than* socialism. It is not merely the most extreme variety, it is also something new. It surpasses the category to which it belongs.

Though this interview appeared under the headline "New Views of Mr.

Oscar Wilde," in it he really only restates some of his established positions. Beginning with poetry ("A glorious passion is poetry") and finishing with education ("A truly ignorant and unsophisticated man is the noblest work of God"), Wilde works his way around to politics, religion, and crime.[26] Here many of his views are familiar from "The Soul of Man under Socialism": Christ is a "marvelous personality," pirates are "very fine fellows," and the prison system is "a perfect fiasco."[27]

In one interesting exchange, Wilde also expressed "considerable sympathy" with burglars: "In nine cases out of ten they only take what we really do not want. . . . The loss of our last guinea is a loss; the loss of a thousand pounds when we have a hundred thousand in the bank is *not* a loss." He goes on to tell of the unhappiness a friend experienced when his house was robbed, only to conclude: "now, had someone fallen downstairs and broken a limb, it would have been reasonable cause for distress; but, really, silver spoons! Japanese curiosities! What good are they?"[28]

The story—a bit surprising from a man whose earliest lectures centered on the need for beautiful things in the home—shows us something of Wilde's attitude toward property.[29] As he wrote in "The Soul of Man":

> In a community like ours, where property confers immense distinction, social position, honour, respect, titles, and other pleasant things of the kind, man, being naturally ambitious, makes it his aim to accumulate this property long after he has got far more than he wants, or can use, or enjoy, or perhaps even know of. Man will kill himself by overwork in order to secure property, and really, considering the enormous advantages that property brings, one is hardly surprised. One's regret is that society should be constructed on such a basis that man has been forced into a groove in which he cannot freely develop what is wonderful, and fascinating, and delightful in him—in which, in fact, he misses the true pleasure and joy of living.[30]

In the details of the interview, then, we find Wilde repeating the points he had made in the earlier essay. The brief mention of anarchism, in this context, suggests not a new philosophy but a new name for his position. It announces, in other words, that Wilde's socialist ideas are, in fact, anarchist and that "The Soul of Man" should be read accordingly.

What the State Is to Do

If there is a case to be made against the anarchism of "The Soul of Man," it must be that Wilde assigned a role to the state. He did so: "The State is to be a voluntary manufacturer and distributor of necessary commodities. The State is to make what is useful. The individual is to make what is beautiful."[31]

A few pages later, he explains in greater detail, "It is clear, then, that no Authoritarian Socialism will do. . . . Every man must be left quite free to choose his own work. No form of compulsion must be exercised over him. If there is, his work will not be good for him, will not be good in itself, and will not be good for others. . . . Of course authority and compulsion are out of the question. All association must be quite voluntary. It is only in voluntary association that man is fine."[32]

A Dangerous Adventure

I noted previously that there were two occasions on which Wilde referred to himself as an anarchist. But there was also a third time, when he came very close. This last is, in some respects, I feel, the most revealing. It's a small story, but it says much about Wilde's attitude and approach.

In August 1894, Wilde wrote to his lover, Lord Alfred Douglas, to tell of "a dangerous adventure." He had gone out sailing with two lovely boys, Stephen and Alphonso, and they were caught in a storm. "We took five hours in an awful gale to come back! [And we] did not reach pier till eleven o'clock at night, pitch dark all the way, and a fearful sea. . . . All the fishermen were waiting for us."

Tired, cold, and "wet to the skin," the three men immediately "flew to the hotel for hot brandy and water." But there was a problem. The law stood in the way: "As it was past *ten* o'clock on a Sunday night the proprietor could not *sell* us any brandy or spirits of any kind! So he had to *give* it to us. The result was not displeasing, but what laws!"

Wilde finishes the story: "Both Alphonso and Stephen are now anarchists, I need hardly say."[33]

Resist Everything

Emphasis and Interpretation

"The Soul of Man under Socialism" has long been accepted into the anar-chist canon. In the first decades of the twentieth century, millions of cop-ies sold in Europe, and revolutionary groups distributed it in the United States.[34] Emma Goldman advertised it in the back pages of her magazine *Mother Earth*, along with works by Peter Kropotkin, Edward Carpenter, William Morris, Thomas Paine, Friedrich Nietzsche, and Leo Tolstoy.[35] George Woodcock considered Wilde's essay the "most ambitious contri-bution to literary anarchism during the 1890s," and his Porcupine Press released a pamphlet version in 1948.[36] Robert Graham includes it in his expansive collection *Anarchism: A Documentary History of Libertarian Ideas*.[37]

But "The Soul" has largely been set apart from Wilde's other work, treated as a single, inexplicable foray into the serious, unironic, political world, having no bearing on and no relationship to his poetry, plays, and fiction. It has thus occupied a somewhat marginal position in the overall body of Wilde studies. And the rest of Wilde's writing has for the most part escaped the attention of anarchist readers. It is thought to be a trivial curi-osity that the author of "The Soul of Man under Socialism" and the author of *The Picture of Dorian Gray* happen to be the same person. In fact, for all the attention given this connection, they might as well have *not* been the same man but instead two men with the same name. This division, I believe, is a mistake, whichever way one looks at it. If we take Wilde's politics seri-ously, if we put "The Soul of Man" first, so to speak, and refuse to sever it from the rest of Wilde's work, then certain important connections inevitably become apparent. The political implications of his drama, verse, fiction, and especially his essays, criticism, and lectures suddenly stand out sharply. And the aesthetic, Hellenic, spiritual, and queer elements of "The Soul of Man" simultaneously take on a new import.

In this volume, I seek to identify the values Wilde advanced in his works, the ideals often implicit in his literary writing and sometimes explicit in his essays. By putting the politics first, it is possible to find a kind of unifying outline for Wilde's thought as a whole. His politics connect to his aestheticism, to his sexuality and nationality, to his humor and irony, and to his deeply tragic view of life. Wilde's political commitments were subtly but centrally present in even his purely aesthetic works; and conversely, his aesthetics, his critical perspective, and even his keen wit and sense of irony had their role in shaping his politics. At the root of Wilde's thought was a deep belief that individual freedom is desirable both for its results and for its own sake, that such freedom requires creativity and pleasure, and that it can only be achieved when our basic needs are met, ideally through an economic socialism that unites a diverse community on terms of fraternal equality.

The following chapters are arranged, broadly speaking, chrono-thematically, grouping Wilde's ideas by subject but ordering them to trace the development of his thought. Put in very simple terms, they cover violence, aesthetics and labor, women, homosexuality, prison, and Wilde's legacy. These subjects are related, in turn, to Wilde's first play, *Vera, or the Nihilists*, and his collection of stories, *Lord Arthur Savile's Crime*; his American lectures and his fairy tales; the society plays; *The Portrait of Mr. W. H.* and the trials; his prison letters and "The Ballad of Reading Gaol"; and, finally, *Salomé* and Wilde's grave.

Wilde's work, it turns out, is dense with politics. If we fail to perceive its political aspects, we misunderstand much of the rest of it. But if we try to isolate the "political"—his views about government policy or economic arrangements—we fail, rather sadly, to comprehend his vision at all. For philosophy, politics, and art—these were not, to Wilde, separate concerns or distinct pursuits. They could not be divided without harm. The principle of their unity is what he would call beauty; the expression of this unity is what might be called art—or life.

Milieu and Entourage

This book is not a biography of Wilde, nor is it a critical exegesis of his major works, though it contains elements of both. What I offer is a way of understanding Wilde, his life, and his work that puts his politics in the forefront. Much of my argument will rely on establishing context, placing various texts in their historical moment and situating Wilde in his social habitat.

That effort leads one to relate *The Happy Prince* to sweatshop labor, to read *Earnest* in connection with the Fenian bombings, at times to treat Wilde's levity seriously. It also leads me to explore the ideas and activities of Wilde's friends, family, and collaborators. As much as he praised individual genius, Wilde was wise enough to see that "an artist is not an isolated fact, he is the resultant of a certain milieu and a certain entourage."[38] In London Wilde was on friendly terms with anarchists like John Barlas, Peter Kropotkin, and Stepniak (Sergei Mikhailovich Kravchinskii).[39] In Paris he sought out both the political and artistic avant-garde, finding himself among a troop of symbolists active in the anarchist movement—Stuart Merrill, Adolphe Retté, Henri de Regnier, Remy de Gourmont, and Francis Vielé-Griffin.[40]

One minor episode—in fact, a nonoccurrence—may say something about Wilde's sympathies for and ties to the world of radical politics. In April 1889 Wilde responded to an invitation from May Morris, daughter of William Morris and a socialist organizer in her own right, regretfully declining her invitation to help organize a series of lectures by Kropotkin on social evolution. "I am afraid I could not promise to attend any committee meetings, as I am very busy," Wilde wrote, bringing to mind the quip often attributed to him that the problem with socialism is that it occupies too many of one's evenings.[41] (He did sometimes attend meetings of the Fabian Society and the Socialist League.)[42] However, he continued, "If you think my name of any service pray make any use of it you like." He goes on to explain that though the magazine he was editing, the *Woman's World*, had already gone to press, he had taken the initiative in placing notices of Kropotkin's talks in the *Daily Telegraph* and the *Pall Mall Gazette*, "as a means of explaining to people that the subject of the lectures was *not* to be 'Anarchy with practical illustrations.'"[43]

Wilde is being either ironic or coy. Evolutionary science, and especially the theory of "mutual aid" (whereby the advantages of cooperation are highlighted), was central to Kropotkin's practical anarchism—and to Wilde's.[44] As Michael Helfand and Philip Smith document in their analysis of "The Evolutionary Turn" in Wilde's criticism:

> Like other radical Darwinists such as A. R. Wallace, [Grant] Allen, Kropotkin, [D. G.] Ritchie, and Patrick Geddes, Wilde believed that science gave a picture of human nature and its development

very different from the dominant Victorian view of a basically self-ish, competitive, and brutal creature who improved through a bloody intraspecies struggle for existence caused by an inevitable scarcity of human necessities. Radical Darwinists believed that individuals were naturally social and creative creatures who cooperated with their fellows to ensure the survival of the human species. In their opinion, the wasteful, inhumane, and brutally competitive "law of the jungle" which supposedly dominated human nature was encouraged by an artificially imposed social and economic system.[45]

Wilde was unabashed in his admiration for Kropotkin, whom he described as "a man with the soul of that beautiful white Christ that seems coming out of Russia."[46] A prince by birth and a scientist by inclination, Kropotkin became a revolutionary by conviction. After witnessing the suffering of the poor, he renounced his career, his position, his title, and much of his personal wealth to devote himself fully to the cause of anarchism, enduring prison and exile as a consequence.[47] Wilde believed this one "of the most perfect lives I have come across in my own experience"[48]

It would have been interesting to hear Wilde's reaction to the lectures. But like so much in the history of anarchism, the planned series never occurred.[49]

Wilde's Sins

My reading is not, of course, the only way of understanding Wilde, and many will argue that it is neither an obvious nor the best way to do so. There remain always other ways of reading, other meanings to discover. As Wilde saw it, "all interpretations [are] true, and no interpretation final."[50] However, I believe that by taking his politics seriously—allowing them a significance and a depth—new and underappreciated aspects of Wilde's thought come to stand out. Viewed from the proper angle, context can be seen not only to contain but also to penetrate the text, and the subversive subtext rises to the surface and may even become the dominant note.

There is certainly a great deal that could be said against Wilde's anarchism. Wilde was, at least at times, snobbish, misogynistic, anti-Semitic, and racist.[51] He was enthralled with the aristocracy, openly admired Queen Victoria, and sympathized with Jefferson Davis and the Lost Cause of the Confederacy.[52] Those who busy themselves by finding motes in their neighbor's eyes will surely find plenty in his. Though Wilde was in many respects a man ahead of his time, he was also very much a man *of* his time, and to accuse a nineteenth-century British gentleman of being elitist, sexist, racist, and anti-Semitic is practically redundant. Of course, recognizing that such faults were general does nothing to excuse them in the particular case, but it may mean that individual indictments are less meaningful than they first seem. As Wilde wrote in "The Rise of Historical Criticism," "On est de son siecle même quant on y proteste." ("A man belongs to his age even when he struggles against it.")[53]

To understand Wilde—perhaps to understand anyone—it is less important to examine the ways in which he was typical than the ways in which he was exceptional. His adherence to the norms and conventions of his society, therefore, is less remarkable than his rebellion against them and his subversion of them. It is not his misogyny but his feminism that compels our attention, not his snobbery but his egalitarianism. One might say that Wilde's anarchistic qualities are more striking *because* of the contradiction: "It is the feet of clay that make the gold of the image precious."[54]

Why Should We Care?

The best argument against reading Wilde politically must surely be his protestations of political indifference.

In a poem celebrating the value of romantic love above all other concerns, he writes from the perspective of one enthralled by a woman and aloof from the injustice and conflict of the society surrounding them.

> And She and I are as Queen and Master,
> Why should we care if a people groan
> 'Neath a despot's feet, or some red disaster
> Shatter the fool on his barren throne?
> What matter if prisons and palaces crumble,
> And the red flag floats in the piled-up street,

When over the sound of the cannon's rumble
The voice of my Lady is clear and sweet?
For the worlds are many and we are single,
And sweeter to me when my Lady sings,
Than the cry when the East and the West world mingle,
For clamour of battle, and the fall of Kings.[55]

These lines from "Love Song" seem to express a resolute quietism, a studied self-involvement, and an air of disdain and disinterest. But even as he declares romance to be greater than politics, the poet nevertheless introduces themes that will gain political significance later in his career—the impermanence of political rule and the concern for the "single" over the mass, for example. And, more subtly, the poem may actually answer its own rhetorical questions, as it returns repeatedly to the violence of politics. Even as the verse insists on the irrelevance of these events—barricade and cannonfire, recalling the Paris Commune—it nevertheless creates a sense of preoccupation; the tone is not one of indifference and careless joy but of encroaching disaster and growing anxiety. "Why should we care?" Perhaps because at every moment the "clamour of battle" threatens to intrude on the "Queen and Master" just as it does the despot and king. The falling of the palace and the opening of the prisons may be delayed, for the moment, but how long can a "fool" survive "on his barren throne" as East and West collide and the people protest against tyranny?

On the Side of Civilization

Civilization Is Socialism, Individualism Is Hellenism

Wilde's evasions often hide the seeds of subversion.

Asked by a Philadelphia newspaper, "What are your politics, Liberal or Conservative, Mr. Wilde?," he coyly replied, "Oh, do you know, these matters are of no interest to me. I know only two terms—civilization and barbarism; and I am on the side of civilization."[56] Asked later, "What is civilization?" he offered this: "That condition under which man most completely realizes the perfection of his own nature. Civilization without beauty or art is an impossibility."[57]

Despite this apolitical pose, Wilde was to pick up this theme again in "The Soul of Man under Socialism" and develop it in more radical directions. He begins the essay by posing the problem of how "a great man of science, like Darwin; a great poet, like Keats; a fine critical spirit, like M. Renan; a supreme artist, like Flaubert" may "realise the perfection of what was in him, to his own incomparable gain, and to the incomparable and lasting gain of the whole world." In answer, he states that socialism "will restore society to its proper condition . . . and insure the material well-being of each member of the community. . . . But for the full development of Life to its highest mode of perfection . . . [what] is needed is Individualism."[58] Wilde then specifies his notion of perfection: "What I mean by a perfect man is one who develops under perfect conditions; one who is not wounded, or maimed, or in danger."[59] Therefore, one "may be a great poet, or a great man of science; or a young student at a university, or one who watches sheep upon a moor; or a master of drama, like Shakespeare, or a thinker about God, like Spinoza; or a child who plays in a garden, or a fisherman who throws his net into the sea. It does not matter what he is, as long as he realises the perfection of the soul that is within him."[60] That is to say, to achieve perfection, one must develop that which makes one unique: "All imitation in morals and life is wrong. . . . There is no one type for man. There are as many perfections as there are imperfect men."[61] Individualism, in fact, "is the perfection that is inherent in any mode of life, and towards which all development tends."[62]

Wilde then ends the essay by equating individualism and civilization: "Man has sought to live intensely, fully, perfectly. When he can do so without exercising restraint on others, or suffering it ever and his activities are all pleasurable to him, he will be saner, healthier, more civilised, more himself. . . . The new Individualism, for whose service Socialism, whether it wills it or not, is working, will be perfect harmony. . . , and through it each man will attain to his perfection. The new Individualism is the new Hellenism."[63]

Ideal and Realization

There is no point in trying to claim that Wilde was always, only, or wholly an anarchist. I doubt that anyone is ever always, only, or wholly *anything*. We human beings are far too complex for that, and Wilde was more complex than most.

Wilde was, like the best of philosophers, always unorthodox and never doctrinaire. His style was such that he preferred bold gestures to careful plans, tantalizing fictions to tedious facts. There are reasons why he came to specialize in the paradox, why he wrote so profitably about double lives, and why he titled one piece of criticism "The Truth of Masks." He did not adhere to a single political line or commit to follow any one school of thought—and this, in itself, is a sign of his anarchism. "Socialism," Wilde wrote,

> is not going to allow herself to be trammeled by any hard-and-fast creed or to be stereotyped into an iron formula. She welcomes many and multiform natures. She rejects none, and has room for all. She has an attraction of a wonderful personality, and touches the heart of one and the brain of another, and draws this man by his hatred of injustice, and his neighbor by his faith in the future, and a third, it may be, by his love of art, or by his wild worship of a lost and buried past. And all of this is well.[64]

Wilde was not a systematic thinker, though he was a deep and serious one. To insist on utter consistency would be foolish and may actually risk suppressing what is original and vibrant in his thought. Inconsistencies, even imperfections, are sometimes a sign of vitality, and in Wilde's case they were as much a part of his character as his hedonism or his delight in epigrams. Still, the overall direction of his thought—and, as importantly, his desires—was toward an ideal of freedom, toward a humane society, and in sympathy with those who fight to free themselves from oppression.

Chapter 1

The Dynamite Policy

*Cosmopolitan Nationalists, Aesthetic
Terrorists, and Nihilist Saints*

Propaganda by the Deed

"I am something of an anarchist," Wilde told an interviewer in 1894 and then added, "but of course the dynamite policy is very absurd indeed."[1]

The association of anarchism with violence, which persists even now, has its origin in Wilde's time.[2] It rests, now as then, partly on actual anarchist practice, partly on slander, and to a disturbing degree, on the work of police provocateurs. It was aided by a persistent conflation of nihilists, populists, separatists, and those from other tendencies similar to anarchism, and an opportunistic impulse among certain criminals to try to politicize their crimes after the fact to win sympathy and public support.[3]

Of course, there was never really a dynamite policy, but there was a theory, called "propaganda by the deed."[4] It consisted of the notion that a heroic act of violence directed against a representative of the ruling order would demonstrate the vulnerability of the state and embolden the masses to revolt. Writing in *Commonweal* in May 1891, David Nicoll prophesied: "Individual assaults on the system will lead to riots, riots to revolts, revolts to insurrections, insurrection to revolution."[5]

In practice, it never worked out that way. But once the cycle of assassination and reprisal took hold, violence became more and more common and less and less discriminate. Albert Camus later described the period: "In the year 1878 Russian terrorism was born." It began with a single attempt, when a "very young girl, Vera Zasulich," tried to murder General Fyodor Trepov of the secret police: "This revolver-shot unleashed a whole series of repressive actions and attempted assassinations, which kept pace with one another and which, it was already evident, could only be terminated by mutual exhaustion. . . . From then on, the nineteenth century abounds in murders, both in Russia and in the West." Specifically, Camus recounts:

> attempts were made on the lives of the Emperor of Germany, the King of Italy, and the King of Spain. . . . In 1879 there is a new attack on the King of Spain and an abortive attempt on the life of the Czar. In 1881, the Czar is murdered by terrorist members of the People's Will. . . . In 1883 takes place the attempt on the life of the Emperor of Germany, whose assailant is beheaded with an ax. . . . In France the 1890's mark the culminating-point of what is called propaganda by action. The exploits of Ravachol, Vaillant, and Henry are the prelude to [President] Carnot's assassination. In the year 1892 alone there are more than a thousand dynamite outrages in Europe, and in America almost five hundred.[6]

The United Kingdom was in the same period facing its own threat from Irish nationalists who likewise resorted to assassinations and bombings, first in Ireland itself, then reaching England in 1881 when the Irish Republican Brotherhood, or "Fenians," attacked a barracks in Lancashire and government offices in London.[7]

Within a relatively short period, doubts were being voiced in radical circles, first privately and then in the press. William Morris's reservations were probably typical: "I cannot for the life of me see how such principles, which propose the abolition of compulsion, can admit of promiscuous slaughter as a means of converting people."[8] Kropotkin as usual had sympathy enough for terrorists and victims alike, confiding, "Personally . . . I hate these explosions, but I cannot stand as a judge to condemn those who are driven to despair."[9]

Perhaps most notable was the first issue of *Anarchist*, dated March 1894 and edited by David Nicoll, who had previously served eighteen months for advocating violence in *Commonweal*.[10] The March 1894 *Anarchist* featured a manifesto that, after "declar[ing] for the complete destruction of the existing society" and advocating instead "free co-operative associations of workmen who shall own land, capital and the means of production," exclaimed, "DYNAMITE IS NOT ANARCHY. It is a weapon of men driven to desperation by intolerable suffering and oppression. Our ideal can be realised without it, if the rich will let us."[11]

When violence was directed against specific individuals responsible for repression under autocratic regimes, it garnered a certain amount of public sympathy. As it took on every appearance of being simply random, however, that sympathy was lost.[12] After the bombing of a Parisian cafe, the anarchist writer Octave Mirbeau commented: "A mortal enemy of anarchism could not have done better" than this "inexplicable bomb," which injured only "peaceful anonymous people who had come to a café to drink a beer before going to bed."[13] Nonetheless, the attack was not the last of its kind, and the terrorist was seen both as a villain and a hero.

Making Sense of Vera

Treason and Plot

Oscar Wilde took up the question of political violence almost from the beginning of his career. Such violence supplies the dramatic theme and the central dilemma of his first play, *Vera, or The Nihilists*.

It must be said at the start that *Vera* is a bad play in nearly every respect. Politically inconsistent, psychologically incoherent, crowded with thin and implausible characters, and notably lacking Wilde's characteristic humor, the plot plods from one melodramatic episode to another, with abrupt reversals substituting for development and escalating, histrionic speeches clumsily mimicking a depth of feeling.

The plot can be summarized thus: A young woman, Vera Sabouroff, is converted to nihilism when her brother is arrested for political activities and exiled to Siberia. Swearing revenge, she joins a conspiratorial cell plotting to assassinate the czar. Unbeknown to the other members of the conspiracy, one of their number is the czar's own son, Alexis, who despite his privileged position is committed to the cause of liberty. Czar Ivan, meanwhile, grows increasingly paranoid and, under the guidance of his wicked prime minister, Prince Paul Maraloffski, prepares repressive legislation of an unspecified but especially draconian type. The czar and his son quarrel; the son declares himself a nihilist; and just as the monarch is ordering his own heir into exile, a shot rings out, and the czar dies. Alexis ascends to the throne and immediately embarks on a series of reforms: "all the convicts in Siberia . . . recalled, and the political prisoners . . . amnestied," the corrupt administrators "banished" and their "estates confiscated to the people," the palace guards dismissed, freedom of speech and conscience established, taxes reduced, and a parliament proposed.[14] In response, the prime minister joins the nihilists, acting as an agent provocateur in order to engineer an assassination before the reforms take effect. Vera, who is also Alexis's lover, is tasked with killing him, but at the crucial moment she kills herself instead, proclaiming, "I have saved Russia!"[15]

All of this is, of course, ridiculous. But despite its faults, the play remains interesting as a cultural artifact, indicating social preoccupations current to its moment in history and offering evidence of Wilde's own political confusion. *Vera* serves as a marker of his attitudes as they transitioned from an early nationalism and republicanism toward socialism and anarchism. Indeed, Elizabeth Carolyn Miller considers *Vera* "a key text in conceptualizing Wilde's politics," aligning feminism, terrorism, and democratic reform through a focus on individual choice, and presenting a critique of British imperialism masked as a critique of Russian imperialism.[16]

Most obviously, the play's plot connects to a different sort of "plot," rumors of which were then thick in Russia, Europe, and the United States.

The idea for *Vera*, and the title, likely came from the real-life Vera Zasulich's attempted 1878 assassination of General Trepov, which, whatever its political dimensions, also had a romantic element: Trepov had ordered the flogging of Vera's lover after he refused to salute.[17] Zasulich then shot Trepov, who survived. At her trial, the defense pointed to the general's cruelty as a justification, and Zasulich was unanimously acquitted.[18] The gallery burst into cheers, "Bravo! Our little Vera!"[19]

Curiously, Wilde did not set his play in his own time but in the 1820s, nearer to the period of the Decembrist uprising, when liberal army officers led a mutiny against the czar. Critics have often complained of this and similar anachronisms—such as mentions of railroads—though they have generally given less attention to the political incoherence characterizing Wilde's band of assassins.[20] Nominally nihilists, they are also called communists, refer to themselves as patriots, talk eagerly of democracy, aim to establish a republic, and appeal to God in their rhetoric. Their slogan is "God save the people!"[21]

But what seems at first a hopeless confusion may have been purposeful. It was common at the time, and indeed deliberate, for authorities and newspapers to conflate the state's enemies and treat Fenians, anarchists, and nihilists all of a piece.[22] Perhaps Wilde sought to take advantage of this ambiguity and turn it to his own ends. Vera's protest at the introduction of martial law—"Without trial, without appeal, without accuser even, our brothers will be taken from their houses, shot in the streets like dogs, sent away to die in the snow, to starve in the dungeon, to rot in the mine. . . . It means the strangling of a whole nation"—may well have reminded audiences of the "coercion acts" used to govern Ireland in times of unrest, sometimes suspending jury trials and producing hundreds of political prisoners.[23] A clumsy substitution allows Wilde to comment on the Irish question without ever mentioning the country of his birth: Ireland becomes Russia, Fenians become nihilists, the eighties become the twenties—but inaccurately, unconvincingly, so as to signal that he is actually talking about something else.

Another possibility is that Wilde had no specific political struggle in mind but just wanted to use the atmosphere of conspiracy and assassination to lend force to his rather wooden melodrama—that is, "modern Nihilistic Russia, with all the terror of its tyranny and the marvel of its martyrdoms, is merely the fiery and fervent background in front of which the persons of my dream live and love."[24] His mistakes then are born of indifference. He is less interested in any historically identifiable revolutionary movement than in the *idea* of political violence and the moment of choice when one's private sympathies and one's political commitments come into conflict.

By the surface reading, Vera dies for love, and Wilde sides with the personal over the political.[25] But what then does she mean when she says that she has "saved Russia"? The obvious and most conservative interpretation identifies the czar with the nation; by sparing the one she has saved the other. However, this is a czar who accepted his crown reluctantly and then immediately "talked of a Parliament . . . and said that the people should have deputies to represent them"; so perhaps she means that she has preserved that democratic program, saving the country from a return to absolutism.[26] Is the lesson then that political violence is foolhardy and self-defeating, that the path to freedom is through reform rather than militant action (a position that Wilde explicitly rejects in "The Soul of Man under Socialism")? Or is it important that the assassination of Czar Ivan opened the space for reform and that the plot against Czar Alexis is forwarded by a reactionary? In that case, the point may be simply that revolutionaries must know when to stop, that their goals are also boundaries, that to go too far ultimately means going backward. Excesses lead to reversals.

In any case, the question arises as to why Vera must die. By the logic of the play, Vera dies so that the czar may live: the nihilists plan to storm the castle if the assassination fails, and Vera is to throw the bloody dagger into the street below to show that she has succeeded. She uses her own blood instead of the young czar's, faking an assassination to forestall the insurrection. But also—symbolically, though not practically—by killing herself, Vera robs the czar of an heir, ending the line of succession and killing the monarchy rather than the monarch.[27]

Rebels and Martyrs

Vera's death also serves a moral purpose. For Wilde elsewhere suggests that such deaths were central to the nihilists' self-conception and moral outlook. The nihilists imagined themselves not merely as avenging heroes but also as martyrs to a cause. The pamphlet *A Death for a Death* by Sergei Mikhailovich Kravchinskii, better known as Stepniak, made this connection explicit: "The terrorist is noble, irresistibly fascinating, for he combines in himself the two sublimates of human grandeur: the martyr and the hero. From the day he swears in the depths of his heart to free the people and the country, he knows he is consecrated to death."[28]

In *The Rebel*, a study of the fraught relationship between philosophical nihilism and political rebellion, Albert Camus writes that the early terrorists,

> were incapable of justifying what they nevertheless found necessary, and conceived the idea of offering themselves as a justification and of replying by personal sacrifice to the question they asked themselves. For them, as for all rebels before them, murder is identified with suicide. A life is paid for by another life, and from these two sacrifices springs the promise of a value. . . . Therefore they do not value any idea above human life, though they kill for the sake of ideas. To be precise, they live on the plane of their idea. They justify it, finally, by incarnating it to the point of death.[29]

This principle of justice—a death for a death—they ultimately apply to themselves. Camus writes: "He who kills is guilty only if he consents to go on living. . . . To die, on the other hand, cancels out both the guilt and the crime itself."[30] By this "double sacrifice of their innocence and their life" they aimed to resolve the contradiction between idealism and violence: "The terrorists no doubt wanted first of all to destroy—to make absolutism totter under the shock of exploding bombs. But by their death, at any rate, they aimed at re-creating a community founded on love and justice, and thus to resume a mission that the Church had betrayed."[31]

Camus comments that, given nihilism's origin in "the rejection of any action that was not purely egoistic . . . , it is surprising not to find the nihilists engaged in making a fortune or acquiring a title." Instead they elevate their very rejection of principles to the level of a principle, and they make a value of negation, a virtue of crime. "[The] defiance they hurled in the face of society" was itself "the affirmation of a value." Dogmatically skeptical, puritanical even in their attack on morality, "their personal solution consisted in endowing their negation with the intransigence and passion of faith."[32] As Mikhail Bakunin remarked, "They are magnificent, these young fanatics. Believers without God, and heroes without phrases."[33]

Revolutionary Catechism

"Purity of heart," Kierkegaard believed, "is to will one thing."[34] By this standard, the nihilist assassin was a model of purity, living an ascetic existence and exhibiting an absolute devotion to his cause. Such selfless dedication, however, can sometimes have perverse results. Sergei Nechaev, once a comrade of Vera Zasulich and later a confederate of Bakunin's, formulated a model of the revolutionary as the single-minded, eternally devoted, ruthless, and fanatical conspirator, whose only aim and only value—indeed only *interest*—is the furtherance of his cause.[35] Nechaev's *Catechism of the Revolutionist* portrays this figure, his life and character: "Tyrannical toward himself, he must be tyrannical toward others. All the gentle and enervating sentiments of kinship, love, friendship, gratitude, and even honor, must be suppressed in him and give place to the cold and single-minded passion for revolution. For him, there exists only one pleasure, one consolation, one reward, one satisfaction—the success of the revolution. Night and day he must have but one thought, one aim—merciless destruction." In consequence of this total devotion, "He has no personal interests, no business affairs, no emotions, no attachments, no property, and no name. Everything in him is wholly absorbed in the single thought and the single passion for revolution."[36]

It is clearly this ideal that spoke to Alexander Berkman as he set himself the mission of murdering Henry Clay Frick, a factory manager responsible for the massacre of striking workers.[37] Berkman imagined the revolutionary as a kind of *Übermensch*: "A being who has neither personal interests nor desires above the necessities of the Cause; one who has emancipated himself from being merely human, and has risen above that, even to the height of conviction which excludes all doubt, all regret; in short, one who in the very inmost of his soul feels himself revolutionist first, human afterwards."[38] Berkman understood that killing Frick could cost him everything—perhaps his life, almost certainly his freedom. Yet rather than a deterrent, that sense of intense sacrifice seems to have supplied his deepest motive. As he later wrote, "It is the test of a true revolutionist—nay, more, his pride—to sacrifice all merely human feeling at the call of the People's Cause. If the latter demand his life, so much the better. Could anything be nobler than to die for a grand, a sublime Cause? Why, the very life of a true revolutionist has no other purpose, no significance whatever, save to sacrifice it on the altar of the beloved People."[39] Berkman's mission failed. Frick survived, and not even the striking workers knew how to understand Berkman's motives. (Many assumed there to be a quarrel over money.)[40] Yet in his almost childish intention of realizing through his own action his ideal of a just world, and seeing himself as a hero and martyr, we may find something to admire.

Nechaev's own career was altogether less laudable. Relying on Bakunin's reputation, Nechaev was the author of numerous elaborate but imaginary conspiracies and the leader of equally imaginary secret committees. The single concrete act of his Moscow cell, "The Axe," was to murder one of its own members, a student named Ivanov who dared to doubt Nechaev's plans and thus question his leadership.[41]

Wilde drew from the *Catechism* in composing the oath for his fictional band of assassins—"To strangle whatever nature is in me; neither to love nor to be loved; neither to pity nor to be pitied; neither to marry nor to be given in marriage, till the end is come"—and in one respect *Vera* is a riposte to the ideal of the revolutionary as a selfless fanatic.[42] Vera does give up everything: she commits suicide. But perhaps her defining characteristic, certainly the thing that distinguishes her from her nihilist cohort, is that she does *not* choose her cause over her attachment to other living human beings. She loves "the people," surely, but she also loves *specific* people. It is her love for her brother that pulls her into revolutionary politics, and it is her love for Alexis that precipitates her break with her nihilist comrades. As Wilde wrote in a letter, "I have tried . . . to express within the limits of art that Titan cry of the people for liberty, which in the Europe of our day is threatening thrones and making governments unstable from Spain to Russia, and from north to southern seas. But it is a play not of politics but of passion."[43] Wilde's biographer Richard Ellmann comments, "Of the two causes for which Vera Sabouroff may be said to die, she no longer believes in nihilism, but she does believe in love."[44]

In an 1883 interview, Wilde explained, "Heretofore the passion portrayed in the drama has been altogether personal, like the love of a man for a woman, or a woman for a man." Wilde wanted to do something new: "I have tried to show the passion for liberty, the Nihilism of Russia, which is akin to the anarchism of old France." Ultimately, however, the theatrical form and the aims of the playwright conflict and provide the dramatic crisis: "The prevailing idea is a conflict between liberty and love."[45]

Sympathy and Sadism

For an alternative to Nechaev's ideal, we might look to Stepniak. The two men would seem to share much in common: both were Russian, influenced by Bakunin, and active in the same period. But judging by either ideals or actions, Stepniak proved far more attractive a figure. Calling himself a nihilist, he assassinated the adjunct general Nikolai Mezentsev in 1878 and fled to London, where he knew Wilde.[46]

Stepniak was famous, however, not merely for his ruthless cunning but also for his kind nature and sense of decency. The *New York Times* offered this brief profile: "Anybody taking a good look at him would say: 'There's a man overflowing with good nature; a warm-hearted sympathetic fellow. He cannot be a Nihilist.' But that is the very sort of man to make a good Nihilist. . . . [A] Nihilist is a man who, touched by the suffering of his people, feels impelled to espouse their cause and to make a martyr of himself, if needs be, to right their wrongs. He may do very bad things, but he does them because he is a very good man."[47]

What motivated Stepniak, and likewise Vera, was a sense of fellow feeling, human sympathy, care for others. What motivated Nechaev was, at best, an intellectual commitment to an idea. Seen more cynically, it was an egotistical drive to self-aggrandizement and a sadistic impulse, which directed outward produces violence, and directed inward, asceticism. Bakunin wrote to Nechaev, concerned: "In your *Catechism* . . . [you] wish to make your own self-sacrificing cruelty, your own truly extreme fanaticism, a rule of life for the community."[48] The results would be not only authoritarian but totalitarian. By excluding consideration of any value except the revolution, Nechaev removes any limit to revolutionary action. By denying the revolutionary any motive or interest of his own, he also justifies any atrocity as disinterested and even altruistic. Nihilism thus becomes its own morality, merciless and exacting, totalizing in its demands. It falls prey, in other words, to precisely those faults that Wilde detected in the more conventional morals of the Victorian bourgeoisie: it "lose[s] all sense of humanity."[49]

Vera, unlike her nihilist co-conspirators, does not lose her sense of humanity; that is the meaning of her sacrifice. Caught between her love and her cause, she kills herself and saves both. Though it destroys her, this final act also completes her. It realizes the perfection latent within her. Had she chosen love over liberty or liberty over love, had she betrayed her cause and saved her lover or advanced the cause but betrayed her lover, either way she would have betrayed herself as well. She sacrifices her life instead and preserves her humanity. She kills herself and remains true to both her cause and her lover. Vera dies for love, she dies for Russia, she dies for liberty. Most of all, though, she dies by her own hand, by her own choice, by her own will.

The True Christian and the New Hellenism

Early in the play, when Vera pledges herself to the nihilist cause, her language—jarring in its context—is unmistakably religious: "O Liberty . . . Thy throne is the Calvary of the people, thy crown the crown of thorns. O crucified mother, the despot has driven a nail through thy right hand, and the tyrant through thy left! . . . The end has come now, and by thy sacred wounds, O crucified mother, O Liberty, I swear that Russia shall be saved!"[50] In her final sacrifice, then, Vera becomes identified both with liberty and with Christ.

Later, in "The Soul of Man under Socialism," Wilde writes, in tones of praise for each, that the nihilist is the truest Christian. Christ, Wilde argues, "is a God realising his perfection through pain"; because "the injustice of men is great," it was "necessary that pain should be put forward as a mode of self-perfection."[51] Though "medieval," such ideals are sometimes still needed.[52] "Even now," he writes, "in some places in the world, the message of Christ is necessary. No one who lived in modern Russia could possibly realise his perfection except by pain. . . . A Nihilist who rejects all authority because he knows authority to be evil, and welcomes all pain, because through that he realises his personality, is a real Christian. To him the Christian ideal is a true thing."[53] Both the nihilist and Christ are figures whose ideals are realized through self-sacrifice and whose ultimate victory is only achievable through martyrdom.

However, Wilde immediately goes further: "Pain is not the ultimate mode of perfection. It is merely provisional and a protest."[54] It is the inevitable response of sensitive people to brutal conditions. And while sympathy with suffering is natural and necessary, on its own it solves nothing and is not a state to which one should aspire. Instead, Wilde urges, "when Socialism has solved the problem of poverty, and Science solved the problem of disease, . . . the sympathy of man will be large, healthy and spontaneous. Man will have joy in the contemplation of the joyous life of others."[55]

Newer, more hopeful ideals arise, ideals of pleasure rather than pain, of bliss rather than sorrow, a "new Individualism, for whose service Socialism, whether it wills it or not, is working"—"an individualism expressing itself through joy." This individualism will be "perfect harmony. . . . It will be complete, and through it each man will attain his perfection. The new Individualism is the new Hellenism."[56]

"I think self-realisation—realisation of one's self—is the primal aim of life," Wilde would later testify at trial: "I think that to realise one's self through pleasure is finer than to realise one's self though pain. That is the pagan ideal of man realising himself by happiness as opposed to the later and perhaps grander idea of man realising himself by suffering. I was, on that subject, entirely on the side of the ancients—the Greeks, I will say—the philosophers."[57]

This shift, from the Christian to the Hellenic, denotes a total change in outlook. It suggests a new moral focus, a new system of virtues, a different ideal for humanity, and ultimately new politics. As Wilde wrote in his Oxford notebooks: "the chief moral agent of antiquity was the sense of human dignity, the sense of sin took its place in modern medievalism—the first produces the qualities of a patriot, the second those of a saint."[58] In proposing a return to Hellenism, Wilde forwards an ethics and a politics centered on autonomy, on human agency rather than the moral law, and, in the Irish context, the virtues of a revolutionary rather than the purity of a saint.

Curtains for *Vera*

Vera was scheduled to open at London's Adelphi Theatre on December 17, 1881.[59]

But luck, fate, or history intervened. On March 13, 1881, Czar Alexander II was assassinated. Facing a certain amount of unofficial pressure—a real concern in an age when the state licensed theaters—the play was canceled while still in rehearsal.[60]

Illustrating Wilde's theory that life imitates art, one of those involved in the real-life conspiracy was named Vera (Vera Figner); the targeted czar was a reformer who had freed the serfs, created local assemblies, modernized the courts and universities, granted limited autonomy to Poland, liberalized treatment of the Jews, and on the very morning of his death ordered the drafting of a new constitution.[61] His closest advisors, however, were reactionaries bent on thwarting his plans. What the assassination accomplished, at least in the short term, was giving the hard-liners the upper hand, forestalling the reforms and introducing a new period of repression.[62]

When the play finally opened in New York in 1883, it disappointed all concerned. The *New York Times*, while seeing much (unrealized) potential in Wilde himself, found that his play only succeeded in making nihilism seem boring: "It comes as near to failure as an ingenious and able writer can bring it."[63]

Wilde's own considered opinion was hardly kinder. Years later, after his trials and the forced auction of his property, a neighbor, Wilfred Cheeson, found some of Wilde's books for sale at a Chelsea bookstore. He bought the family Bible, a copy of Shakespeare's sonnets (with Wilde's annotations), and original drafts of *Vera* and the *Duchess of Padua*; he then traveled to France and offered them as gifts to the exiled poet. Wilde gratefully accepted them all—except for *Vera*, about which, he said, he could not "profess the slightest interest."[64]

Nationalist Contexts and
Contentious Identities

A Daughter of Ireland, and Her Son

Oscar Wilde's ambivalence concerning revolutionary violence was born not of direct experience but nevertheless of a deep and formative tie to the Irish nationalist movement.

His mother, Jane Francesca Elgee, was in her youth a prominent writer aligned with the cause of Young Ireland. Never one for humility or moderation, she cast herself as "the acknowledged voice in poetry of all the people of Ireland" and declared, "I express the soul of a great nation."[65] One of her early poems, "The Faithless Shepherds," written in the midst of the Great Famine and published under the pseudonym "Speranza" ("Hope" in Italian), laid the blame for the crisis on her own class, the landlords.[66] Another poem, "France in '93," compared the conditions of the famine to those producing the bread riots in the early days of the French Revolution.[67] In one verse she recollects or foretells:

Royal blood of King and Queen
Streameth from the guillotine;
Wildly on the people goeth,
Reaping what the noble soweth.[68]

Writing in the journal *Nation*, on July 8, 1848, she put forward the case for revolution in forthright terms, arguing that since "a government is not organised to control, but to execute a people's will," if it fails in that obligation and instead "stands in the path of the people," then, simply, "that government must be overthrown." Such was the case, she said, in Ireland. "The country, therefore, is now in a position which . . . would *justify* armed resistance to tyranny, and an armed enforcement of the people's rights."[69]

A week later, on July 15, one of the paper's founding editors, Charles Gavan Duffy, was arrested under the Treason Felony Act, with Speranza's work cited as evidence.[70] Duffy refused to name Elgee or to call her as a witness in his defense. Desperate to intervene, she bravely visited the solicitor general and announced herself to be Speranza. When that failed to change the course of the prosecution, she tried to interrupt the trial by speaking from the balcony, but court officers acted quickly to silence her. Belatedly and anticlimactically, the charges against Duffy were dropped, but the ordeal left Elgee shaken. She wrote to a friend that "the lesson was useful—I shall never write sedition again."[71]

In 1851 Jane Elgee married William Wilde, a man whose accomplishments were later commemorated with a plaque marking their home at 1 Merrion Square, Dublin: "Aural and ophthalmic surgeon, archeologist, ethnologist, antiquarian, biographer, statistician, naturalist, historian, and folklorist."[72] Together they had two sons, Oscar and Willie, and a daughter, Isola, who died in childhood. In addition to his professional and intellectual interests and his remarkable family, Sir William Wilde also had his own set of political concerns, including an acute personal interest in liberalizing the laws governing the legitimacy of children (he had three illegitimate children himself), the conditions in asylums and the treatment of the mentally ill, freedom of speech, and the desperate poverty then so prevalent in Ireland.[73]

Lady Wilde did her best to instill her own nationalist fervor in their boys. She dedicated a collection of her poetry "to My Sons, Willie and Oscar Wilde," stating that she had "made them indeed, Speak plain the word COUNTRY" and "taught them, no doubt, That a country's a thing men should die for at need!"[74]

Touring the United States in 1882, Oscar Wilde spoke at a Saint Patrick's Day commemoration in Minnesota. A local priest introduced him as the son of "one of Ireland's daughters . . . who in the troublous times of 1848 by the works of her pen and her noble example did much to keep the fire of patriotism burning brightly."[75] Wilde gave a short speech, which began by acknowledging "with a pleasure and a pride" the praise paid to "the efforts of my mother in Ireland's cause." He then recalled the country's former greatness in the "time before the time of Henry II," when it "stood at the front of all the nations of Europe in the arts, the sciences, and genuine intellectuality" and served as "the university of Europe." He lamented the Saxon invaders' destruction of cathedrals, monasteries, and other centers of culture and noted that, though "art could not live and flourish under a tyrant," nevertheless "the artistic sentiment of Ireland was not dead in the hearts of her sons and daughters." He predicted then that once the country won its independence, its culture would be revived: "Ireland will regain the proud position she once held among the nations of Europe."[76]

In Sacramento, too, Wilde spoke on Irish poetry, reading some of his mother's work.[77] In San Francisco, he again lectured on "Irish Poets of '48," reading a long poem by Speranza along with other similarly patriotic verse.[78] He also voiced his admiration for the revolutionaries it had been his pleasure to know. Duffy, Wilde stated proudly, "one of my friends," was one of those poets "who had made their lives noble poems also, men who had not merely written about the sword but were ready to bear it, who not only could rhyme to Liberty, but could die for her also, if need had been so." Likewise, he recalled, "The earliest hero of my childhood was [William] Smith O'Brien," a leader of the Young Ireland Rebellion in 1848, convicted of sedition and for a time exiled. "I remember [him] so well, tall and stately, with the dignity of one who had fought for a noble idea and the sadness of one who failed." However, Wilde was ready to add, "such failures are at least often grander than a hundred victories."[79]

Liberty with Bloody Hands

As the nineteenth century wore on, "the Irish question" tremored beneath the foundations of the empire, a major fault line in British politics, and not even the Irish were agreed as to how to answer it. The Land League, advocating nationalization, took up the slogan "The Land for the People," while Charles Parnell sought the more moderate course of tenant ownership. The Fenians, meanwhile, opposed agrarian reform altogether, being committed to the larger aim of national independence. Questions of means were likewise disputed, with Fenians condemning indiscriminate violence and adhering to principles of "honourable warfare," while groups like the Skirmishers and the Clan na Gael, inspired by the continental anarchists and Russian Narodniks, undertook terrorist bombings.[80] William Gladstone, the British prime minister, cannily mixed reforms and repression to undercut support for more radical solutions, passing both a coercion act and a land act in 1881. Parnell's opposition led Gladstone to imprison him and Lady Wilde to praise him (with her typically Romantic exuberance) as an "agrarian martyr," "man of destiny," and "predestined saviour."[81]

From prison, Parnell negotiated with Gladstone what became known as the Kilmainham Treaty, under which Land League prisoners were released, tenants could appeal to the courts for fair rent, and nationalist leaders promised to use their influence to curb political violence. Clearly not everyone was satisfied with the results, however. Michael Davitt, leader of the Land League, departed for the United States in a sort of self-imposed exile. On the other side, W. E. "Buckshot" Forster, the chief secretary of Ireland and a hard-line reactionary, resigned in protest of the treaty's concessions. He was replaced by Lord Frederick Cavendish, who was then assassinated almost as soon as he arrived in the country. Cavendish and the undersecretary Thomas Burke (both, ironically, personal friends of the Wildes) were stabbed to death in Phoenix Park by a mysterious group called the Invincibles.[82]

It was under these circumstances that Wilde remarked to a reporter, "When liberty comes with hands dabbled with blood it is hard to shake hands with her." He quickly turned, though, to address the context of the outrage: "We forget how much England is to blame. She is reaping the fruit of seven centuries of injustice."[83] His equivocation angered Irish militants, though one doubts that it especially pleased the English either.[84]

Later the *Times* claimed it had correspondence from Parnell expressing support for the Invincibles. The government convened a special commission to investigate the allegations, along with his party's involvement in other violence. Oscar Wilde, who had previously announced himself "strongly in sympathy with the Parnell movement," attended the hearings, and his brother Willie reported on them for the *Daily Telegraph*.[85] Oscar was also present for Parnell's speech before "The Eighty Club" advocating autonomy for Ireland. A copy of that speech, along with the investigating commission's final report, found a home on Wilde's shelves.[86]

Parnell was cleared when the letters in question were revealed to be forgeries. His vindication was soon eclipsed by other controversies, however. In 1890 he was caught up in an adultery scandal, ending his political career. He died in October the following year; Wilde spent a fortnight in mourning.[87]

Contentious Identities

As the Irish movement became increasingly radical, and as Oscar Wilde grew wary of political violence (especially against family friends), his mother noted her own apprehension about the shift from the relatively patrician Young Ireland to the more proletarian Fenians. She wrote in a letter from 1866, "The Fenian rebellion engages all our thoughts—but I am not a Fenian. I disapprove highly of their prospects—It is decidedly a democratic movement—the gentry and aristocracy will suffer much from them."[88]

Enmeshed in this class difference was also an important difference of worldview. The Fenians' nationalism tended toward the chauvinistic and provincial; the Wildes' was pluralistic and cosmopolitan.[89] Sir William, for example, in his opening remarks at the 1874 meeting of the anthropological section of the British Association, specifically posited diversity as a source of social progress and advocated increased cultural and racial mixing.[90] And Oscar Wilde noted the invigorating influence of emigration, to the United States especially, on Irish culture: "To mature its powers, to concentrate its action, to learn the secret of its own strength and of England's weakness, the Celtic intellect has had to cross the Atlantic."[91] There was a growing concern that Ireland, rather than asserting its place among the cultures of the world, might instead close itself off and shut the world out.

If Oscar Wilde's nationalism was rather fluid, that may well be because his national identity was far from stable. Wilde described himself as "French by sympathy" and "Irish by race," though "the English . . . have condemned me to speak the language of Shakespeare."[92]

Wilde often, especially in London, insisted that he was Irish rather than English—"which is quite another thing"—but, as Terry Eagleton notes, "several of the characteristics that make him appear most typically upper-class English—the scorn for bourgeois normality, the flamboyant self-display, the verbal *brio* and iconoclasm—are also, interesting enough, where one might claim he is most distinctly Irish."[93] Wilde was already something of an outsider in Dublin. For one thing, his family was Protestant and of a class that gave them as much in common with the English grandees as with the Gaelic peasants. Then he was educated at Oxford (where "my Irish accent was one of the many things I forgot") and took a "double first" in Greats, which is to say Classics.[94] He therefore read Latin and Greek,

French and Italian, a bit of German, and likely some Gaelic and Spanish, as well as English.[95] In his own work he took inspiration, ideas, motifs, and styles from any place he could find them. ("The true artist is known by the use he makes of what he annexes," he said, "and he annexes everything.")[96] Thus we can find in his writing traces of Shakespeare and the Bible, Irish fairy tales and English pulp novels, Russian anarchism and German philosophy, the Ancients and the Decadents.

Toward the end of his life he even showed signs of a kind of Anglophilism—throwing a party for neighborhood children to celebrate Victoria's jubilee and privately expressing support for the the Second Boer War.[97] From a certain point of view, such attitudes are quite understandable. Surely the impulse must have been very strong to forcefully assert, perhaps even to prove, that he belonged to the society that had condemned him. To assert, after all, one's Englishness, to express the feeling that one's fate is, despite everything, tied to the fate of that country which has rejected you is also, in a way, to insist on that country's responsibility for you and its responsibility for what it has done to you.[98]

A Principle of Autonomy

An ambivalence about nationalism has long been a characteristic of anarchist politics. As the historian Peter Marshall explains, "In general, [anarchists] have supported national liberation struggles as part of a wider struggle for freedom, but they have opposed the statist aspirations and exclusive loyalties of the nationalists."[99] Nationalism offers an expression of self-determination but also limits it by applying the principles exclusively to "nations" and exercising it through the creation of states.

For Oscar Wilde, the principle in common between nationalism and anarchism was that of autonomy, and his move from the one view to the other suggests that it was this concern with self-determination that animated his nationalism in the first place. In 1887 Wilde reviewed *Greek Life and Thought*, by his former tutor J. P. Mahaffy. In his review, Wilde accuses Mahaffy of allowing his feelings about the British Empire to color his reading of the Classics and vehemently objects to the book's attack on the Hellenic system of autonomous city-states. Wilde argues, as it were, in the opposite direction, and takes from his reading of the Classics lessons to inform his critique of empire. He notes, for instance, that "the imperialism of Rome, which followed the imperialism of Alexander, produced incalculable mischief, beginning with intellectual decay, and ending with financial ruin."[100] He further discerns from the Greek example "the doctrine of Autonomy . . . [and] as a principle of political economy, the curious idea that people should be allowed to arrange their own affairs!"[101] It may be that this connection—between Irish Home Rule and the independence of the Greek city-states—led Wilde to think deeply about the ideal of autonomy, pushing the notion far beyond his mother's revolutionary nationalism.

What was important to Wilde was the notion that people—including whole groups of people—have the right to determine their own affairs without being ruled by others. Which is to say that his concern represented a universal principle of autonomy, not a chauvinistic interest in Celtic purity. Wilde's nationalism was cosmopolitan rather than parochial. Its tendency was not toward isolation but toward connection. Internationally and cross-culturally, as well as interpersonally, identity is formed in large part in relation to others. Thus self-discovery is facilitated by coming to understand other people, which in turn requires an exercise of imagination.[102] It is the same imaginative sympathy that allows one to identify with one's *own* tradition—to encompass "the dreams, and ideas, and feelings of myriad generations"—that allows us to connect with those different from us: "To know anything about oneself one must know all about others. There must be no mood with which one cannot sympathise, no dead mode of life that one cannot make alive. . . . [N]o form of thought is alien, no emotional impulse obscure."[103] Characteristically, in the same dialogue, Wilde also reverses this formulation: "If you wish to understand others you must intensify your own individualism."[104]

Wilde envisioned Ireland as a nation in a community of nations, neither isolated nor subjugated. He conceived of the national culture as distinctive and unique but open rather than closed—participating in and contributing to an international culture. "The political independence of a nation," he argued in one lecture, "must not be confused with any intellectual isolation."[105] He pictured Ireland as generous, gregarious, and open-hearted, not suspicious, sullen, and hard.

This attitude and the exchange it can facilitate between cultures, Wilde thought, held the key to international peace. "It is Criticism that makes us

cosmopolitan," he writes. "The Manchester school [of laissez-faire econom-
ics] tried to make men realise the brotherhood of humanity by pointing out
the commercial advantages of peace. It sought to degrade the wonderful
world into a common marketplace for the buyer and the seller. It addressed
itself to the lowest instincts, and it failed." The pressures of the market did not
bring peace, any more than did "mere emotional sympathies, or to the shallow
dogmas of some vague system of abstract ethics . . . , [or the] Peace Societies
. . . and their proposals for unarmed International Arbitrators." What Wilde
sought instead was critical engagement, leading to "the peace that springs
from understanding." He theorized, "It is only by the cultivation of the habit
of intellectual criticism that we shall be able to rise superior to race-prejudices.
. . . Criticism will annihilate race-prejudices, by insisting upon the unity of the
human mind in the variety of its forms. If we are tempted to make war upon
another nation, we shall remember that we are seeking to destroy an element
of our own culture, and possibly its most important element."[106]

Wilde's community of nations, and his view of the role of one nation
among them, found an analogy in his thinking about the relationship
between socialism and individualism. And his thinking on the latter was
likely shaped by his thinking on the former. In both cases he saw that the
point of any sort of collectivism was to help the individual members to
develop and prosper, not merely in a material sense but also in an artistic
and even spiritual sense. We do that, whether as individuals or as nations,
not in isolation but in communication and cooperation with one another.
Likewise, the healthy and happy community does not try to limit and control its individual members, or to suppress what is unique in each of them,
but to encourage and aid them in their development, to gain what we can
from their special talents, and to learn what we can from each one's unique
point of view. In his lecture on the Irish poets, Wilde reflected, "I do not
know anything more wonderful or more characteristic of the Celtic genius
than the quick artistic spirit in which we adapted ourselves to the English
tongue. . . . The Saxon took our lands from us and left them desolate—we
took their language and added new beauties to it."[107] This sense of cultural
rather than political mastery likely supplies the meaning of Wilde's suggestion, wittingly inserted in the midst of a debate between his son Cyril, then
only eight years old, and a house guest over the question of Home Rule.
"My own idea," Wilde offered, "is that Ireland should rule England."[108]

The Critic as Anarchist

Small Explosions

The political context must surely inform our reading of *Vera*, and Elizabeth Carolyn Miller proposes that a political reading of *Vera* forces a reevaluation of Wilde's later plays as well. For instance, in *The Importance of Being Earnest* the revelation that Jack was found in an unattended bag in a railway cloakroom may have been slightly alarming to attentive audiences: the Fenian bombing of Victorian Station was achieved by leaving the explosive in the cloakroom.[109] Likewise, when Jack admits that he can no longer sustain the fiction of an invalid friend named Bunbury, he regretfully murmurs that "Bunbury has been quite exploded." Aunt Augusta takes this utterance as literal and asks, "Was he the victim of a revolutionary outrage?"[110]

Jokes about explosions were common in radical circles, a kind of teasing over the panicked association of socialism and violence. Walter Crane recalls an occasion when William Morris was visited by Lord Richard Grosvenor, who broke with the Liberal Party over their support for Irish Home Rule. As Grosvenor was looking for a seat among the books and papers piled on every surface, Morris reassured him, "Oh, you can sit there all right—there's not dynamite under the papers."[111] It is hard to know who caught the barbed end of such jests—the bourgeoisie, who imagined every land reformer a secret assassin and every Fabian lecture a dynamite plot—or the radicals themselves, who too often did display an unhealthy preoccupation with secret committees, homemade bombs, and high-profile murders, and who with surprising frequency tried to bring such boyish fantasies into fruition, often ineptly.

Killing people is hard work, and bomb-making is not a pastime suitable for dilettantes. It took multiple attempts before Czar Alexander II was finally killed. In 1879, he was spared when the assassin's bomb failed to ignite. Soon thereafter, another bomb *did* go off but missed its target as the czar had unexpectedly changed trains. In February 1880 an explosion in the Winter Palace killed eleven soldiers and injured fifty others, but the czar was away.[112]

Britain was relatively quiet, compared with Russia and the continent, and its anarchist adventurers proved more tragicomic than terroristic in their effect. In early 1892 four men received long prison sentences on conspiracy charges relating to a bombing that never occurred; evidence suggests the influence of an agent provocateur.[113] In 1894 a young anarchist died in Greenwich Park, outside the Observatory, when a bomb he was carrying exploded prematurely.[114] Wilde's remark about "the dynamite policy" came a month later.[115]

Wilde caricatured this record, though not cruelly, in "Lord Arthur Savile's Crime." Cheekily subtitled "A Study of Duty," the story depicts the misadventures of a young aristocrat who, informed by a palm reader that he is destined to commit a murder, resolves to do so right away so that he may marry with (as it were) a clear conscience and pure intentions, without some future crime looming over him. After failed attempts at dispatching elderly relations (being careful to choose targets without the moral complications of mixed motives, whether "personal pique" or "vulgar monetary advantage"), Lord Arthur resolves his dilemma by throwing the fortune-teller himself off a bridge, thus fulfilling his destiny while symbolically rejecting it, satisfying his duty by committing a crime, and enacting a sort of poetic justice in the form of a capital offense.[116] All of this is treated as a kind of delightful nonsense, anticipating the graceful absurdity of *The Importance of Being Earnest*. In each work, Wilde's light tone and sparkling wit contrast favorably with the serious attitude that certain central characters adopt with regard to their most ridiculous predicaments.

Anarchists are implicated in "Lord Arthur Savile's Crime" from the very first page. The story begins at "Lady Windermere's last reception before Easter," where, we are told, "Gorgeous peeresses chatted affably to violent Radicals, popular preachers brushed coat-tails with eminent sceptics, a perfect bevy of bishops kept following a stout prima-donna from room to room, on the staircase stood several Royal Academicians, disguised as artists, and it was said that at one time the supper-room was absolutely crammed with geniuses."[117] In this dense mix of artists, anarchists, and aristocrats, it can be difficult to discern who occupies which role, and identities sometimes blur together. "People are so annoying," Lady Windermere complains: "All my pianists look exactly like poets; and all my poets look exactly like pianists; and I remember last season asking a most dreadful conspirator to dinner, a man who had blown up ever so many people, and always wore a coat of mail, and carried a dagger up his shirt-sleeve; and do you know that when he came he looked just like a nice old clergyman, and cracked jokes all evening? Of course, he was very amusing, and all that, but I was awfully disappointed."[118] Her smooth transition from poet to pianist to dynamiter (the types divided by a mere semicolon) implies a kind of equivalence, while the real contrast is that between her expectations and reality.

Lady Windermere's image of the "conspirator" is, of course, a comic stereotype. With the addition of chain mail it becomes an exaggeration of an exaggeration, a kind of *reductio ad absurdum* to the cloaked, bearded, foreign-looking, wild-eyed, bomb-toting anarchist of the popular imagination.[119] The reality of the "nice old clergyman" is one rebuke to the stereotype, and the rhetorical proximity to the poet-pianists and pianist-poets is another. For it is clearly ridiculous to think that there is something that poets or pianists or conspirators or clergymen *must* look like, though we cannot help thinking that there is. (And it would be a sorry conspirator who *looks* like a conspirator; one might even conclude that a conspirator should look like a clergyman.) But then, having written off such stereotypes at the outset, Wilde introduces one again a few short pages later—a slovenly foreigner, in the poor quarter of the city, animated by a monomaniacal obsession with explosives.[120]

In Lord Arthur's first attempt he tries to poison an elderly aunt. Poison, for Wilde, is a powerful symbol linking aesthetics and crime. He explores this connection most fully in his essay "Pen, Pencil, and Poison," a meditation on the life of the dandy, author, artist, forger, and serial killer Thomas Griffiths Wainwright and more broadly an exploration of the relationship between art and morality, or lack of same. ("The fact of a man being a poisoner is nothing against his prose. . . . There is no essential incongruity between crime and culture.")[121] Wilde repeatedly returns in his work to this use of poison: Dorian Gray was "poisoned, or made perfect," by a book.[122] Baudelaire was the "most perfect and the most poisonous of all modern French poets."[123] Saltus's book on Mary Magdalene was "so poisonous, and so perfect."[124] And Swinburne, Wilde wrote, "once set his age on fire by a volume of very perfect and very poisonous poetry. Then he became revolutionary, and pantheistic, and cried out against those who sit in high places both in heaven and on earth."[125] Despite such rich resonances, however, poison, for Lord Arthur, "proved a complete failure," and so "dynamite, or some other form of explosive, was obviously the proper thing to try."[126]

To procure the explosives, Lord Arthur approached his friend Count Rouvaloff, "a young Russian of very revolutionary tendencies," who was "generally suspected . . . [of being] a Nihilist agent." Rouvaloff provides a reference to a "famous Conspirator," "Herr Winckelkopf, as he was called in England." Lord Arthur asks for "an explosive clock," and Winckelkopf provides him a device of his own invention, "a pretty little French clock," featuring "an ormolu figure of Liberty trampling on the hydra of Despotism" and "a round cake of dynamite about the size of a penny." Interestingly, political considerations seem of secondary importance to Winckelkopf, since Lord Arthur informs him the device is for use in "a purely private matter"; and the bomb-maker refuses all payment above the cost of materials: "I do not work for money; I live entirely for my art."[127]

Unfortunately for Lord Arthur, Winckelkopf's enthusiasm exceeds his skill. The bomb is sent anonymously to the Dean of Chichester, "a man of great culture and learning," a political reactionary, and Lord Arthur's uncle.[128] Days pass, and Lord Arthur scours the papers for news of the explosion, without satisfaction. At last his mother receives a letter from the Dean's daughter, cheerily describing the "great fun" the family has had with "a clock that an unknown admirer sent papa." They placed it on the hearth and, the next day, in the words of the Dean's daughter, "just as the clock struck twelve, we heard a whirring noise, a little puff of smoke came from the pedestal of the figure, and the goddess of Liberty fell off . . . it looked so ridiculous that James and I went into fits of laughter, and even papa was amused. When we examined it, we found it was a sort of alarm clock, and that, if you set it to a particular hour, and put some gunpowder and a cap under a little hammer, it went off whenever you wanted." The Dean, his daughter writes, forbid it in the library, "as it made a noise," and so his young son "carried it away to the schoolroom, and does nothing but have small explosions all day long."[129]

Winckelkopf, of course, is embarrassed and "full of elaborate apologies," explaining that "everything is so adulterated nowadays, that even dynamite can hardly be got in pure condition." However, he also recalls an earlier mishap, in which "a barometer that he had once sent to the military Governor at Odessa, . . . though timed to explode in ten days, had not done so for something like three months." And then, unfortunately, "it merely succeeded in blowing a housemaid to atoms."[130]

Being a man of his word, Winckelkopf "offered to supply [Lord Arthur] another clock free of charge, or with a case of nitro-glycerin bombs at cost price." But it was no use. Lord Arthur "had lost all faith in explosives."[131]

The parody, again, finds its basis in fact. The history of late-Victorian terrorism is replete with plots that miscarried. Bombs went off too late, too soon, or not at all. They killed too many people, the wrong people, or no people. Assassins missed their mark, lost their nerve, or succumbed to conscience. Fugitives failed to get away. And trusted comrades turned out to be lunatics, incompetents, or police.[132]

Even when such plots were successful—a royal assassination or a public explosion—the results, especially in the aggregate, were not what was desired. Assassinations might inspire other assassins, and bombings encourage other bombings. But the public as a whole—the masses, the people, the working class, the oppressed—did not in general find themselves emboldened to resist tyranny, especially when it was *their* cafés where such explosions occurred. Instead anarchism became permanently identified in the public mind with arbitrary and even senseless violence; and rather than open the way to a revolutionary upheaval, the bombings served to justify repression.[133]

Too Many Martyrs

In *Anarchy and Culture*, David Weir tracks the portrayal of anarchism in the novels of the late nineteenth and early twentieth centuries, finding: "As anarchism develops from benign theory to outright terror, novelists treat it critically but sympathetically at first (Turgenev's *Rudin*, 1860), then with increasing anxiety (Dostoevsky's *The Possessed*, 1872), then with irony (James's *The Princess Casamassima*, 1886), and finally as the target of satire (Conrad's *The Secret Agent*, 1907) and even comedy (Chesterton's *The Man Who Was Thursday*, 1908)."[134] Wilde's shift in tone, from *Vera*'s ponderous melodrama to "Lord Arthur Savile's" comic absurdity, to *Earnest*'s almost Dadaist abstraction, proceeds along something of the same line, though at a quicker pace.

Nevertheless, despite his reservations and jests, Wilde was realistic enough to recognize that violence was sometimes rational, necessary, and even justified. In "The Soul of Man under Socialism," he explained, "It is often said that force is no argument. That, however, entirely depends on what one wants to prove. Many of the most important problems of the last few centuries, such as the continuance of personal government in England, or of feudalism in France, have been solved entirely by means of physical force."[135] And, when the movements demanding change clashed directly with the defenders of the existing order, there could be no question as to where Wilde's sympathies lay.

In a letter to Wilde's friend and biographer Frank Harris, George Bernard Shaw recalled an attempt to circulate a petition on behalf of "the Chicago anarchists," who were at that time facing execution. The men were convicted of a bomb attack against the police as they moved to break up a demonstration at Haymarket Square. The accused were manifestly innocent of the bombing. Most had not even been at the demonstration, and those present were on the speaker's platform when the bomb was thrown. Nevertheless, the prosecution argued that as agitators and propagandists they were responsible for any action their ideas might inspire. The trial was farcical, with biased jurors, perjured testimony, and fabricated or irrelevant evidence. Yet eight anarchists were convicted and seven sentenced to hang. Four ultimately did hang, and another committed suicide in his cell. After an international outcry and an investigation by the governor, the survivors were ultimately pardoned.[136]

History has vindicated the Haymarket martyrs, but at the time many on the left wanted to distance themselves from any association with violence or extremism. Thus, Shaw's efforts to circulate his petition were largely frustrated. As he recalled: "I tried to get some literary men in London, all heroic rebels and skeptics on paper, to sign a memorial asking for the reprieve of these unfortunate men. The only signature I got was Oscar's."[137]

Showing Contempt

Then, on New Year's Eve 1891, a poet named John Evelyn Barlas fired a pistol at the houses of Parliament. When a police constable arrived, Barlas handed over his revolver and told him, "I am an anarchist, and I intended shooting you; but then I thought it a pity to shoot an honest man. What I have done is to show my contempt for the House of Commons."[138]

When Barlas appeared in court on January 7, he was supported by Wilde and two friends. Nine days later, Wilde provided half of the £200 required for bail; the other half came from H. H. Champion, a former president of the Social Democratic Federation (SDF). Champion hadn't known Wilde previously but went to his Tite Street home to ask for help. Wilde obliged, though his court appearance made him late for a reading of *Lady Windermere's Fan*.[139]

Barlas, the son of a Scottish merchant and a descendent of the national hero Kate Douglas, had known Wilde at Oxford, and Wilde served as reference for him to be admitted to the Reading Room at the British Museum. Between 1884 and 1893 he had published eight volumes of love poetry under the name Evelyn Douglas and anonymously published *Holy of Holies: Confessions of an Anarchist*. In 1887 he had been beaten by police at a demonstration in Trafalgar Square—the first of many "Bloody Sundays." At the time he was a member of the Marxist SDF, though he soon followed Champion out of the organization and into the Labour Electoral Association. By May 1891 he had further moved to the Socialist League, and from there he moved on to anarchism.[140]

After his attack on Parliament, Barlas was deemed incompetent and therefore not prosecuted. He was briefly held and then released. He wrote Wilde a note of thanks, to which Wilde replied, addressing him as "My dear friend and poet": "Whatever I did was merely what you would have done for me or for any friend of yours whom you admired and appreciated. We poets and dreamers are all brothers. . . . We will have many days of song and joy together when the spring comes, and life shall be made lovely for us, and we will pipe on reeds."[141]

The promised spring never came for John Barlas. As he grew older he became increasingly unstable. Some of his friends attributed it to the concussion he received at the hands of the police, but his deterioration may also have been caused by syphilis. In any case, he was arrested once more, for an unprovoked assault. He was first confined to an asylum for a few months in 1892 and 1893 and later institutionalized for longer periods. He died in Gartnavel Asylum, Glasgow, in 1914.[142]

Barlas never forgot Wilde, what he had done for him and, perhaps above all, what he represented. In 1905 Barlas wrote to his son that Wilde "was and remains my ideal of a man of genius in this generation; his words and writings . . . half-concealing under an appearance of sportive levity unheard of profundity and thought."[143]

Bloody Sunday

The effects of Bloody Sunday are better remembered than the causes. The demonstration has variously been described as a protest against unemployment in England, the colonial policy in Ireland, and the execution of the Haymarket defendants in the United States. But the central issue was the right of the public to assemble for purposes of protest at all.[144]

What is notable is the number of Wilde's friends who were involved in the events surrounding the day, Shaw among them.[145] Walter Crane, a socialist and one of the illustrators of Wilde's collection *The Happy Prince*, recalled the atrocities of November 13, 1887:

> Large contingents of workmen with bands and banners marched from every quarter of London and made for the square, but Sir Charles Warren with an enormous force of police, which he used as an army, issued orders to stop every procession half a mile before it reached the square, and to break it up. Morris at the head of his Hammersmith League was thus stopped. . . . At another point the cordon was broken by a determined rush headed by R. B. Cunninghame Graham, H. M. Hyndman, and John Burns, but all these were instantly taken into custody, the former being struck on the head by the truncheon of one of "our admirable police" (a phrase used by Mr. Gladstone). The next business of the police was to clear the sides of the square. . . . I never saw anything more like real warfare in my life—only the attack was all on *one* side.[146]

Over 150 people were arrested, 200 were treated in area hospitals, and one person—Alfred Linnell, a bystander caught in a charge by mounted police—died from his injuries.[147] A large funeral march was arranged, with many prominent socialist leaders in attendance. William Morris wrote a song for the occasion, with music by Malcolm Lawson. Printed as a pamphlet with a cover by Walter Crane, it sold for a penny to benefit Linnell's family. It was sung as the procession moved through London.[148] Tens of thousands participated. Graham and Morris served as pall bearers, and the Reverend Stewart Headlam delivered the sermon.[149]

Though Graham was seriously injured, his friends and family conveyed their contempt for the authorities by sustaining an ironic air of levity. His wife had cards printed to invite friends to the trial:

Mrs. Cunninghame Graham
At Home
Bow Street Police Court.[150]

Wilde wrote to George Percy Jacomb-Hood (Crane's collaborator on the illustrations for *The Happy Prince*), promising to "come round and see your young anarchist Cunninghame Graham" and commenting, "I hope they won't cut his nice curly hair in prison, or clip that amazing mustache!"[151]

Graham was no anarchist, though it is interesting that Wilde would describe him that way. Instead he was the first socialist elected to the House of Commons and a founding member of both the Scottish Labour Party and what would become the Scottish National Party.[152] Aside from his steadfast opposition to capitalism, his nearest resemblance to an anarchist was likely found in his anti-imperialism. Rather than loot the world in exchange for imposing a European standard of civilization, Graham argued, "it is better to let others follow their destiny as it best pleases them." He declared that "progress"—which in the context of colonialism "means tramways and electric light"—is "a crime against humanity."[153]

Graham ultimately served six weeks for his part in the Bloody Sunday demonstrations.[154]

Vengeance and Punishment

In France the vendetta-like cycle of lawful punishment and radical vengeance to which Camus referred in *The Rebel* took hold on May Day 1891, when police broke up a small anarchist demonstration in the Paris suburbs and later attempted to arrest the leaders. A shoot-out ensued; three anarchists were arrested and given long sentences as a result. In retaliation, a young dandy going by the name Ravachol bombed the homes of the trial judge and the prosecuting attorney, as well as a royal residence and an army barracks. When Ravachol was executed in July 1892—legally speaking, for the unrelated murder of an elderly hermit—a young activist named Émile Henry responded with a bomb that killed several police and an office boy.[155]

In short order, the motives for such attacks became more obscure and the targets more arbitrary. In December 1893, Auguste Vaillant, a writer, translator, and bohemian associated with the avant-garde theater, threw a bomb into the Chamber of Deputies. Aside from Vaillant himself, the attack injured only a single politician; it did not even halt the hearing then underway, a debate over proposals to censor the press.[156] Vaillant was executed just the same. Again Henry sought revenge, this time bombing an ordinary working-class café with the too-tempting name of Terminus. Twenty were injured, and one man died. Henry would in his turn also be executed, but in this case the avenger was quicker than the executioner. Henry was still awaiting trial when a bomb hidden in a bunch of flowers exploded at a restaurant across the street from the Palais de Luxembourg. The restaurant was a regular haunt for politicians, but the only person actually injured in the blast was Laurent Tailhade, a poet with anarchist sympathies.[157]

The bomber turned out to be a friend of Tailhade as well as of Henry—the anarchist writer and art critic Félix Fénéon. Fénéon, who contributed regularly to *Le Revue Anarchiste*, *Le Revue Libertaire*, and *L'En Dehor*, was also an acquaintance of Wilde, having been introduced to him by Stephane Mallarmé some years before, and Wilde's influence is apparent by the fact that his epigrams often appeared at the start of Fénéon's articles.[158] Fénéon had initially tried to dissuade Henry from violence but then loaned him a dress to use as a disguise while placing the explosives, and he ultimately took on the role of terrorist himself after Henry was captured. By day, Fénéon worked in the Ministry of Defense, where he hid the explosives in his desk.[159]

The terrorist campaign set off a panic among the authorities—especially after a member of an anarchist group called the Hearts of Oak stabbed and killed President Carnot in retaliation for Ravachol's death.

Nearly eight hundred people were arrested on suspicion of anarchist activities, and special laws were passed forbidding any advocacy of, or even association with, anarchism. Many writers and artists sympathetic to the movement, Camille Pissarro and Paul Adam among them, left the country in some haste. Thirty were charged with subversive conspiracy, and twenty-five went to trial. This was too much for French justice to bear, however, and even Fénéon—who had been caught with explosives and was clearly guilty—was acquitted at trial.[160]

Ravachol and Vaillant, meanwhile, enjoyed a posthumous vindication, or even canonization. The anarchist Charles Maurin painted Ravachol as a kind of saint, a Christ-figure awaiting crucifixion.[161] The symbolist Paul Adam likewise praised him as "a saint" and "violent Christ."[162] Groups made pilgrimages to Vaillant's grave where, David Sweetman tells us, "poets read out their verses and . . . the wicker basket that was said to have contained his severed head was displayed like a medieval relic, in which the faithful dipped their handkerchiefs hoping to stain them with his saintly blood."[163]

The violence of the state, like that of the anarchists, was symbolic in its aims and ironic in its effect. When anarchists took to terrorism, a philosophy of universal freedom became identified with indiscriminate destruction; and when the state executed those responsible, it converted murderers into martyrs.

Aesthetic Terrorism

The ties between this set of terrorists, Ravachol to Fénéon, and the artistic avant-garde is important, and they likely informed public interpretations of their actions. It was not uncommon for an attentat to be described, even justified, in aesthetic terms—a beautiful act, a grand gesture, a work of art. Zola referred to the "eternal dark poetry" of terrorism. Mallarmé wrote of the "decorative explosion" created by dynamite.[164] Oscar Wilde wrote in "The Soul of Man under Socialism," "The very violence of a revolution may make the public grand and splendid for a moment."[165] Tailhade had said of Vaillant's attack, "What matter the victims, if the gesture is beautiful!"[166] The historian Alex Butterworth therefore detects a touch of "poetic justice" in the fact that Fénéon's bombing took out Tailhade's eye.[167]

An aesthetic element was always implied by this kind of political violence. Indeed, the "propaganda" aspect of propaganda by the deed requires that its purpose be in part communicative. It was never simply a means of eliminating undesirable people but also of demonstrating their vulnerability, of illustrating by example the possibility of striking against an oppressive system. Kropotkin, for one, argued explicitly that the intended effect was mainly psychological: "Above all, it awakens the spirit of revolt; it breeds daring. . . . [S]oon it becomes apparent that the established order does not have the strength often supposed. . . . The people observe that the monster is not so terrible as they thought."[168] In that sense the violence was always "symbolic"—the word Vaillant's attorney used to describe his attack.[169] The symbolism was more important than the violence itself.

From prison, Berkman said as much. "As far as my purpose and aims were concerned," he wrote, "it mattered very little whether my shots were fatal or not; indeed, viewed from the true anarchistic standpoint, it did not make the slightest difference what the outcome, the physical results of my attempt were. . . . It was my aim, first and last, to express, by my deed, my sentiment toward the existing system of legal oppression and industrial despotism; to attack the institution of wage-slavery in the person of one of its most prominent representatives, to give it a blow—rather morally than physically—this was the real purpose and significance of my act."[170]

The primacy of the idea over the effect led some anarchists to choose violent symbolism over violent action. In 1881 anarchists bombed a statue of Adolphe Thiers, in symbolic retribution for his role in the bloody defeat of the Paris Commune. (The statue was not damaged by the explosion, and the government declined to prosecute the culprits.)[171] Decades later, in 1968, American radicals likewise bombed a statue of a policeman, erected in remembrance of those officers killed in the Haymarket bombing.[172]

Of course, some militants find this privileging of symbolic over strategic action utterly ridiculous. It seems to value personal expression over political effect, symbols over substance, image over actuality, aesthetic choice over military necessity. It seems shallow, a trivialization of politics. And so Johann Most privately joked that Berkman had used a toy pistol in his attack on Frick.[173] Ironically, most of a century later, a young punk rocker *did* use a toy pistol in a mock attack on the Queen.[174] As with Barlas's assault against Parliament, the *idea* of violence, not the violence itself, was the important feature. The point was not to injure in a physical sense but to show contempt and, perhaps, by its very triviality, by its satirical form and playful tone, to undercut the reverence for authority, to render ridiculous the object of a ridiculous attack, to simultaneously demonstrate the vulnerability of important personages and mock their exaggerated concerns for security. Perhaps, in other words, by substituting the symbols of violence for violence itself, the terrorists were attacking the idea of authority rather than simply the individual who exercised it. By its mercy as well as its violence, such a gesture may remind us that our rulers are, after all, only human.

The Urge to Destroy

The interplay—dialectical, paradoxical, or symbolic—between creation and destruction, between terrorism and utopia, between violence and aesthetics, seems a permanent and at times defining feature of anarchism as a philosophy. In Alan Moore's Thatcher-era graphic novel *V for Vendetta*, the anarchist V, an aesthete and terrorist, tells his young protégé, "Anarchy wears two faces, both *creator* and *destroyer*. Thus destroyers topple empires; make a canvas of clean rubble where creators can then build a better world."[175]

The usual formulation of this duality appears in the slogan "The urge to destroy is a creative urge," a paraphrase of this passage from Bakunin: "Let us put our trust in the eternal spirit which destroys and annihilates only because it is the unsearchable and eternally creative source of all life. The passion for destruction is also a creative passion!"[176]

Decades later, Alexander Berkman likewise wrote:

> We mean both: To destroy *and* to build. For, socially speaking, Destruction is the beginning of Construction. Superficial minds speak sneeringly of destruction. O, it is easy to destroy—they say—but to build, to build, that's the important work.
>
> It's nonsense. No structure, social or otherwise, can endure if built on a foundation of lies. Before the garden can bloom, the weeds must be uprooted. Nothing is therefore more important than to destroy. Nothing more necessary and difficult. . . . To destroy the Old and the False is the most vital work. We emphasize it: to blast the bulwarks

of slavery and oppression is of primal necessity. It is the beginning of really lasting construction.[177]

Wilde took this urge to destroy and transmuted it into the realm of ideas. In "The Critic as Artist," he wrote, "What has been done up to now has been chiefly the clearing of the way. It is always more difficult to destroy [than] it is to create, and when what one has to destroy is vulgarity and stupidity, the task of destruction needs not merely courage but contempt. Yet it seems to me to have been, in a measure, done. We have got rid of what was bad. We have now to make what is beautiful."[178] In this sense, criticism and creation are united. Wilde takes his destructive impulses and, rather than satisfy this side of his personality with the explosions of dynamite, does so instead with the subtle subversion of irony and the devastating blast of paradox.[179]

John Barlas wrote a short essay on Wilde, which, as it draws to a close, compares his weapons to those of the terrorists and assassins: "He does not use dynamite, but the dagger—a dagger whose hilt is crusted with flaming jewels, and whose point drips with the poison of the Borgias. That dagger is the paradox. No weapon could be more terrible. He has stabbed all our proverbs, and our proverbs rule us more than our kings."[180]

Chapter 2

The Basis for a New Civilization

Art and Labor, Artists and Workers, Aestheticism and Socialism

Useless Beauty

Young Ambition

At Oxford, a fellow undergraduate asked Oscar Wilde, "What you are going to do with your life? . . . What is your real ambition in life?" Wilde replied, "God knows. . . . I won't be a dried-up Oxford don, anyhow. I'll be a poet, a writer, a dramatist. Somehow or other I'll be famous, and if not famous, I'll be notorious."[1]

A few years later, he was asked much the same thing by the *Omaha Weekly Herald*: "You have plans for future work, I presume?" Wilde replied, "For my life, do you mean? . . . Well, I'm a very ambitious young man. I want to do everything in the world. I cannot conceive of anything that I do not want to do. I want to write a great deal more poetry. I want to study painting more than I've been able to. I want to write a great many more plays, and I want to make this artistic movement the basis for a new civilization."[2]

Fresh from school, with only a slim volume of poetry and a bad play to his credit, yet determined to become "if not famous . . . notorious," Oscar Wilde made a name for himself by saying startling, outrageous, and occasionally absurd things about art, its social significance, and its place in life. In his lecture, "The English Renaissance of Art," he outlined his philosophy:

> For the good we get from art is not what we learn from it; it is what we become through it. Its real influence will be in giving the mind that enthusiasm which is the secret of Hellenism, accustoming it to demand from art all that art can do in rearranging the facts of

common life for us—whether it be by giving the most spiritual interpretation of one's own moments of highest passion or the most sensuous expression of those thoughts that are the farthest removed from
sense; in accustoming it to love the things of the imagination for their
own sake, and to desire beauty and grace in all things.[3]

This was the philosophy of aestheticism, most famously summed up in the
slogan "art for art's sake."[4] These ideas were elaborated, or perhaps encoded,
in a series of axioms comprising the preface to Wilde's novel, *The Picture of
Dorian Gray*:

> Those who find ugly meanings in beautiful things are corrupt without
> being charming. This is a fault.
> Those who find beautiful meanings in beautiful things are the
> cultivated. For these there is hope.
> They are the elect to whom beautiful things mean only beauty. . . .
> We can forgive a man for making a useful thing as long as he
> does not admire it. The only excuse for making a useless thing is that
> one admires it intensely.
> All art is quite useless.[5]

The Moral Economy

Wilde's views on art, strange as they were striking, both enticed and scandalized Victorian society. They elicited gossip in the salons, ridicule in
Punch, and denunciations from the pulpit.[6] Even his style of dress was, in its
way, a protest against the values of the age. During his American tour, his
knee breeches and pointed shoes were much commented upon in the press,
revealing deep anxieties over gender, national identity, bourgeois notions
of equality, personal restraint and serious-mindedness, and the indus-
triousness suited to a capitalist economy. "Display of any kind is foreign
to our modern notion of the perfectly well-bred man," the *Nation* commented reproachfully, "but display in women we expect and like. Democracy is against the aristocratic beau. Time, in the modern community, has
commercial value."[7] The dandy as a figure and Wilde as an individual were

each judged against the serious, hardworking, modern American man and stood rebuked as archaic, elitist, ostentatious, frivolous, impudent, imprudent, foreign, and, perhaps above all, effeminate. What is remarkable is the peculiarly moral tone of the journalists' disapproval, driven it seems by the identification of personal virtue with economic production, and of capitalism with democracy. There is a whole worldview contained in this disdain for dress sense, to which Wilde by his very appearance represented a challenge.[8]

Victorian society was likewise dominated—perhaps, defined—by values of propriety, respectability, practicality, industry, and self-restraint. In short, the culture was ruled by what sociologist Max Weber would later term the Protestant Ethic. As Weber explained, elements of Protestant, especially Calvinist, theology encouraged habits of hard work, sobriety, discipline, and thrift and at the same time invested material success with a sense of moral import.[9] It thus prescribed a fully ordered and planned life, encouraging discipline and restraint as virtues and treating all spontaneous joy as suspect, if not actually sinful.

No less a figure than John Wesley had advised, "Avoid all manner of passions," and Sunday school teachers were instructed to "tame the ferocity of their [charges'] unsubdued passions—to repress the excessive rudeness of their manners—to chasten the disgusting and demoralising obscenity of their language—to subdue the stubborn rebellion of their wills—to render them honest, obedient, courteous, industrious, submissive, and orderly."[10] The effect was the cultivation of those habits that, in workers, make labor profitable for their masters. Indeed, work was treated as a duty—or a *pure act of virtue*," as Andrew Ure put it in his 1835 treatise *The Philosophy of Manufactures,* which included a chapter on the "Moral Economy of the Factory System."[11]

Yet this moral economy made no additional demands of the well-off, except that they continue to show God's favor through further prosperity.[12] As Weber recounted in *The Protestant Ethic and the Spirit of Capitalism,*

> A specifically bourgeois economic ethic had grown up. With the consciousness of standing in the fullness of God's grace and being visibly blessed by Him, the bourgeois business man, as long as he remained within the bounds of formal correctness, as long as his moral conduct

was spotless and the use to which he put his wealth was not objectionable, could follow his pecuniary interests as he would and feel that he was fulfilling a duty in doing so. The power of religious asceticism provided him in addition with sober, conscientious, and unusually industrious workmen, who clung to their work as to a life purpose willed by God.

Finally, it gave him the comforting assurance that the unequal distribution of the goods of this world was a special dispensation of Divine Providence.[13]

A hymn dated 1848 intones,

> The rich man in his castle,
>   The poor man at his gate,
> God made them high and lowly,
>   And order'd their estate.[14]

This theology offered justifications for the rule of the wealthy, reassurances to ease the conscience of the middle class, demands for order with which to control the workers, and rigid strictures to condemn the poor.[15] That hard work, frugality, and self-restraint were the seeds of all success was taken as obvious. Poverty, then, said nothing of the injustice of society or the greed of the capitalists; it merely revealed the moral failings of the lower orders. By this view, the poor suffered not from bad luck, bad prospects, or a bad economy—but from their own bad character. The solution lay in a combination of discipline and austerity, to be cultivated by the individual and imposed by society. If the Sunday sermon failed to instill it, the penitentiary would take up the task.[16]

Wasted Days

Wilde rejected this entire way of seeing things and did what he could to subvert it. He struck at capitalism not only on the basis of economics but also at the level of values. He wrote in "The Soul of Man under Socialism": "The virtues of the poor may be readily admitted, and are much to be regretted." He specifies: "For a town or country labourer to practice thrift would be absolutely immoral. Man should not be ready to show that he can live like a badly fed animal." Instead, Wilde declared, "A poor man who is ungrateful, unthrifty, discontented, and rebellious, is probably a real personality, and has much in him. As for the virtuous poor, one can pity them, of course, but one cannot possibly admire them."[17] Thus Wilde praised not thrift but indulgence, not industry but pleasure, not humility but pride, not self-restraint but self-assertion, not deference but dignity.

Richard Le Gallienne recalled an incident in which he and Wilde were out for a walk, and a beggar approached. "He had, he said, no work to do and no bread to eat." Wilde cried out, "Work! . . . Why should you want work? And bread! Why should you eat bread?" He put his hand on the man's shoulder, and confided, "Now, if you had come to me and said that you had work to do, but you couldn't dream of working, and that you had bread to eat, but couldn't think of eating bread—I would have given you half-a-crown. . . . As it is, I give you two shillings."[18]

Wilde celebrated leisure, excess, earthly joy, physical pleasure, and beauty—beauty most of all. He found in beauty a whole other system of values, outside of considerations of morality or utility, independent of the demands of social discipline or the capitalist marketplace. For instance, his poem "Wasted Days," written in reply to a painting by his acquaintance Violet Troubridge, offers a subversive revaluation of conventional wisdom.

Troubridge's painting features two panels. The first shows a young boy sitting cold and hungry on the stoop of a house, excluded from the feast inside. This image is contrasted with the same boy lounging by the field while others bring in the harvest. In case the viewer might miss the moral, the artist has included an inscription: "He must hunger in frost that will not work in heate."[19]

Wilde responds first by praising the boy's physical beauty—"A fair slim boy not made for this world's pain, With hair of gold thick clustering round his ears"—and then worries that his youth and his beauty are wasted:

Pale cheeks whereon no kiss hath left its stain,
Red under-lip drawn in for fear of Love, . . .
Alas! alas! if all should be in vain.

In this lament the boy is likened rather than contrasted with the "reapers, all a-row," who spend their day "In heat and labour toiling wearily, To no sweet sound of laughter or of lute." In each case, the lovely summer day is spoiled by lack of joy.

Wilde ends with a traditional poetic admonishment (purposely echoing Robert Herrick) that time is short, and we must grasp our pleasures where we find them:

> The sun is shooting wide its crimson rays,
> Still the boy dreams: nor knows that night is nigh,
> And in the night-time no man gathers fruit.[20]

Night will come for the workers and the dreamer alike. Better then to seize the day. And if winter is harsh, all the more reason that summer should be filled with laughter and song and love and kisses.

The Price of Everything

"Work," Wilde once quipped, "is the curse of the drinking classes."[21] Reversing the usual formulation, he made clear his disdain for the condescending, sermonizing attitude well-meaning people often took toward the poor.[22] Wilde could see at once what the moralists could not, that the problem of poverty lay not with the pleasures of the poor but with their misery.[23] And likewise he could grasp what economists could not, that the problem of work was not that there was too little of it to go around but that the need to earn a living takes up too much of each of our lives.

He therefore decried the capitalist-class philistines and what passed for their virtues—"their heavy inaccessibility to ideas, their dull respectability, their tedious orthodoxy, their worship of vulgar success, their entire preoccupation with the gross materialistic side of life, and their ridiculous estimate of themselves and their importance."[24] As Lord Henry Wotton observed in *Dorian Gray*, "When they make up their ledger, they balance stupidity by wealth, and vice by hypocrisy."[25]

Wilde complained that such people "lived without making life worth living for—without any cultivation of the sense of pleasure, the beautiful. To me the life of the businessman who eats his breakfast early in the morning, catches a train for the city, stays there in the dingy, dusty atmosphere of the commercial world, and goes back to his house in the evening, and after supper to sleep, is worse than the life of the galley slave—his chains are golden instead of iron."[26] Wilde saw in the ascetic, utilitarian, anti-cultural philistinism of his day not only an unnerving deadness of spirit but also an effort to stifle precisely what was best in humanity, to suppress all the joy of life. "[If] our days are barren without industry," he warned, "industry without art is barbarism."[27]

It was just this barbarism that reduced all value to the economically productive and socially useful. The tendency is to quantify always, to weigh everything on a single scale and judge according to a unifying standard. Where money provides that standard, it becomes easy to assume that nothing matters unless it can be bought and sold.[28] As Wilde complained, "Nowadays people know the price of everything, and the value of nothing."[29]

Wilde then reversed the utilitarian presumption and praised the superfluous: "A work of art is useless as a flower is useless. A flower blossoms for its own joy. We gain a moment of joy by looking at it. That is all that is to be said about our relations to flowers. Of course a man may sell the flower, and so make it useful to him, but this has nothing to do with the flower. It is not part of its essence. It is accidental. It is a misuse."[30] A flower—the symbol here of beauty—has value both in and for itself. There is "a moment of joy" in our appreciation. But beauty is to some extent independent even of our concern. It follows its own course, it "blossoms for its own joy." And so it is a mistake to try to reduce the value of beauty to that of mere utility or to commodify it and measure it by the price that it might fetch. Such exercises seek to judge the beautiful object according to "accidental" factors and not by its "essence." This is, in Wilde's terms, not only a mistake but a "misuse." Hence, the *Cincinnati Enquirer* praised Wilde as "a young apostle of beauty against a decaying age of trade and swap."[31]

Pursuing "art for art's sake" means that art is an end in itself. It is not *for* anything. There's no greater purpose that it must serve. And human beings, Wilde says, must become like art, must treat themselves as objects of beauty—that is, as ends (an almost Kantian argument, derived from separate premises). Socially this view does tend to support the extravagance of obsolete aristocrats, but it also supports the claims of dignity of those society throws away—the unemployed, the elderly, the criminal, the insane. What it clearly does *not* support—in fact, what it explicitly repudiates—is the bourgeois presumption that a person adds to his worth simply by adding to his bank account.

Every Worker an Artist

The Poets and the People

Given Wilde's refusal to subordinate art to any definite purpose, one might be surprised to find him writing in "The Poets and the People" as "One of the Latter" to remind the former of their social responsibilities.

"Who," Wilde demands, "in the midst of all our poverty and distress, that threatens to become intensified, will step into the breach and rouse us to the almost super-human effort that is necessary to alter the existing state of things?" He states frankly that "the hour has come when the poets should exercise their influence for good, and set fairer ideals before all than the mere love of wealth," and he faults the leading lyricists for indulging in "melancholy pessimism," "unintelligible jargon," and "literary hocus-pocus," while "a nation . . . is heroically struggling against the injustice of centuries and panting for national freedom," a quarter of the population is "struggling against poverty," and "we are in danger of having all that is idealistic and beautiful crushed out of us by the steam engine and the manipulations of the stock exchanges."[32]

It must be said that this short polemic—more like a sermon—does not sound very much like Wilde at all. In place of the cool air of practiced sophistication and the elegiac praise of beauty, we find a fiery urgency and the repeated, insistent invocation of duty. It is likely significant that the piece was published anonymously, for "man is least himself when he talks in his own person. Give him a mask, and he will tell you the truth."[33]

"The Poets and the People" appeared in the *Pall Mall Gazette* in February 1887. Two years later, the question Wilde ends with—"where is the poet who is the one man needful to rouse the nation to a sense of duty and inspire the people with hope?"—had been answered, and the answer was not what Wilde might have expected, though perhaps it was more than he had dared to hope.[34] It was not "one man" but many, and the job of "inspir[ing] the people with hope" was largely taken up by the people themselves. In February 1889 Wilde reviewed *Chants of Labour: A Song-Book of the People*. He begins his review by paraphrasing the Christian socialist Stopford

Brooke on the promise of socialism for art, "that Socialism and the Socialist spirit would give our poets nobler and loftier themes for song, would widen their sympathies and enlarge the horizon of their vision, and would touch with the fire and fervour of a new faith lips that had else been silent, hearts that but for this fresh gospel had been cold."[35]

He goes on to note the striking diversity of the contributors to the volume at hand and the "curious variety of their several occupations." In addition to well-known figures like Edward Carpenter, William Morris, and Walter Crane, one also finds a "science lecturer," "a draper and a porter," "two late Eton masters, and then two bootmakers," "an ex-Lord Mayor of Dublin, a bookbinder, a photographer, a steelworker and an authoress," "a journalist, a draughtsman, and music teacher," "a Civil servant, a machine-fitter, a medical student, a cabinet-maker and a minister of the Church of Scotland." The songs themselves are just as varied: "Some of them, to quote from the editor's preface, are 'purely revolutionary; others are Christian in tone; there are some that might be called merely material in their tendency, while many are of a highly ideal and visionary character.'" All of this Wilde finds "very promising." He feels that the ecumenical reach of such a collection, across divisions of class and tendency, is itself a kind of political victory: "Clearly, it is no ordinary movement that can bring in close brotherhood men of such dissimilar pursuits." And it is the very broadness of the socialist movement that supplies at once its strength and its appeal. "She welcomes many and multiform natures. She rejects none, and has room for all."[36] This plurality finds its way into both the form and the production of its music. Wilde notes approvingly the socialist movement's "confidence in the art instincts of the people," and he quotes a few lines to illustrate the point:

> They say that the people are brutal
> > That their instincts for beauty are dead
> Were it so, shame on those who condemn them
> > To the desperate struggle for bread.
> But they lie in their throats when they say it,
> > For the people are tender at heart,
> And a well-spring of beauty lies hidden
> > Beneath their life's fever and smart.[37]

It is Wilde's assessment, then, that "socialism starts well-equipped. . . . If she fails it will not be for lack of expression. If she succeeds, her triumph will not be a triumph of mere brute force. . . . [S]hould the Revolution ever break out in England we shall have no inarticulate roar, but rather pleasant glees and graceful part-songs." He hopes that this gentleness and beauty might color the new society as well as the present movement, as "it is for the building up of an eternal city that the Socialists of our day are making music."[38]

Ruskin's Road

Wilde's interest in the condition of the working class likely originated at Oxford, under the tutelage of John Ruskin, the moralist, art critic, hater of industrialism, advocate for economic justice, and enthusiast for Gothic architecture.[39] The product of a strict Christian upbringing, Ruskin considered himself both a Tory and a communist.[40] Though devoted to art's specifically moral mission, he became a defender of the Pre-Raphaelite Brotherhood and an inspiration to the Aesthetic movement.[41]

Beauty, in Ruskin's analysis, can only result from specific social conditions. It must be produced by skilled workers who are treated not as mere instruments for the ends of others but as creators in their own right and participants in the design of the works they produce.[42] Likewise, it is the duty of the idealists and visionaries to take an active, practical hand in the work of improving the world, not only to guide and instruct but also to participate directly in the construction and completion of the realized product. The idea was to ease the hierarchical division of labor, under which, Ruskin complained, "it is not, truly speaking, the labour that is divided; but the men;—Divided into mere segments of men—broken into small fragments and crumbs of life."[43] The industrial system of production requires

> one man to be always thinking, and another to be always working . . .
> whereas the worker ought often to be thinking, and the thinker often
> to be working, and both should be gentlemen in the best sense. As it
> is, we make both ungentle, the one envying, the other despising, his
> brother; and the mass of society is made up of morbid thinkers and

miserable workers. Now it is only by labour that thought can be made healthy, and only by thought that labour can be made happy, and the two cannot be separated with impunity. It would be well if all of us were good handicraftsmen in some kind, and the dishonour of manual labour done away with altogether.[44]

And so it happened (as Wilde told the story) that at one of Ruskin's Oxford lectures "he spoke to us not on art this time but on life. . . . He thought, he said, that we should be working at something that would do good to other people, at something by which we might show that in all labour there is something noble." Soon after, Ruskin "went out round Oxford and found two villages, Upper and Lower Hinksey, and between them there lay a great swamp, so that the villagers could not pass from one to the other without many miles of a round." Ruskin recruited a group of undergraduates, Wilde among them, to gather in the mornings and build a flower-lined lane to connect the towns.[45] Calling themselves the "diggers"—coincidentally, perhaps, a name they shared with a sect of proto-anarchist Christian utopians who reclaimed the commons on St. George's Hill during the English Civil War—the young men went out every morning, "day after day, and learned how to lay levels and to break stones, and to wheel barrows along a plank."[46] Together they "worked away for two months at our road." Only, at last, "like a bad lecture it ended abruptly—in the middle of a swamp." The school term over, Ruskin left for Venice, and the project was abandoned. But the experience planted in Wilde the idea "that if there was enough spirit amongst the young men to go out to such work as road-making for the sake of a noble ideal of life," then it might also be possible to "create an artistic movement that might change . . . the face of England."[47]

William Morris and the Pleasure of Life

As much as he admired Ruskin, ultimately Wilde's views on handicraft, labor, workers, and socialism were shaped more by his acquaintance with another of Ruskin's disciples, William Morris.[48] Wilde's early lectures contain much that is straight Morris. His focus on the decorative arts and the beauty of everyday objects, his disdain for the gaudy and the ill-made, his insistence that art become popular and that all classes of society be educated in practical craftwork, the desire to see art and labor joined, and his faith in the artisan as a rejuvenating element of society—all of these he learned from Morris.[49]

Morris was a Marxist of a peculiarly artistic, humane, and libertarian variety—both a romantic and a revolutionary, a craftsman and a communist, a man celebrated for his individual genius and his public spirit.[50] Morris was a kind of latter-day Renaissance man, a poet, a political visionary, a designer and manufacturer, a skilled artisan, and a spokesman for both the Arts and Crafts movement and the Socialist League. Wilde called him "a master of all exquisite design and of all spiritual vision" and credited him with "giv[ing] to our individualized romantic movement the social idea and the social factor also."[51]

Morris's vision of socialism was "a condition of society in which there should be neither rich nor poor, neither master nor master's man, neither idle nor overworked, neither brain-sick brain workers, nor heart-sick hand workers." Instead, he foretold, "all men would be living in equality of condition, and would manage their affairs unwastefully, and with the full consciousness that harm to one would mean harm to all—the realization at last of the meaning of the word COMMONWEALTH."[52]

Wilde and Morris met in 1881.[53] Morris was initially less than impressed with the younger poet, writing in a letter that though Wilde was "certainly clever" he remained nevertheless "an ass."[54] Despite the inauspicious start, the two men soon became friends. Their ideas grew enough alike that ten years later, in 1891, Morris's essay "The Socialist Ideal" appeared together in a pamphlet with Wilde's "Soul of Man under Socialism."[55] In his essay, Wilde protested the effect of coercion on the worker, his labor, and the eventual product: "An individual who has to make things for the use of others, and with reference to their wants and their wishes, does not work with interest and consequently cannot put into his work what is best in him."[56] In the same pamphlet, Morris argued that "instead of looking upon art as a luxury incidental to a certain privileged position, the Socialist claims art as a necessity of human life which society has no right to withhold from any one of its citizens." Therefore, once socialism is established, "people shall have every opportunity of taking to the work which each is best fitted for; not only that there may be the least possible waste of his effort but also that

that effort may be experienced pleasurably. For . . . the pleasurable exercise of our energies is at once the source of all art and the cause of all happiness; that is to say, it is the end of life."[57]

What is important and valuable, for Wilde as for Morris, is the *creative* aspect of work, not the strictly *productive* element or the constitutive effect on the moral character of the individual worker. Both men valued labor in the service of life, not toil for toil's sake. On this point, the socialists were at odds with both the moralists and the sentimentalists. As Wilde wrote in "The Soul of Man under Socialism," "A great deal of nonsense is being written and talked nowadays about the dignity of manual labour. There is nothing necessarily dignified about manual labour at all, and most of it is absolutely degrading. It is morally and mentally injurious to man to do anything in which he does not find pleasure, and many forms of labour are quite pleasureless activities, and should be regarded as such."[58] By way of example he pointed to a common occupation among the very poor, including sometimes children: that of waiting at street corners with a broom in hand and, as respectable people approached to cross, with their polished shoes and their long skirts, walking ahead of them in the lanes and brushing out of their path the collected dirt, trash, and horse manure, in hopes that they might spare a few pennies in gratitude.[59] Wilde comments, sensibly: "To sweep a slushy crossing for eight hours on a day when the east wind is blowing is a disgusting occupation. To sweep it with mental, moral, or physical dignity seems to me impossible. To sweep it with joy would be appalling. Man is made for something better than disturbing dirt."[60]

Morris likewise held that "no work which cannot be done without pleasure in the doing is worth doing."[61] As he explained elsewhere, "If a man has work to do which he despises, which does not satisfy his natural and rightful desire for pleasure, the greater part of his life must pass unhappily and without self-respect." Such joyless drudgery, economically exploitative and morally degrading, can be contrasted with what Morris termed "real art," defined as "the expression by man of his pleasure in labour. I do not believe he can be happy in his labour without expressing that happiness; and especially is this so when he is at work at anything in which he especially excels."[62] Morris believed that this melding of art and labor, and the aestheticization of daily life, was neither a utopian dream nor a dilettante's trifle but an urgent social necessity, with radical implications: "The beginning of Social Revolution must be the foundation of the rebuilding of the Art of the People, that is to say: of the Pleasure of Life."[63]

The Best Classes of Society

In 1882, when asked about the effect of the Aesthetic movement, Wilde replied: "It has had the widest influence among the best classes of society." He then clarified: "The real strength of our movement lies in the great spread of beautiful designs among the handicraftsmen of the various cities."[64] Elsewhere he elaborated, arguing that the pursuit of beauty "must begin not in the scholar's study—not even in the studio of the great artist, but with the handicraftsmen always. And by handicraftsman I mean a man who works with his hands; and not with his hands merely, but with his head and his heart."[65]

The sense of engagement in skilled labor, the care in creating a beautiful object, calls on the artisan to bring his sense of individuality into the work process—in contrast to mass production and industrialization, which stifles the individual spirit, produces shoddy goods, and "makes men themselves machines also. Whereas we wish them to be artists, that is to say men."[66]

This concern with the role and status of the worker—in ontological as well as social terms: not merely artisan or proletarian, but man or machine, author or instrument, ends or means—led Wilde to declare aestheticism "the most democratic impulse in the history of the world." He explained: "The people, the artisan class, have toiled long enough in unloved labor and amid unlovely, hard, repulsive surroundings. A man's work should be a joy to him. Make him an artist, make him a designer, and you render it so. What a man designs he delights in bringing to completion." Thus, Wilde concludes, "you see the political-economic importance of aestheticism."[67]

Travels in America: Democracy Underground

Wilde spent an entire year crossing the North American continent by train, lecturing, giving interviews, and visiting notable political and cultural figures from Walt Whitman to Oliver Wendell Holmes—as well as meeting ordinary working people. He went to lecture on art and expound the principles of aestheticism—and he received unanticipated lessons in social equality.[68] "I met a railroad-repairer," he recalled, "a man working out on the line at a hard, laborious task. It was his daily business. He talked with me, wanted to know what we [aesthetes] are trying to do. Why, that man quoted Pope to me, analyzed his method, discussed my positions with me, understood me, and where he doubted gave his reasons in homely phrases, but unmistakably and clearly. He took an interest in the best of life; was keen, kindly, receptive and pugnacious in need, withal—altogether a charming fellow."[69]

Later, in Leadville, Colorado, Wilde lectured miners on ethics in art and read passages from the silversmith Benvenuto Cellini.[70] Afterward, the mayor and the mine superintendent took Wilde "to descend a mine in a rickety bucket in which it is impossible to be graceful." Then, at "the heart of the mountain," he was invited to dine with the workers, "the first course being whisky, the second whisky, and the third whisky."[71] Wilde was later to comment, "I found these miners very charming and not at all rough."[72] Instead, he said, "They were great, strong, well-formed men, of graceful attitude and free motion. Poems every one of them. A complete democracy under ground."[73]

Wilde was greatly encouraged by such encounters: "Here I learn that a man is fairly representative of a myriad," he said. "It is to the mechanics and workers of your country that I look for the triumph that must come."[74]

Fine China: Nothing That Is Not Beautiful

It undoubtedly surprised Wilde's audiences that among those to whom he looked for models to emulate were the members of a broadly despised community—the Chinese immigrants.

"Of course I have no desire to enter into a political discussion," he began coyly. "[However], in my opinion, the Chinese have a decided artistic value, which I think Congress should consider in discussing the Chinese question." (The legislature was in the midst of debating what would become the Chinese Exclusion Act, which subsequently barred immigration from the country and triggered a series of pogroms in the western states.)[75] "I learned many things from the Chinese," Wilde said.[76]

This opinion marked an explicit reversal. Just days before, when approaching San Francisco, he had declared, "Chinese art . . . possesses no elements of beauty; the horrible and grotesque appearing to be standards of perfection."[77] Then, lecturing in the city, he advised his audience, "Don't borrow any Chinese art, for you have no need of it any more than you have need of Chinese labor"—a position in line with that of the Workingman's Party of California, which demanded shorter hours, honest government, the abolition of national banks, and the expulsion of Chinese immigrants.[78]

But Wilde's prejudice did not survive contact with its object. The very next day he visited Chinatown, its stores, restaurants, theaters, and opium dens. He said afterward that he "delighted in the Chinese quarters. They fascinated me. I wish these people had a quarter in London. I should take pleasure in visiting it often."[79] He recalled, "I enjoyed going down into the Chinese quarter and sitting on a pretty latticed balcony and drinking my tea out of a cup so dainty and delicate that a lady would handle it with care. Yet this was not an expensive place for wealthy people to go to. It was for the common people. The laborers on the railroad came here, with pick and shovel, and drank their refreshing beverage out of a pretty cup of the two beautiful colors blue and white"[80]—"A little cup," he added later, "as delicate in texture as the petal of a flower."[81] And then, "When the Chinese bill was presented it was made out on rice paper, the account being done in Indian ink as fantastically as if an artist had been etching little birds on a fan."[82]

By the time he returned to England, Wilde was willing to declare, "China Town, peopled by Chinese labourers, is the most artistic town I have ever come across. The people—strange, melancholy Orientals, whom many people would call common, and they are certainly very poor—have determined that they will have nothing about them that is not beautiful."[83] Wilde urged that we follow their example: "Beautiful things for everyday use are what we want. . . . Beauty should be as free as the air and water, and then it cannot fail to leave its impression on all minds."[84]

Everyday Beauty

And so Wilde instructed his audiences, "Have nothing in your house that is not useful or beautiful"—an abbreviation of Morris's "golden rule": "Have nothing in your houses that you do not know to be useful, or believe to be beautiful."[85]

A beginning may be made by applying artistic principles to everyday objects. Wilde advised, "It is all very well to devote time to little flower vases; they do for ladies' drawing-rooms, but that is not touching the people. It is the people we want to touch, and this can only be done by beginning with the simple things. The least things, every household article should be made beautiful, and I had far rather that, instead of designs for flower vases, a good design should be produced for a simple jug and basin, instead of the coarse pottery, inartistic in color and outline, which is now so common."[86] The point was to make an art of necessities rather than reserve it for luxuries. "The moment art becomes a luxury it loses," Wilde warned. "Luxury gives us the gaudy, the ugly, the transient."[87]

However, Wilde also clarified that the motive force of aestheticism was not possessive but creative, and therefore that its truest disciples were to be found among the working, not the owning, classes. "We do not want the rich to possess more beautiful things, but the poor to create more beautiful things," he said, concluding, "for every man is poor who cannot create."[88]

He told the *Recorder-Union*, "I hope the masses will come to be the creators of art . . . that art will soon cease to be simply the accomplishment and luxury of the rich. . . . All that is artistic must begin in handicraft. . . . I would dignify labor by stripping it of its degradation and by developing all that is beautiful in the laborer's surroundings and opening his eyes to it."[89] The paper responded by declaring the aesthete "the poor man's friend."[90]

The social message appealed to Wilde's audience as well. People attended Wilde's lectures, sometimes to learn, sometimes to mock, sometimes out of pure curiosity, but in any case expecting, as one spectator put it, to hear art described "as a thing quite apart" from the commonplaces of daily life, a world "wherein the true aesthetic alone can languish in a cultivated scorn of [the] real workers of the world." Instead, to "our delight," Wilde had conveyed the idea "that beauty was inwrought with homely, honest, workaday life, that labour can be elevated and the labourer thereby raised from ignorance and degradation into the true beauty of history."[91]

Fairy Tale Economics

A Common Heritage

Though present in his lectures on art, Oscar Wilde's concern for the lower classes appears most clearly in his fairy tales. Despite its childish association, the form of the fairy tale was, in one sense, perfectly suited to Wilde's socialistic message, the genre itself marking the story as a piece of community property that each new telling works and renews in the spirit of stewardship.[92] Thomas Wright characterizes Wilde's concept of "literacy tradition" as constituting "a sort of communism of ideas and motifs."[93] Such an attitude was shaped importantly by Wilde's Irish background.

Oscar's father, Sir William Wilde, was a noted physician and a folklorist whose collections of traditional Irish tales—the "poetry of the people," as he called them—remain authoritative resources for scholars today.[94] Sir William was known in the community for his practice of treating the indigent, accepting a story as his fee. These stories eventually appeared in his published collections.[95] The political significance of this exchange is multiple: It allowed the preservation of a part of the culture in danger of dying out under the pressures of colonial modernity.[96] It extended first-rate medical care to the very poor without the sting of charity. And it treated the tale as a thing of value, the telling as a kind of labor, and the storyteller as both a worker and an artist.[97] Growing up in a household where a world-class physician would treat penniless peasants and gladly accept a story as his reward—surely this influenced Oscar Wilde's views on the relative importance of art and money.

Giants and Gardens

The simplest of Wilde's fairy tales, in terms of plot, though the most complex in terms of allegory, is "The Selfish Giant." The story begins with children playing in a giant's garden. When the giant returns home, he drives them out and puts up a wall: "'My own garden is my own garden,' said the Giant; 'anyone can understand that, and I will allow nobody to play in it but myself.'

So he built a high wall all round it, and put up a notice-board. 'TRESPASSERS
WILL BE PROSECUTED.'"[98] Winter then descends on the garden, with snow
and frost and cold wind. "[And] spring never came, nor the summer."[99] No
flowers bloomed, no birds sang. The spell is only broken when the children
sneak in again. Once they do, "the trees were so glad to have the children
back again that they had covered themselves with blossoms, and were wav-
ing their arms gently above the children's heads. The birds were flying about
and twittering with delight, and the flowers were looking up through the
green grass and laughing."[100] The giant is happy at this scene and regrets his
earlier selfishness. He knocks down the wall and announces, "It is your garden now, little children." One boy in particular the giant had a fondness for,
and he lifts him up into a tree, "and the little boy stretched out his two arms
and flung them round the Giant's neck, and kissed him."[101]

Years pass, and children continue to come and play. But the giant grows
old, and on the day that he dies he sees his special friend again, now recog-
nizable as Christ. "For on the palms of the child's hands were the prints of
two nails, and the prints of two nails were on the little feet." The giant, no
longer selfish, is rewarded in heaven: "The child smiled on the Giant, and
said to him, 'You let me play once in your garden, to-day you shall come
with me to my garden, which is Paradise.'"[102]

The religious theme is obvious, with the garden, the exclusion, and the
ultimate reconciliation through Christ. Curiously—heretically—it is not
only the children who suffer from the separation but also the garden itself.
More interesting still is the social analogy. For the giant's wall replicates in
miniature the enclosures by which the common land was claimed by the
gentry as their exclusive property and the common people were deprived
of their traditional rights to use it. Peter Linebaugh informs us, "Between
1725 and 1825 nearly four thousand enclosure acts appropriated more than
six million acres of land, about a quarter of cultivated acreage [in England],
to the politically dominant landowners."[103] Between 1800 and 1815 alone,
approximately three million acres were seized.[104] The legal battles over these
enclosures continued into the 1870s.[105]

In the background too there is the colonization of Ireland and its resultant system of rule by absentee land owners. As G. C. Campbell reported in
1869, in his book *The Irish Land*, "Rare as evictions now are, there seems to
be present in every Irishman's mind the image of the typical case: a peasant

farmer who has built his home, improved the land, begotten his children, and is then turned out on the roadside at the arbitrary will of a landlord."[106] In Wilde's telling, the land, being denied for the use of the common people, is deprived also of its natural purpose. Spring never comes; nothing blooms; it is barren and without beauty.

This political reading gains support from the recent film by Clio Barnard titled *The Selfish Giant* and purportedly inspired by Wilde's story. That film is virtually the opposite of a fairy tale. There is no giant, no Christ-child, no flora that blooms with delight at the laughter of children. Barnard's *Selfish Giant* is instead realistic and relentlessly bleak, a story of poverty and social exclusion. Instead of a giant, there is a bullying and exploitative scrap metal dealer, the archetype of all absent/domineering father figures and simply capitalism. Likewise, the children—adolescent boys who find themselves rejected by society and struggling to survive in a semi-criminal postindustrial piecework economy—never are admitted into the garden to play among the flowers and climb in the branches of the trees. The walls that keep them out prove completely unbreachable. Barnard thus treats literally the themes that Wilde engaged symbolically, and the film insists on tragic reality where the story offered redemptive fantasy.[107]

What Luxuries Cost

In another of Wilde's tales, "The Young King," an aesthete who is due to inherit the crown suffers a series of dreams in which he is shown the source of the beautiful things he loves and the symbols of his wealth and power. He sees Black slaves diving for the pearl that will adorn his scepter, some dying in the process. He sees men dig "deep pits in the ground . . . and cleft the rocks with great axes," searching for rubies to ornament his crown, while Avarice and Death quarrel over their fates.[108] And, closer to home (for the boy king and for Wilde's readers), he sees his coronation robe being woven in "a long, low attic, amidst the whir and clatter of many looms. The meagre daylight peered in through the grated windows, and showed him the gaunt figures of the weavers bending over their cases. Pale, sickly-looking children were crouched on the huge cross-beams. . . . Their faces were pinched with famine, and their thin hands shook and trembled."[109]

It is in this gloomy sweatshop that the king receives a lesson in political economy. A weaver says to him,

> In war . . . the strong make slaves of the weak, and in peace the rich make slaves of the poor. We must work to live, and they give us such meagre wages that we die. We toil for them all day long, and they heap up gold in their coffers, and our children fade away before their time, and the faces of those we love become hard and evil. We tread out the grapes, and another drinks the wine. We sow the corn, and our own board is empty. We have chains, though no eye beholds them; and we are slaves, though men call us free.[110]

Taking this message to heart, the king refuses the traditional vestiges of his office and goes instead to claim his throne dressed as a simple shepherd. There, as he "stood before the image of Christ" and "bowed his head in prayer," the golden sunlight became his robe, and his shepherd's staff blossomed with lilies—flowers notable for both aestheticist and biblical associations—and he wore for a crown a wreath of roses.[111]

"The Happy Prince"—published a few months earlier, with illustrations from the socialist Walter Crane—proceeds along much the same line, another story of a royal personage who, learning to see suffering, becomes a kind of saint. In this case the prince has been immortalized in a statue overlooking the city. He is covered in gold, with sapphire eyes and a ruby in the hilt of his sword. He recalls how, as a living prince, "I did not know what tears were, for I lived in the Palace of Sans-Souci, where sorrow is not allowed to enter. . . . Round the garden ran a very lofty wall, but I never cared to ask what lay beyond it, everything about me was so beautiful." Upon his death, however, the prince was transformed into a work of art and placed "so high that I can see all the ugliness and all the misery of my city."[112]

As with the young king, the happy prince's sympathy is stirred by a vision of a garment worker: "'Far away,' continued the statue in a low musical voice, 'far away in a little street is a poor house.'" In it there is a woman and a little boy. "Her face is thin and worn, and she has coarse red hands, all pricked by the needle, for she is a seamstress. She is embroidering passion-flowers on a satin gown for the loveliest of the Queen's maids-of-honour to wear at the next Court-ball." In the same room as she is working, her little boy lies in bed, sick with fever. He "is asking for oranges," but his mother "has nothing to give but river water, so he is crying."[113] The prince asks a little bird, a swallow that has sheltered between his feet, to take the ruby from his sword and give it to this family.

The story goes on like that. The swallow plucks out the prince's sapphire eyes and gives them to a young playwright freezing in a garret and to a little match girl who has dropped all of her matches.[114] Newly blind, the prince asks the little bird to serve as his eyes: "So the Swallow flew over the great city, and saw the rich making merry in their beautiful houses while the beggars were sitting at the gates. He flew into dark lanes, and saw white faces of starving children looking out listlessly at the black streets. Under the archway of a bridge two little boys were lying in one another's arms to try to keep themselves warm. 'How hungry we are!' they said. 'You must not lie here,' shouted the watchmen, and they wandered into the rain."[115] All this the bird reports to the prince, who then resolves, "I am covered in fine gold. . . . you must take it off, leaf by leaf, and give it to my poor."[116] When he has nothing left to give, the statue, now dull and gray, is melted down by the city officials. And the swallow, who has stayed in the north too long into the winter, dies of cold. In the end, both the prince and the little swallow are honored in heaven.

The Seamstress and the Season

The appearance of a dressmaker's shop in both "The Happy Prince" and "The Young King" may have served to spur the conscience of Wilde's readers. During "the Season"—that period between April and August when Parliament was in session and the social elite hosted innumerable elaborate parties with which to display their wealth, solidify class loyalties, marry off their daughters, and increase their prestige—nearly a million workers found temporary employment as servants, cooks, and entertainers at such parties. The Season further demanded the skills of about twenty thousand seamstresses, mostly young women, who for the duration worked between twelve and seventeen hours a day.[117]

As one needle worker relayed, "I got a job in Hanover Square on Court dresses, and we used to do the sequin work on the dresses for the ladies who were being presented. There were about fourteen of us, seven [on] either side of the table, working on each dress, and when the Court dresses were finished we were all told, 'no more work, off you go.'" Unemployment, ironically, would sometimes bring the workers into contact with the customers:

> We used to go up to the West End every so often to see if there was any work, and if there wasn't, that was expensive paying the fare up, so we'd amuse ourselves while we were up there, and we used to go to the theaters and banquets to watch them all going in. They were all dressed up in their diamonds, jewelry and beautiful clothes, and we used to stand there, bitter, thinking to ourselves, "fancy, they're all dressed up and there's us, we can't even get a job to live on. They don't care a hang what becomes of us."[118]

These fancy people attending the theater in the West End—they were Wilde's audience, and Wilde parodied their callous attitude. In "The Happy Prince," a beautiful girl at the palace worries aloud, "I hope my dress will be ready in time for the State-ball. . . . I have ordered passion-flowers to be embroidered on it; but the seamstresses are so lazy."[119]

The truth was quite the reverse, as several dressmakers attested in their appearance before the Children's Employment Commission: "The great cause of these long hours," one seamstress explained, "is that no one will refuse an order; they make a promise for any time a lady wishes." By way of illustration, another worker recalled, "I was several times asked by ladies, late on Saturday night, to let them have a dress home the very first thing on Monday morning. I have taken orders at tea-time—4 o'clock—for a ball-dress to be sent home that same night, 'any time before 12 would do.'" This haughty indifference among the clients—precisely what Wilde's tale rebuked in passing—was a common source of complaint among the garment workers. One remembered, "a dress ordered at 12, fitted on at 6 p.m., finished the same night, and sent home the next day. The lady who ordered it said, 'I suppose you work till 11, and begin at 6 in the morning'. She did not care how long we worked. We were very much hurt at the way in which it was said."[120]

Delight and Discontent

Wilde may have included the dressmakers in these stories not only as an emblem of the evils of wage labor, but also as a sign of more hopeful possibilities. Toward the end of his life, Wilde spoke to the anarchist Thomas Bell about collective ownership and worker self-management, referring to a pair of novels, Nicolai Chernyshevsky's *What Is to Be Done?* and Walter Besant's *All Sorts and Conditions of Men*. Both books include descriptions of dressmakers establishing a co-op.[121]

Written in 1863 while Chernyshevsky was imprisoned in the dreaded Peter and Paul Fortress, *What Is to Be Done?* is a strikingly modern novel about a young woman, Vera Rozalsky, who escapes the control of her family, embarks on a series of egalitarian experiments in both her personal life and her work, and is blessed in a dream with the vision of a future utopia. About midway through the novel, there appears a detailed description of a dressmakers' co-op, democratically run, with profits shared equally among the workers. Gradually its mission expands as the workers discover new advantages within cooperative enterprises. Soon they are living near to one another, on the same streets or even in the same apartments, buying in bulk, and offering no-interest loans to help one another through emergencies. "And so, step by step they moved toward a communal arrangement."[122]

More complex was Wilde's relationship to Walter Besant's *All Sorts and Conditions of Men*. Wilde was familiar with the novel from early on, noting in "The Decay of Lying" that the People's Palace—a cultural center and technical school for the working class in London's East End—"rose out of the *débris* of a novel," finding its origin in the imagination of one of Besant's characters.[123] In fact, traces of Besant's influence can be found in several places in Wilde's work, and at times it almost feels as though their views are in dialogue.

Besant's protagonist, the unsubtly named Angela Messenger, seeks to civilize the lower orders by exposing them to fine culture and grand ideas, not out of simple philanthropy but as a subversive ploy to raise expectations and stimulate the desire for more of the best things in life. One element of this strategy is the founding of a center for education, recreation, and culture, sometimes called the Palace of Delight. Angela reflects:

There should be, for all who chose to accept it, a general and standing invitation to accept happiness and create new forms of delight. She would awaken in dull and lethargic brains a new sense, the sense of pleasure; she would give them a craving for things of which as yet they knew nothing. She would place within their reach, at no cost whatever, absolutely free for all, the same enjoyments as are purchased by the rich. A beautiful dream.

They should cultivate a noble discontent; they should gradually learn to be critical; they should import into their own homes the spirit of discontent; they should cease to look on life as . . . a daily mechanical toil. . . . To cultivate the sense of pleasure is to civilize. With the majority of mankind the sense is undeveloped, and is chiefly confined to eating and drinking. To teach the people how the capacity of delight may be widened, how it may be taught, to throw out branches in all manner of unsuspected directions, was Angela's ambition. A very beautiful dream.[124]

The theory here is that if the poor are exposed to a little of the good, they will want, and ultimately demand, more and better. The idea was expressly *not* to pacify them but to agitate, to stimulate new desires and broader ambitions.

The other half of Messenger's scheme is the founding of a dressmakers' association, a sewing shop "in which there was to be no mistress, but to be self-governed," and where the workers "share the proceeds among them all in due order and with regard to skill and industry." In addition to shorter hours and higher pay, the co-op also incorporates common meals, a gymnasium with hours set aside for daily exercise, plus singing and dancing in the evenings.[125]

Despite the project's reliance on a wealthy benefactor, the book emphasizes the need for the lower classes to act on their own initiative and in their own interests. In one of the novel's several dramatic speeches, an orator chides his audience: "You think that Government can do everything for you. You FOOLS! Has any Government ever done anything for you? Has it raised your wages? Has it shortened your hours? . . . Will it ever try to better your position? Never, never, never." He goes on to list a series of failed reforms concerning housing, sanitation, and the quality and purity of food. Then, abruptly, his argument pivots: "You have the Power—all the Power there is. . . . You expect the Government to use your Power—to do your work. My friends, I will tell you the secret—whatever you want done you *must do for yourselves*—no one else will do it for you."[126]

But action requires motive, and thus the novel returns repeatedly to the essential importance of stoking desire, of raising expectations. "I am endeavoring to make such people as I can get at discontented as a first step," Angela admits. "Without discontent, nothing can be done."[127]

Wilde too believed that "discontent is the first step in the progress of a man or a nation."[128] And he may have had something like Angela's mission in mind when he wrote in "The Soul of Man under Socialism" that "agitators are a set of interfering, meddling people, who come down to some perfectly contented class of the community and sow the seeds of discontent amongst them. That is the reason why agitators are so absolutely necessary. Without them . . . there would be no advance towards civilisation."[129] Indeed, Wilde seems to have embarked on a strategy not that distant from Angela Messenger's when he took to lecturing the large public on aesthetics. Wilde himself drew this connection. In 1886, the year before the opening of the People's Palace—the real-world institution modeled on the fictional Palace of Delight—Wilde wrote to offer himself "as a candidate for the Secretaryship" of the organization, noting that "since taking my degree, in 1878, I have devoted myself partly to literature and partly to the spreading of art-knowledge and art-appreciation among the people." He concludes the letter: "This People's Palace will be to me the realisation of much that I have long hoped for, and to be in any way officially connected with it would be esteemed by me a high and noble honour."[130]

The reply to Wilde, if any, is not known.[131]

From Aestheticism to Anarchism

Her Own Laws

In art, Wilde could theorize an area of life and a system of values exempt from the demands of commerce, government, and morality. Art does not need to be practical, useful, or virtuous—so long as it is beautiful. It is an end, and, if it is also a means, it is clearly a means to its own ends: "Art has no other aim but her own perfection, and proceeds simply from her own laws."[132]

Wilde told us, "Life itself is an art, and has its modes of style no less than the arts that seek to express it."[133] Further, "To become a work of art is the object of living."[134] It is this ideal that led Wilde to rebel against the moralism of his time, against established doctrine and common sense, and against the whole practical, material, shopkeeper side of life. Sometimes his rebellion took the tone of flippancy and irony; sometimes it took the form of tragedy, and sometimes that of utopia. But beneath it all was a deeply human faith that we *are* better than this, and the hope that life can be richer, fuller, more beautiful. "For there never was an age that so much needed the spiritual ministry of art as the present," Wilde lectured.

> Today more than ever the artist and a love of the beautiful are needed to temper and counteract the sordid materialism of the age. In an age when science has undertaken to declaim against the soul and spiritual nature of man, and when commerce is ruining beautiful rivers and magnificent woodlands, and the glorious skies in its greed for gain, the artist comes forward as a priest and prophet of nature to protest, and even to work against the prostitution or the perversion of what is lofty and noble in humanity and beautiful in the physical world, and his religion in its benefits to mankind is as broad and shining as the sun.[135]

Life realizes its meaning in the pursuit of beauty, and each of us in our lives must seek our own perfection and develop according to our own laws.

From the point of view of aesthetics, a good life would be one that is full and fulfilling, brimming with experience. It would not be arduous and drab. It would be expansive and enriching, not narrow and repressed. And what is more, if life is to be made beautiful, it must be judged by the standards of beauty, not those of morality or utility or economics. Wilde establishes art not merely as an end but as an *ideal*. It is not simply a source of value for life; it is also a *mode* of value.

Whereas the Victorians were obsessed with concepts like duty and sin, Wilde imagines a universe in which nothing is prohibited and nothing is obligatory, yet some things still are better than others.[136] In this he was clearly looking back to the Hellenic age, but he was also looking ahead to a new Renaissance and a period of unprecedented freedom. Lecturing in New York, he foretold a "new birth of the spirit of man . . . in its desire for a more gracious and comely way of life, in its passion for physical beauty, its exclusive attention to form, its seeking for new subjects for poetry, new forms for art, new intellectual and imaginative enjoyments."[137] Wilde thought that art would prepare us for "a new history of the world, with a promise of the brotherhood of man, of peace rather than war, of praise of God's handicraftsmanship, of new imagination and new beauty."[138]

A New Hellenism

Wilde's aesthetic philosophy provided the theoretical foundation for his more overtly political work. What economics were for Marx, aesthetics were for Wilde. His aestheticism set out his feelings about what was valuable— that is, not only about what people desire but also about what we must come to respect and cherish if we are to flourish, to live rather than merely survive. "The supreme object of life is to live. Few people live. It is true life only to realize one's own perfection, to make one's every dream a reality. Even this is possible."[139]

Wilde's views on life, on its worth and ultimate ends, were at first largely borrowed from Walter Pater's *Studies in the History of the Renaissance*. Wilde knew Pater personally at Oxford and referred Pater's book as "the golden book of spirit and sense, the holy writ of beauty."[140]

In one often-quoted passage, Pater wrote,

Not the fruit of experience, but experience itself is the end. . . . To burn always with this hard, gemlike flame, to maintain this ecstasy, is success in life. . . . While all melts under our feet, we may grasp at any exquisite passion, or any contribution to knowledge that seems by a lifted horizon to set the spirit free for a moment, or any stirring of the senses, strange dyes, strange colours, and curious odours, or work of the artist's hands, or the face of one's friend. Not to discriminate every moment some passionate attitude in those about us, and in the very brilliancy of their gifts some tragic dividing of forces on their way, is, on this short day of frost and sun, to sleep before evening. . . . The theory or idea or system which requires of us the sacrifice of any part of this experience, in consideration of some interest into which we cannot enter, or some abstract theory we have not identified with ourselves, or of what is only conventional, has no real claim upon us.[141]

Compare that with this, from Wilde's lecture "The English Renaissance of Art":

[For those] who seek for experience itself and not for the fruits of experience, who must burn always with one of the passions of this fiery-coloured world, who find life interesting not for its secret but for its situations, for its pulsations and not for its purpose; the passion for beauty engendered by the decorative arts will be to them more satisfying than any political or religious enthusiasm, any enthusiasm for humanity, any ecstasy or sorrow for love. For art comes professing primarily to give nothing but the highest quality to one's moments, and for those moments' sake.[142]

Wilde's ideals posed a challenge to the piety of puritanism and the degradations of the marketplace, but aestheticism was meant to be more than a reaction to the systems against which it dueled. Wilde announced the coming of an "English Renaissance" and with it "a great revolution in English life and art."[143] As he writes in "The Soul of Man under Socialism," "For what man has sought for is, indeed, neither pain nor pleasure, but simply Life. Man has sought to live intensely, fully, perfectly. When he can do so without exercising restraint on others, or suffering it ever, and his activities are all pleasurable to him, he will be saner, healthier, more civilized, more himself."[144]

As Pater's influence is evident in Wilde's aestheticism, so too can traces of Wilde's thought be discerned in the writing of anarchists in the years immediately following. Emma Goldman argued, "Anarchism, being a philosophy of life, aims to establish a state of society in which man's inner make-up and the conditions around him, can blend harmoniously, so that he will be able to utilize all the forces to enlarge and beautify the life about him."[145] Edward Carpenter—a self-described "Socialist . . . with a drift, as was natural, toward Anarchism"—argued similarly in his essay "The Art of Life": "*Life is expression.* . . . To obtain a place, a free field, a harmonious expansion, for your activities, your tastes, your feelings, your personality, your Self, in fact, is to Live."[146]

Alexander Berkman put it simply, in his "ABC of Anarchism," when he prophesied, "The man of the coming day will see and feel existence on an entirely different plane. Living to him will be an art and a joy. . . . He will grow and develop according to his nature. He will scorn uniformity, and human diversity will give him increased interest in, and a more satisfying sense of, the rich ways of being. Life to him will not consist of functioning but in living."[147] Therefore, Berkman believed, "Life in freedom, in anarchy, will do more than liberate man merely from his present political and economic bondage. . . . Far greater and more significant will be the *results* of such liberty, its effects upon man's mind, upon his personality." It will mark "the birth of a new culture, of a new humanity."[148]

Individualism as Unifying Principle

Wilde turned to the aesthetic to provide a mode of life and a system of values that would elevate rather than degrade the individual. The challenge of aesthetics, as Wilde explained it, was to cultivate the personality and make life beautiful. This has almost nothing in common with "the vulgar standard of goodness" propagated by Victorian moralism, but it *is* rather close to the Aristotelian project of ethics—itself a branch of politics.[149] The best political system for Wilde, as for Aristotle, would be that which would allow people to develop their best characteristics, though one thinker described these in terms of virtue and the other in terms of beauty. Wilde wrote in his copy of the *Nichomachean Ethics*: "Man makes his end for himself out of himself: no end is imposed by external considerations, he must realise his true nature, must be what nature orders, so must discover what his nature is."[150]

The principle here is one of self-development, self-realization, even self-creation. This individualism was the principle underlying Wilde's aestheticism, and it was also the ideal to which his aestheticism pointed. As he wrote in "The Soul of Man under Socialism," "Art is the most intense form of Individualism that the world has ever known," perhaps even "the only real mode of Individualism that the world has known."[151] Art pits creativity always against authority—whether church, state, or the tyranny of public opinion.[152] It shows us the possibility of perfection and the necessity of freedom.

Another Factor

One of those who appreciated Wilde's blending of socialism and individualism was that most prominent representative of anarcho-communism, Peter Kropotkin. Indeed, Kropotkin seems to have adopted the central ideas of "The Soul of Man under Socialism" (which he described as "that article that O. Wilde wrote on Anarchism—in which there are sentences worth being engraved, like verses from the Koran are engraved in Moslem lands.")[153] In the conclusion to his book *Mutual Aid*, after examining the role of cooperation in both animal and human societies and positing it as "a factor of evolution," often decisive in the survival of a species, Kropotkin offers this important caveat: "There is, and always has been, the other current—the self-assertion of the individual, not only in its efforts to attain personal or caste superiority, economical, political, and spiritual, but also in its much more important although less evident function of breaking through the bonds, always prone to become crystallized, which the tribe, the village community, the city, and the State impose upon the individual. In other words, there is the self-assertion of the individual taken as a progressive element."[154]

Wilde had written, in "The Soul of Man," "Individualism is a disturbing and disintegrating force. Therein lies its immense value. For what it seeks to disturb is monotony of type, slavery of custom, tyranny of habit, and the reduction of man to the level of a machine."[155] He put the same point more dramatically, and in language more nearly anticipating Kropotkin's, in "The Critic as Artist": "What is termed Sin is an essential element of progress. Without it the world would stagnate, or grow old, or become colourless. By its curiosity Sin increases the experience of the race. Through its intensified assertion of individualism it saves us from monotony of type. In its rejection of the current notions of morality, it is one with the higher ethics."[156]

In 1902, the same year that *Mutual Aid* was published in its book form, Kropotkin also wrote a long letter to Max Nettlau in which he contrasted the "petty and false" selfishness of elitists, economists, egoists, and Nietzscheans with what he called "true individualism"—defined as "the full development of the individuality."[157] Kropotkin's biographers Woodcock and Avakumovic suggest Wilde's essay as a likely source for this distinction and summarize the argument thus: "What Kropotkin clearly means is that real individualism, in the sense of an enrichment of personality, will only arise from a society where co-operation in the material factors of life has removed those causes of strife and oppression which in any other order relegate individualism to a privilege of the few who live at the expense of the toiling many."[158]

By the same reasoning, Kropotkin also believed, like Wilde, that by ensuring a measure of material security, socialism would produce greater individuality and thus greater diversity, with beneficial implications for art and culture. He wrote, "As soon as [one's] material wants are satisfied, other needs, which, generally speaking, may be described as of an artistic nature, will thrust themselves forward. These needs are of the greatest variety; they vary with each and every individual; and the more society is civilized, the more will individuality be developed, and the more will desires be varied."[159]

However, there were also profound differences between Kropotkin's individualism and Wilde's, as revealed by Kropotkin's ambivalent response to Wilde's confession letter, "De Profundis." Though he "read it with the deepest sympathy" and found "passages and pages in it which are sublime," Kropotkin worried that it evinced too much "'Christian' humility," and he wrote in a letter, "I cannot help thinking, that it is this humility wh. brought O. W. to end so miserably after his release."[160] It seems at first an ironic charge against a man so commonly accused of egotism, and doubly ironic coming from a figure sometimes described as saintly.[161] But Kropotkin goes on, explaining: "Such a humility is life-destroying, a life-killing force, because it is too *personal*, too *egotistic*, while to *live* after a great suffering one ought to have an aim much higher and wider—and such an aim could only be *mankind*."[162]

We see here, in this letter, both the likeness and also the difference between Wilde's philosophy and Kropotkin's. As much as Wilde may have taken from Kropotkin's communism, and as much as Kropotkin seems to have learned from Wilde's egoism, their views on each half of the anarchist ideal—individualism and socialism, freedom and equality, personal development and mutual aid, the unique and the common—were quite different.[163] For Kropotkin, the great cause of humanity, and its struggle for freedom, was what gave individual life its purpose and its meaning, while for Wilde, the *point* of socialism was as an aid to individualism. Wilde hoped that beauty might supply the basis for a new society, a new civilization, both creative and free—a socialism in the service of individual development and expression, one that prizes the unique over the uniform, and an individualism that is not selfish and petty but expansive in its sympathies and egalitarian in its commitments.

Egoism, Altruism, and Rebellion

Wilde's disdain for the cult of work has often been interpreted as inveterate snobbery—and not without some cause. Wilde had expensive tastes, a luxurious temperament, and the aristocrat's admiration of idleness. He was fascinated by titles, valued good manners, and prized breeding. He taught that the only excuse "for being occasionally a little over-dressed" was to be "always absolutely over-educated," and (following Matthew Arnold) he identified the philistine element of British society with the respectable middle classes rather than the aristocracy, who at least had taste enough to be decadent.[164]

That truly was one dimension of Wilde's character. But another encompassed a deep sympathy and an effortless generosity. When a working-class district in London flooded, Wilde went to help the people displaced by the deluge.[165] Sir James Rennell Rodd later recalled, "A number of the houses of the very poor were wrecked, [and] we went together to see what we could do to help the unfortunate families who were camping in the street." Wilde, he said, "penetrated into a miserable tenement and talked to an old bed-ridden Irish woman, cheering her with his merry humours and assisting her with little necessities." Rodd concludes his recollection: "He was generous and reckless, with no thought for the morrow and indeed indolent until a desperate obligation to work came home to him. I would like this side of his nature to be known."[166]

Edgar Saltus, likewise, recalls walking with Wilde on a very cold night and encountering a beggar, who opened his jacket to show that he had nothing on underneath. Saltus gave the man a coin, but Wilde took off his own overcoat and wrapped it around the poor and shivering man.[167]

More mysterious is a letter dated April 28, 1891, from a person who has not been identified, expressing gratitude for Wilde's assistance in saving the home of an unnamed family.[168] Such incidents were not uncharacteristic. His friend Robert Sherard explained: "Oscar Wilde was at once a supreme egotist and the least selfish of men—that is to say, that he combined indi-vidualism with a large and generous altruism. . . . He could not go against his own nature to oblige another. He would not have divided his last shilling with a friend, but, what is infinitely more rare, he was always ready to give away his superfluity."[169]

"You know I have no sense of property," Wilde told Sherard.[170] And he liked to quote Proudhon, "La propriété, c'est le vol." ("Property is theft.")[171] Wilde saved nothing but gave away much—and he always expected that the same generosity would be shown to him when he was in need.[172]

"His politics," biographer Richard Ellmann comments, "were grounded in such sympathies."[173] But, more than that, in a strange way so was his very snobbery. Wilde was offended by the degradations of poverty and by the vulgarity of the poor, not simply because of the striking difference between the classes but more so because he could see the humanity common among them. He wrote in one of his dialogues, "We are all of us made of the same stuff. . . . Where we differ from each other is purely in accidentals: in dress, manner, tone of voice, religious opinions, personal appearance, tricks of habit and the like. . . . Indeed, as any one who has ever worked among the poor knows only too well, the brotherhood of man is no mere poet's dream, it is a most depressing and humiliating reality."[174] It is an illuminating passage.

Because we share a common nature, "It is only shallow people who don't judge by appearances."[175] For the same reason, our highest aspiration can only be to make ourselves, and our lives, beautiful. Yet by this thinking, no real elitism can be justified, since we do all share a common nature. If, as Wilde observes in "The Soul of Man under Socialism," "all Humanity gains a partial realisation" through those who "in consequence of the existence of private property . . . are enabled to develop a certain very limited amount of Individualism" and thus "have realised themselves"—specifically, "the poets, the philosophers, the men of science, the men of culture"—then all humanity is likewise degraded owing to the vastly larger numbers of people who are denied these same opportunities of self-development and self-realization, who are oppressed and exploited.[176]

The worker, Wilde says, is treated not as a unique individual but as "the infinitesimal atom of a force that, so far from regarding him, crushes him: indeed, prefers him crushed, as in that case he is far more obedient." Wilde preferred the workers when they were rebellious: "Disobedience, in the eyes of any one who has read history, is man's original virtue."[177]

Thus, on September 1, 1889, Constance and Oscar attended a demonstration in Hyde Park in support of striking dockworkers.[178] The strike, which demanded sixpence an hour in wages, began at a single job site but quickly spread to all the London docks, then to other industries. Soon students were walking out of East End schools, and tenants began withholding rent. Altogether 130,000 workers downed their tools. The conflict threatened, but never quite managed, to become a general strike.[179] William Morris described it in terms of class warfare: "a revolt against oppression . . . a strike of the poor against the rich."[180] Several of Wilde's friends—Morris, Shaw, Cunninghame Graham, Kropotkin—delivered speeches at the strikers' rallies.[181]

A Reconstruction

Wilde understood that the problems of poverty—the filthy conditions, the slum housing, the hunger—were only the outer manifestation of a system that treated people essentially as tools. Such a system could not be corrected through policy reforms, which merely sustain the underlying condition.

What was wanted was to "reconstruct society on such a basis that poverty will be impossible."[182]

Wilde's solution to the problem of work lay in his marriage of socialism and individualism. He is vague on the details, exhibiting his usual disregard for practical matters, but the principle he lays out is that the necessities of life should be socialized, provided by a state that is not a government but "a voluntary manufacturer," leaving every individual free to pursue such work as one finds interesting and enjoyable.[183] The worst jobs would be automated, and we may infer that those remaining would be greatly altered by the new social arrangements—transformed from drudgery to artistry, from tedious toil to creative adventure.[184]

Every worker would be like an artist in his field. The benefits then would be double: society being blessed with skilled, engaged, creative, and satisfied workers, and at the same time with well-crafted and beautiful handiworks. Labor may at last find its dignity by becoming art, which in turn becomes indistinguishable from the pleasurable activities of life.[185]

Chapter 3

Love Is Law

The New Woman, the Society Plays, and
the Transvaluation of Values

The Woman Question

Petticoat Anarchists

If capitalism regarded workers as tools, the bourgeois family treated women as little more than property.

Questions of sexual morality, family life, and, at bottom, the role of women in society were being forcefully posed and fiercely contested in the late nineteenth century. Central to the debate was the figure of the "New Woman"—imagined by both advocates and adversaries as independent, assertive, no longer bound by convention or tradition.[1] The novelist Eliza Lynn Linton characterized the New Woman as "aggressive, disturbing, officious, unquiet, rebellious to authority and tyrannous . . . the most unlovely specimen the sex has yet produced." (She preferred those "sweet girls still left among us who have no part in the new revolt, but are content to be dutiful, innocent, and sheltered.")[2] The May 2, 1894, *Woman* likewise denounced the New Women as "petticoat anarchists who put a blazing torch to the shrine of self-respect and feminine shame."[3] These women, and their refusal of prescribed roles, cast doubt on some of the deepest assumptions ruling Victorian society, and repercussions were felt in every area of social life, including those far outside women's traditional sphere.

Visiting the Woman's World

For most of two years, from November 1887 to September 1889, Wilde's attention was concentrated on these issues at least two mornings a week at his job editing the *Woman's World*. Before he took charge, the *Lady's World* was a failing fashion and gossip magazine. Changing the name and recruiting an impressive collection of contributors, Wilde set out to make it "the recognized organ for the expression of women's opinions on all subjects of literature, art, and modern life" and to "deal not merely with what women wear, but with what they think, and what they feel."[4]

Arthur Fish, Wilde's assistant at the *Woman's World*, later recalled, "The keynote of the magazine was the fight of woman to equality of treatment with man, with the assertion of her claims by women who had gained high position by virtue of their skill as writers or workers in the world's great field of labour. Some of the articles on women's work and their position in politics were far in advance of the thought of the day, and . . . [Wilde] would always express his entire sympathy with the views of the writers and reveal great liberality of thought with regard to the political aspirations of women."[5]

Contributors included numerous feminists, suffragists, and trade unionists, the anti-racist and anti-imperialist agitator Olive Schreiner, and the anarchist poet Louise S. Bevington.[6] ("We are all creatures of circumstance," Bevington wrote, "and man's will or whim is woman's chief circumstance the world over.") The very first issue under Wilde's watch included a long article, "The Position of Women," advocating changes in marriage law and describing the existing institution as "a hopeless and bitter slavery."[7]

As might be expected, women's suffrage was a recurring topic. Millicent Garrett Fawcett wrote to advocate the vote for women, predicting that it would mean an end to war. One issue featured, under the headline "On Women's Work in Politics," a speech by the suffragist Lady Margaret Sandhurst, then campaigning for London County Council.[8] (Sandhurst won the election, but the courts vacated the results.)[9] Officially, however, the *Woman's World* had "no creed of its own, political, artistic, or theological."[10] So it did sometimes give space to reactionary views as well. Lucy M. J. Garnett, for instance, responded to Laura McLaren's "The Fallacy of the Superiority of Men" with her own "Fallacy of the Equality of Women." She similarly provided "Reasons for Opposing Women's Suffrage." (However, Eleanor

Fitzsimons suggests that the "arguments were so gratuitously insulting" that they could only "elicit sympathy for the other side"—which "one suspects" may have been "Oscar's intention.")[11]

The magazine featured numerous articles about poverty in Britain and Ireland and about the economic prospects for women. Emily Faithfull, a member of the Society for Promoting the Employment of Women, advocated training girls in the trades and professions. Clementina Black, a founding member and secretary of the Women's Trade Union Association, highlighted the plight of needleworkers, and Charlotte O'Conor-Eccles documented the conditions among Irish weavers.[12] Helena Sickert—a dear friend of Wilde and later a noted journalist, suffragist, and pacifist—wrote "The Evolution of Economics" (an article whose title she would misremember as "Competition—Combination—Co-operation").[13] Wilde himself reviewed the book *Women and Work* in January 1888.[14]

Of Wilde's effect on the magazine there can be no question. Its entire tone and direction changed when he took control, and it changed again once he departed. After Wilde left the editor's desk, the *Woman's World* unfortunately reverted to its earlier form—less politics, more fashion—and soon ceased publication altogether.[15] The magazine's influence on Wilde, on the other hand, is perhaps less clear. At the very least we may say that it gave him the opportunity to consider a range of ideas that would show up later in his own writing—the economic issues in his fairy tales, the gender issues as the very basis for his most successful plays.

Trivial Comedies?

Like a Pistol Shot

It is perhaps notable that Wilde's plays continue to be performed more than a century after his death. More remarkable is the fact that they remain funny. Wilde's wit is famous, and it is a testament to his skill as a writer how well his jokes hold up, despite changes in social norms, dramatic technique, and audience expectations. Even today his plays come across as bold and inventive—but once they also seemed slightly dangerous.

Individually and together, Wilde's four society plays—*Lady Windermere's Fan*, *A Woman of No Importance*, *An Ideal Husband*, and *The Importance of Being Earnest*—represent critiques of careerist ambition, the sexual double standard, puritanism, and hypocrisy. With a careless ease, they deconstruct gender norms, class divisions, and moral law. They propose instead an anarchic code—at once classical, Christian, and queer—emphasizing the role of love, acceptance, forgiveness, and individuality. In effect they assert the precious uniqueness of each single personality above the demands of any rigid formula or system of laws.[16]

For Victorian audiences, the inversion of a platitude was also the subversion of an ideal, and Wilde knew it. Contained within these plays are a series of challenges to the most cherished of Victorian values. When a friend stated that a comedy should be like a piece of music, Wilde was adamant in his denial. "No," he said, "it must be like a pistol shot."[17]

Everyone His Own Way

The first of Wilde's society plays, *Lady Windermere's Fan*, depicts a fallen woman, Mrs. Erlynne, seeking after a long absence abroad to reclaim her position in society. Her scheme relies on gaining the public approval of the morally upright Lady Windermere, while at the same time blackmailing Lord Windermere. He is paying Mrs. Erlynne and cooperating with her plot in exchange for her promise not to reveal that she is Lady Windermere's mother. But when Lady Windermere discovers the blackmail, she naturally misinterprets its cause. In anger, she decides to avenge herself by leaving her family and running away with Lord Darlington, an amoral dandy who has long and openly admired her. Mrs. Erlynne intervenes, assures Lady Windermere that her husband is blameless, and persuades her to change her mind about leaving. But it may be too late. Lady Windermere's plan is about to be uncovered—through a theatrical device involving the discovery of her titular fan—when, at the crucial moment, Mrs. Erlynne steps forward to claim the fan, sacrificing her newly refurbished reputation to save that of her still-unacknowledged daughter. The play ends happily: Lady and Lord Windermere are reconciled, her faith in him restored and her own moment of wavering morals undiscovered; Mrs. Erlynne finds a rich and foolish husband, and they retire together abroad.[18]

This outcome seems at first entirely conservative. Marriage is affirmed, the virtues of motherhood showcased, men and women returned to their distinct positions, and the disturbing figure of Mrs. Erlynne removed again to a kind of exile. The ending restores the condition present at the start. But much has changed as well, if only inwardly. Lady Windermere has discovered for herself what it means to succumb to temptation, however briefly and ineffectually, and she has learned from Mrs. Erlynne a surprising lesson about what it means to be a good woman. (Wilde's original title was *The Good Woman*.) She learns about frailty, the need for forgiveness, and the value of compassion over exactitude. A new morality is hinted at, by which the fallen woman might also be the good woman. For Lady Windermere (and presumably the audience), the "good" at the end of the play is not the same "good" as at the start.

The overall tone is one of moral ambiguity. Mrs. Erlynne is not reformed; Lady Windermere is not punished. Lady Windermere hypocritically guards her respectability; Mrs. Erlynne cannot regain her reputation. Social morality still has its force, but society's rules are also revealed to be shallow, wrong, and needlessly cruel. Society is mistaken in its judgment of Mrs. Erlynne, just as Lady Windermere was mistaken in her judgment of her husband. The suggestion is that such judgments are wrong, not only on the facts but also on the basis of the criteria they employ, the values they invoke. The prejudices of Victorian society suffer a sustained attack all through the dialogue and then a final assault in the plot. Richard Ellmann described the moral logic of the play as a "transvaluation of values, by which the bad woman appears in a good light, and the good woman in a bad one, and society in the worst light of all."[19] Emma Goldman thought the play displayed the "revolutionary spirit of modern drama."[20]

At a meeting of the Royal General Theatrical Fund, Wilde identified the "one particular doctrine" advanced by the play as "that of sheer individualism." In brief: "It is not for anyone to censure what anyone else does, and everyone should go his own way, to whatever place he chooses, in exactly the way he chooses."[21]

No Law for Anybody

Wilde's next play, *A Woman of No Importance*, is much more direct. It employs many of the same dramatic conceits—a fallen woman, an amoral dandy, unacknowledged parentage and illegitimate children, the quest for respectability. Again the dialogue is jeweled, or perhaps barbed, with Wilde's famous epigrams. Verbal volleys strike against polite society, conventional morality, and the class system, but the moral of the play is more precise. The play is an attack on the sexual double standard, whereby, in consequence of an illicit affair, "[t]he woman suffers" while "[t]he man goes free."[22] This disparity provides the premise of the plot and its central question.

The play is concocted from the ingredients of melodrama. A fallen woman, Mrs. Arbuthnot, learns that her son Gerald is taking a position as the private secretary to the very man "who spoiled [her] youth, who ruined [her] life, who has tainted every moment of [her] days."[23] Unaware of this history, Gerald is eager to establish himself in a respectable position so that he may propose to Hester Worsley, a young American with a distinctly puritan streak. Fearing the influence of Lord Illingworth—Gerald's mentor, her seducer— Mrs. Arbuthnot urges her son to decline the position. But when she tells the story of her seduction—disguised as that of another young woman—Gerald heartlessly and conventionally replies that "the girl was just as much to blame as Lord Illingworth." Gerald is determined; Arbuthnot is despondent. But at just the right moment Illingworth tries to make good on an earlier dare and attempts to kiss young Hester. Enraged, Gerald moves to attack him. But Arbuthnot intervenes: "Stop, Gerald, stop! He is your own father!"[24]

Learning the truth, yet still serving as the voice of Victorian respectability, Gerald insists that Lord Illingworth and his mother marry. Illingworth agrees, hoping to win his son's loyalty—but Arbuthnot indignantly refuses. Gerald is perplexed and scandalized: "but, mother . . . you must become my father's wife. You must marry him. It is your duty." Hester Worsley, however, unexpectedly abandons her puritan views and rushes to Arbuthnot's defense: "You cannot love me at all unless you love her also. You cannot honour me, unless she's holier to you. In her all womanhood is martyred."[25] In the end, Gerald is persuaded, Worsley agrees to marry him despite his lack of position, and they depart, Mrs. Arbuthnot with them, to start again in America. Illingworth is left alone and rejected—"a man of no importance"—and Arbuthnot is relieved of a lifetime of shame. The fallen woman is vindicated; the corrupting male banished.[26]

In one interview about the play, a journalist commented on "the monstrous injustice of the social code." Wilde agreed, "it is indeed a burning shame that there should be one law for men and another law for women."[27] However, against the demands of the purity crusaders and a certain sort of feminist, who argued that marriage should bind man as well as woman—one law for both—Wilde offered this alternative: "I think that there should be no law for anybody."[28]

Yet in the play itself he offers a different conception of law, one outside the framework of prohibition and punishment. Mrs. Arbuthnot, struggling to let go of her sense of tragic shame, thinks the stigma of her past inescapable. "But we are disgraced," she cries, "We rank among the outcasts. Gerald is nameless." What is worse, she deeply feels they *deserve* society's scorn, even her son: "The sins of the parents should be visited on the children. It is God's law." But Hester, repentant now of her puritanism, and taking a position closer to that of Wilde's Christ, gently corrects her: "God's law is only Love."[29]

No More Idols

Compared to *A Woman of No Importance* or even *Lady Windermere's Fan, An Ideal Husband* is complex and confounding.

The plot concerns a conflict between two of the strongest impulses in Victorian culture: severe and demanding moralism and the vulgar worship of success. In the outcome, Wilde suggests that idealism is in fact the alibi and accomplice to corruption.

Sir Robert Chiltern, a promising young member of Parliament famous for his integrity, is caught in a blackmail scheme. He owes his wealth and subsequent career to "a clever, unscrupulous" action he took as a very young man—selling a state secret to a stock market speculator—and now he is being coerced to support a canal project that he knows to be a swindle.[30] If he refuses, Mrs. Chevely will reveal the shameful origin of his fortune. He will, of course, be ruined, but more importantly he will also lose the esteem, and even the love, of his wife, who openly idolizes him.

At first he surrenders to the blackmail. But then Lady Chiltern learns his secret. She is apoplectic in her disapproval—not merely disappointed but devastated. "You sold a Cabinet secret for money!" she rails, "You began your life with fraud! You built up your career on dishonour! . . . And how I worshipped you! You were to me something apart from common life, a thing pure, noble, honest, without stain. The world seemed to me finer because you were in it, and goodness more real because you lived. And now—oh, when I think that I made of a man like you my ideal! The ideal of my life!" Her image of her husband, her ideal of a man, has been shattered, and she desperately demands that he restore the illusion: "Oh, tell me it is not true! Lie to me! Tell me it is not true!"[31]

But it is true, and she pronounces their love dead. Sir Robert then reverses course and publicly declares against the canal, thinking it means the end of his career. Instead, the blackmailer is herself blackmailed, being fortuitously outmaneuvered by Chiltern's friend and confidant Lord Goring. Goring is a romantic posing as a cynic, a dandy who pretends frivolity but actually serves as the conscience of the play. He believes in love, forgiveness, and personal integrity; he disdains ambition, disapproves of marriage, and dismisses the ideal of purity as a dangerous illusion.

Though Sir Robert has redeemed himself in his wife's eyes, she nevertheless insists that he resign his seat in Parliament. He agrees, albeit reluctantly. But Goring intervenes again, this time with an astonishingly sexist speech, appealing to Lady Chiltern's duty as wife and persuading her to put her scruples aside.[32] "A man's life is of more value than a woman's," he tells her. "It has larger issues, wider scope, greater ambitions. . . . A woman who can keep a man's love, and love him in return, has done all the world wants of women, should want of them."[33] Lady Chiltern then uses her influence to sway her husband, who all too quickly sets aside his reservations to claim again the rewards of his corruption.

The conflict of the play is one of values, manifest in a pair of dilemmas. Wilde explained, "Its entire psychology—the difference in the way in which a man loves a woman from that in which a woman loves a man; the passion that women have for making ideals (which is their weakness) and the weakness of a man who dares not show his imperfections to the thing he loves."[34] Faced with the end of his marriage, Robert Chiltern laments:

> Why can't you women love us, faults and all? Why do you place us on monstrous pedestals? We have all feet of clay, women as well as men; but when we men love women, we love them knowing their weaknesses, their follies, their imperfections, love them all the more, it may be, for that reason. . . .
>
> Women think that they are making ideals of men. What they are making of us are false idols merely. You made your false idol of me, and I had not the courage to come down, show you my wounds, tell you my weaknesses. I was afraid that I might lose your love. . . .
>
> Let women make no more idols of men! Let them not put them on altars and bow before them, or they may ruin other lives as completely as you—you whom I have so wildly loved—have ruined mine![35]

One lesson to be taken from *An Ideal Husband* is that to be idealized can be as oppressive, in its own way, as to be stigmatized, vilified, and shunned. One inevitably disappoints one's disciples; and when one does, they become the most terrible persecutors. It is better to be loved than worshipped.

Yet there is a real irony to this pair of speeches, Chiltern's and Goring's. Robert's complaints of being placed on a pedestal would equally describe the typical attitude assumed by a Victorian husband with regard to his wife. And if, as Lord Goring asserts, a man's life had "larger issues, wider scope, greater ambitions" than a woman's, it could only be because the lives of respectable women were so constrained and confined. Robert may feel ensnared by Gertrude's image of him as "a thing pure" and "without stain," but that image survives because he has held her too apart from the realities of life and preserved her illusions in the name of protecting her innocence. Idealism is a trap that they have built for one another.

Lady Chiltern has made her husband into an ideal, and so she has attached her love to an illusion. To keep her love, he tries to preserve the illusion. When she threatens to withdraw her support—at exactly the time when he most needs it—she makes it impossible for him to do the right thing. She tells him, "All your life you have stood apart from others. You have never let the world soil you. To the world, as to myself, you have been an ideal always. Oh! Be that still." Having spelled out this imperative, she goes on to ask a question she does not really want answered. "I know there are men with horrible secrets in their lives. . . . —Oh! Don't tell me you are such as they are! Robert, is there in your life any secret dishonour or disgrace? Tell me, tell me at once, that— . . . that our lives may drift apart. . . . That they may entirely separate. It would be better for us both." He responds, simply and falsely, "Gertrude, there is nothing in my past life that you might not know."[36]

Lady Chiltern is wrong to tie her love to her husband's perfection. ("It is not the perfect, but the imperfect, who have need of love.")[37] If she would not insist on his perfection, then perhaps he could confess his faults; perhaps he could even withstand Mrs. Chevely's blackmail. Though it might mean his career, his integrity would be restored, and he would be safe at least in the love of his wife. But because he knows that she, like the public, would not forgive his lapse, he must forever act dishonestly to cover it up. The truth would force Lady Chiltern to choose between her morality and her love, just as her morality forces Sir Robert to choose between his love for her and the truth. The dramatic crisis compels not merely a choice but also a transformation: their values must change. If love is to survive, it must be above morality, beyond it; it must be strong enough to face the truth and large enough to absorb it. Gertrude must love the real Robert, not her imagined ideal.

Sir Robert's dilemma pits his public duty against the love of his wife; in the end, thanks to good luck and Lord Goring, these prove to be aligned. Gertrude's dilemma is between her morality and her marriage, between idealism and love. At the beginning, she values purity above all else, makes love a matter of moral judgment, sees ambition as a reflection of virtue, and worships her husband as an ideal; forgiveness has no place in her moral schema. "She stands apart as good women do—pitiless in her perfection—cold and stern and without mercy." Goring changes her mind, first by making a case that the essence of love is forgiveness, second by arguing that too great a sacrifice might kill their love. "Rather than lose your love," he tells Gertrude, "Robert would do anything, wreck his whole career, as he is on the brink of doing." But if he does, "he would lose everything, even his power to love."[38]

Gertrude relents. Husband and wife are reunited, though their love has changed. Lady Chiltern starts out thinking that love demands perfection; she learns that what it really needs is forgiveness. In having her ideal shattered and surrendering her moral demands, she has at last learned real love. Idealism and morality are only obstructions.[39] For when the object of love is an illusion, love itself is an illusion. In the course of the play, Lady Chiltern learns to let go of this fantasy and forgive her husband. She finally sees Robert as he is and not as an idol of her own fashioning.

The Institution Is Wrong

By the surface reading, *An Ideal Husband* is a critique of the ideals of moral purity and a plea for us to be more humane in our judgments, especially of those we love. But this rather Christian message of forgiveness is also co-opted by the institutions of power—money, family, and the state. Robert, strangely unchanged by the ordeal he has just endured, is ready as always to silence his conscience for political expediency. Gertrude, no longer the moralist, becomes instead his enabler and consoler. It is, one critic objected, "not the triumph of love . . . but the triumph of money, ambition and corruption."[40]

Seen this way, the play seems cynical and conservative. Corruption is rewarded. Power is desirable for its own sake. A lifetime of deceit is forgiven in the name of patriarchal duty. Blackmail is a neutral political tactic. Hypocrisy is universal. Money, power, and position are the only measures of success, and success justifies anything.

Under this interpretation, the outcome is discomfiting. The play values love over morality; but in urging forgiveness, it also licenses hypocrisy. Chiltern's scruples force him to risk exposure but not to admit his own culpability. He denounces one swindle while continuing to profit from another. In fact, he does not even feel guilty. ("I don't say that I suffered any remorse. I didn't.")[41] He justifies his crime partly by pointing to the needs of the empire, partly by self-pity over the poverty of his youth, partly by pure Machiavellian opportunism.[42] He lectures his friend, Lord Goring, as he was once lectured by his own mentor:

> One night after dinner at Lord Radley's the baron began talking about success in modern life as something that one could reduce to an absolutely definite science. With that wonderfully fascinating quiet voice of his he expounded to us the most terrible of all philosophies, the philosophy of power, preached to us the most marvelous of all gospels, the gospel of gold. . . . he told me that luxury was nothing but a background, a painted scene in a play, and that power, power over other men, power over the world, was the one thing worth having, the one supreme pleasure worth knowing, the one joy one never tired of, and that in our century only the rich possessed it. . . . Wealth has given me enormous power. It gave me at the very outset of my life freedom, and freedom is everything.[43]

Lord Goring does not sympathize with this view or excuse his friend's corruption. He dismisses the cynical power-worship as a "thoroughly shallow creed" and pities his friend the loss of his integrity. "[Do] you despise me for what I have told you?" Chiltern asks. To which Lord Goring replies, "*with deep feeling in his voice*," "I am very sorry for you, Robert, very sorry indeed." The difference in their perspectives is made clear in their dialogue: "I did not sell myself for money," Chiltern insists; "I bought success at a great price. That is all." To which Goring replies "*gravely*," "Yes, you certainly paid a great price for it." Chiltern believes that by winning wealth and power he has gained his freedom; he cannot see that freedom is precisely what it has cost him. "I felt that I had fought the century with its own weapons, and won," he says. Goring can only repeat "*sadly*," "You thought you had won."[44] Goring does not approve of such careerism in any case, describing it as both degrading and demoralizing: "I think that in practical life there is something about success, actual success, that is a little unscrupulous, something about ambition that is unscrupulous always. Once a man has set his heart and soul on getting to a certain point, if he has to climb the crag, he climbs the crag; if he has to walk in the mire . . . he walks in the mire."[45] Yet Goring also believes that one is greater than the sum of one's flaws. Chiltern's crime, he argues, did not reflect "his real character. It was an act of folly done in his youth, dishonorable, I admit, shameful, I admit, unworthy of him, I admit, and therefore . . . not his true character."[46]

In the end, the frivolous aesthete and amoral dandy, Lord Goring, is more decent and humane than either of the representatives of bourgeois respectability, the legislator or his sanctimonious wife. It is Goring who can see Robert's crime as an offense not against some abstract moral system but against own best nature, a self-betrayal. ("And, after all," Chiltern asks, rhetorically, "who did I wrong by what I did? No one." Lord Goring, "*looking at him steadily*," responds, "Except yourself, Robert.")[47] And so it is also Goring who speaks up for love, for the importance of generosity and forgiveness. "[P]erhaps you are a little hard in some of your views on life," he tells Lady Chiltern. "All I know is that life cannot be understood without much charity, cannot be lived without much charity."[48]

We, the readers and the audience of the play, can see in Goring the representative of a different kind of ethics, not a system of law but a practice of friendship and forgiveness. The Chilterns, however, seem incapable of recognizing him as such. Gertrude and Robert learn very little. As much as their attitudes change over four acts, as much as their standards relax, they cling to a certain self-perception—Lord Chiltern as the honest political leader; Lady Chiltern as the dutiful wife; themselves together as the picture of respectable domesticity.

A sensible, happy alternative is presented by Robert's sister, Mabel, who at the end becomes engaged to Lord Goring. She is a kind of female dandy, with "the fascinating tyranny of youth, and the astonishing courage of innocence." She is not interested in ambition or idealism. She knows nothing of corruption. Integrity and forgiveness seem to her very much things to be taken for granted. She loves Lord Goring, and she loves him as he is. "I delight in your bad qualities," she tells him. "I wouldn't have you part with one of them." She loves him as much *for* his faults as despite them, and, in the play's penultimate scene, she says that she would rather be "a real wife" than have "an ideal husband."[49]

She does not, however, go quite as far as Mrs. Allonby in *A Woman of No Importance*. "The Ideal Husband?" she exclaims. "There couldn't be such a thing. The institution is wrong."[50]

Cheerful Nihilism

Wilde's final and most famous play, *The Importance of Being Earnest*, is the least clear in terms of its message. Delighting in nonsense to almost Dadaist levels, its plot develops arbitrarily, and its characters exhibit neither plausibility nor depth. The play progresses by catching its protagonists in impossible situations and then seeing them out again, safe but no wiser—all while delivering the rapid-fire witticisms that assail every treasured value of Victorian society.

Ordinarily it must sound like a criticism to say that a play's plot is insane and its characters nothing more than transparent vessels for the author's wit. But these are exactly the qualities that lend *Earnest* its buoyancy and charm. The drama is driven entirely by the dialogue; everything else is mere pretext. Like light, *Earnest* is all velocity and no mass. That is why it shines so brilliantly.

"What can a poor critic do," William Archer wrote in mock exasperation, "with a play which raises no principle, whether of art or morals, creates its own canons and conventions, and is nothing but an absolutely wilful expression of an irrepressibly witty personality?" *The Importance of Being Earnest*, he declared, "imitates nothing, represents nothing, means nothing, is nothing."[51] What Archer failed to recognize, or declined to confess, is that this forceful, willful, paradoxically affirming negation may be a kind of politics in itself. The play is a philosophical assault on common sense and an intellectual siege against conventional morality, disguised—or adorned—as a purely formal exercise in dramatic irony and verbal slapstick. It is serious in its lack of seriousness; it is nihilism played for laughs.

The plot concerns a pair of idle aristocrats—Jack and Algernon—each leading a double life. They escape the responsibilities of the town by fleeing to the country, or vice versa, creating elaborate pretenses and alter egos to facilitate their irresponsible freedom. Each man becomes romantically entangled with a young woman—one to Gwendolyn, the other to Cecily—and the plot proceeds through a series of lies followed by unmaskings that often as not reveal the lies to be the truth—until the final, inevitable, neatly orchestrated (and thus self-evidently artificial) happy ending.

The central conflict turns on the exaggerated significance assigned to the idea of a good name. The prospects of marriage—and all of the emotional, social, and economic benefits that it entails—depend narrowly and implausibly on the name "Ernest." But "Ernest" can be seen to stand in for the notion of 'a good name' in two respects: a *good name* in the sense of a good reputation, this being implied by the punning title that identifies a name with a moral quality, and a good *name* in the sense of coming from a notable or at least respectable family, having a certain kind of background and pedigree, and therefore also an elevated social position. Thus, when Jack is revealed to be a foundling, discovered as an infant in a handbag at a railway station, his beloved's Aunt Augusta is aghast: "To be born, or at any rate bred, in a handbag, whether it had handles or not, seems to me to display a contempt for the ordinary decencies of family life that reminds one of the worst excesses of the French Revolution." She sternly advises (which is to say commands), "Try and acquire some relations as soon as possible, and . . . make a definite effort to produce at any rate one parent, of either sex, before the season is quite over."[52]

What is being mocked in *Earnest* is, simply, *everything*. Eric Bentley supposes that the "margins of an annotated copy of *The Importance of Being Earnest* would show such headings as: death; money and marriage; the nature of style; ideology and economics; beauty and truth; the psychology of philanthropy; the decline of aristocracy; nineteenth-century morals; the class system."[53] The snob and the prude are caricatured in the female authorities, Lady Bracknell and Miss Prism. The deference of servants is turned back against their superiors as ironic displays of disdain. Gender roles are reversed: "the women in the play read heavy works of German philosophy and attend university courses, while the men lounge elegantly on sofas and eat dainty cucumber sandwiches."[54] The clergy are shown as harmless and ineffectual, and sacred rituals—baptism, marriage, burial—are trivialized and parodied.[55] Romance is exposed as a confusion of fact and fiction, of sentimental three-volume novels and fraudulent diaries cited as authorities. Morality is confounded and hypocrisy disarmed as identities divide, multiply, and subsequently collapse—or "explode."[56] People are always turning out to be somebody else. Truths and lies are constantly turning into one another.

Wilde even gently mocks his own earlier themes. When Jack mistakes the prudish spinster Miss Prism for his long-lost mother, she "recoil[s] in indignant astonishment" and protests, "Mr. Worthing, I am unmarried!" He is taken aback: "Unmarried!" He considers the matter gravely. "I do not deny that is a serious blow." After just a moment, however, he rises to the occasion: "But after all, who has the right to cast the first stone against one who has suffered? Cannot repentance wipe out an act of folly? Why should there be one law for men, and another for women? Mother, I forgive you."[57]

The very silliness serves a serious purpose. Weighty subjects are lightened, grand themes reduced. Ellmann observes:

> In *The Importance*, sins accursed in *Salomé* and unnamable in *Dorian Gray* are transposed into a different key and appear as Algernon's inordinate and selfish craving for—cucumber sandwiches. The substitution of mild gluttony for fearsome lechery renders all vice innocuous. There *is* a wicked brother, but he is just our old friend Algernon. The double life which is so serious a matter for Dorian or for the *Ideal Husband*, becomes Bunburying—playing Jack in the country and Ernest in town, and only to avoid boring engagements. . . . Yet amusing as the surface is, the comic energy springs from the realities that are mocked.[58]

In the *St. James's Gazette*, Wilde explained the moral of *Earnest*: "that we should treat all the trivial things of life seriously, and all the serious things of life with a sincere and studied triviality."[59] In other words, the dominant values are all wrong, society has its priorities reversed. It cares too much about the wrong things and too little about the things than truly matter. Its absolutes are arbitrary and absurd. Its great pretensions can be deflated with laughter, and in place of the established values, Wilde offers, as Emer O'Sullivan put it, "Lightness, cheerfulness, frivolity, irony—art saying yes to the world."[60]

The Chorus Line

Along with the constant theme of duplicity and the moral subversion of morality, Wilde's dramatic method seems calculated to produce a considerable confusion.

"Wilde is a difficult writer to judge," George Orwell thought. "The dialogue of his plays and stories consists almost entirely of elegant witticisms in which the notions of right and wrong which ruled Victorian society are torn to pieces; but their central theme, curiously enough, often points [to] some quite old-fashioned moral."[61] Orwell noted that the plot of *Lady Windermere's Fan* was utterly conventional by the standards of the time: "Yet that is not the impression it gives when one reads it or sees it acted, and we may guess that that was even less the impression it gave at the time. So far from seeming sentimental and edifying, the play appears frivolous and what used to be called 'daring.' Why? Because in addition to the central characters there is a kind of chorus of worldly 'sophisticated' people who keep up a ceaseless running attack upon all the beliefs current in Wilde's day—and in our own day, to a great extent."[62] Treating the background dialogue as a kind of chorus represents a good insight. As Wilde recorded in his notebook at Oxford: "in Greek tragedy the choruses express attitudes of thought, and turns of mind which it is difficult for us to sympathise with: while the actors deal more with problems that concern ourselves."[63]

There is, further, a third level of meaning present in the plays. The very artificiality of the drama confronts the audience with the artificiality of its "old-fashioned moral"—sometimes by breaking with convention, sometimes by adhering to it implausibly. Of *Windermere*, Julia Prewitt Brown writes: "As the plot proceeds along conventional lines, the audience is made to laugh at the characters' constrained relation to it, deriding its own expectations and coming upon them as illusions." Brown argues that Wilde employs the tropes of Victorian melodrama—"the hidden past, the idealistic heroine, the self-sacrificing mother, the fallen woman," as well as the theme of "crisis-resolved-through-sacrifice"—but undermines the audience's faith in what it sees by combining it with the epigrammatical inversions. "Such lines beat like butterfly wings against the Christian Victorian edifice of the action, making the audience laugh again and again at the very conventions supporting the play's structure."[64] Thus, Karl Beckson notes, "Wilde was most subversive when seeming to conform to Victorian conventions."[65]

It is worth recalling here Wilde's own maxim that "all [art]work criticises itself."[66] The subversive dialogue is layered atop a conventional plot; the radical critique contained in the aphorisms is not usually supported by the action on stage; but then, as Orwell observed, the juxtaposition tends to favor the epigrams. Wilde's plays thus lead double lives, rather like their author. Adding to this complexity is the fact that the movement of the plays, the development of the characters, the enlightenment of the audience, always depends on a transvaluation of values: "good" never means the same thing at the end of the play as at the beginning—by the end of *Earnest* we may wonder whether it means anything at all. If we consider *Lady Windermere's Fan*, for the moment, according to its original title, *The Good Woman*, then each play contains a value-laden term in its title—*Good, Importance, Ideal, Earnest*—which announces in advance exactly the moral or social concept that will undergo this transformation. The end of each play then circles back around to declare the transvaluation complete: Mrs. Erlynne is praised as "a very good woman"; Lord Illingworth is dismissed as "A man of no importance"; Mabel Chiltern asserts, "An ideal husband! Oh, I don't think I should like that"; and, of course, Jack quips at the end of the play, "On the contrary, Aunt Augusta, I've now realised for the first time in my life the vital Importance of Being Earnest."[67]

Where Nietzsche's strategy was a frontal attack, Wilde's was one of infiltration and subversion. By provoking but not antagonizing, he disarmed the audience with his wit and made them complicit with their laughter. "The lighter his touch," Seamus Heaney remarked, "the more devastating his effect."[68]

Marriage, Family, and Legitimacy

Lawless Love and Loveless Marriage

Central to all four of these plays is the intersection between class society and family life—or, seen differently, the nexus of church, state, and commerce.

Questions of legitimacy feature prominently in three of the four. This was a matter of active agitation in Wilde's day—by his own father, Sir William Wilde, who himself had three illegitimate children, and by the radicals of the Legitimation League, whose American branch was founded by the anarchist Moses Harman and led by his daughter Lillian.[69] At issue were questions of social acceptance, the duty of paternal support, and the rights of inheritance. The mere existence of children outside marriage struck at the heart of the legal, social, and economic construction of the "family." Both law and custom therefore sought to preserve the class system by legitimizing some births but not others and to enforce sexual morality by punishing inconvenient children. It was practically assumed that the children must share in the sin of the parents, as well as their disgrace, and that the status of one's birth should be treated as a mark against one's character. This presumption explains the anxiety over the parentage of some of Wilde's characters and the lengths taken to hide the truth of Gerald Arbuthnot's and Lady Windermere's origins, even from themselves.

The other crucial issue—central to all four plays—is the critique of marriage. The angles of attack here are numerous. In *Lady Windermere* marriage is a means to gain a fortune and serves as the emblem of respectability, though its respectability is shown to rely on sacrificing others for one's own sins. For the Chilterns (in *An Ideal Husband*) marriage is first an exercise in mutual (and self-) deception; then, when the couple come to understand and accept one another, it becomes the mask and shelter for hypocrisy. For Mrs. Arbuthnot, that "woman of no importance," marriage is something holy and therefore unattainable—"a sacrament for those who love each other . . . not for such as him or such as me."[70] Her son Gerald sees it as a duty, necessary even if undesirable. For Lord Illingworth is it simply a means to an end. For Lady Bracknell, marriage is a kind of financial speculation; for Cecily, it is a daydream imposed on reality; by the end of *Earnest*, it is reduced to a dramatic convention.

Throughout the plays, and earlier in *Dorian Gray*, marriage provides a reliable target for Wilde's barrage of epigrams: "How marriage ruins a man! It is as demoralising as cigarettes, and far more expensive."[71] "Twenty years of romance make a woman look like a ruin; but twenty years of marriage make her look something like a public building."[72] "Men marry because they are tired; women, because they are curious; both are disappointed."[73] "In married life, three is company and two none."[74] "The proper basis for marriage is a mutual misunderstanding."[75]

The humor of such remarks relies, first, of course, on their defeating our expectations—but then too on the shock of recognition. Such quips point to the difference between the ideals of romantic love and the realities of married life—or, more particularly, to marriage as a social institution.[76] That such a gap exists, that the institution can become not the guardian but the jailer of romantic feeling, suggests that marriage serves purposes distinct from, and at time at odds with, the wants and interests of the individuals it binds together. Wilde's plays, while giving the formal appearance of conventional romance, are frank in their treatment of the institution as a means of managing economic and social stratification.

Logically enough, Wilde argues in "The Soul of Man under Socialism" that in an egalitarian society the institution would serve no purpose and cease to exist: "With the abolition of private property, marriage in its present form must disappear."[77] Wilde saw that marriage, like the other institutions of capitalist society, had a deleterious effect on the individuality of those it constrained. Lord Henry Wotton's critique in *Dorian Gray*—"The real disadvantage to marriage is that it makes one unselfish. And unselfish people are colorless. They lack individuality"—perfectly anticipates Wilde's opening remarks in "The Soul of Man," that "socialism would relieve us of the sordid necessity of living for others."[78] Instead of a system of "legal restraint," our relationships would take on "a form of freedom that will help the full development of a personality, and make the love of man and woman more wonderful, more beautiful, and more ennobling."[79]

These ideas, somewhat scandalous even now, were perfectly in line with the program of "free love" commonly put forward by anarchists before Wilde's time and since. Bakunin, for instance, argued, "With the abolition of the right of inheritance and the education of the children assured by society, all the legal reasons for the irrevocability of marriage will disappear." Instead he proposed both that the "union of a man and a woman must be free" and that *within* such unions "man and woman must enjoy absolute liberty." Such, he said, was not only a matter of rights and justice, but also "the indispensable condition for moral sincerity."[80] Freedom, in other words, is what makes love possible.

The American individualist anarchist Ezra Heywood, in his 1876 pamphlet *Cupid's Yokes*, likewise made that case that marriage was an affront to individual freedom, and the autonomy of women in particular. Taking the foundation of marriage to be economic in nature, he argued that the low wages paid to women forced them to turn to men for support, becoming in essence one or another type of prostitute—either one "who receives a buyer for the night," or else one "who, marrying for a home, becomes a 'prostitute' for life."[81] Furthermore, Heywood surmised that the institution, with its "visible bonds," "tends to destroy [the] Magnetic Forces" of spontaneous attraction that might otherwise "induce unity" between lovers. Our relationships, he believed, should be regulated solely by "mutual discretion—a free compact, dissolvable at will." Love should not be governed by church or state but must stand on its own as "the essential principle of Nature" and ultimately "a law unto itself."[82]

After the century's turn, Emma Goldman continued this tradition of thought: "The popular notion about marriage and love is that they are synonymous," she wrote; that is, "they spring from the same motives and cover the same human needs." Instead, she declared, "Marriage and love have nothing in common; they are as far apart as the poles; are, in fact, antagonistic to each other." She saw the harm that marriage did, first, in its assault on individuality, especially for the woman, who pays "with her name, her privacy, her self-respect" and is then condemned "to life-long dependency, to parasitism, to completely uselessness."[83] In consequence, wedlock "incapacitates her for life's struggle, annihilates her social consciousness, paralyzes her imagination, and then imposes its gracious protection, which is in reality a snare, a travesty on human character."[84] Second, Goldman saw that marriage entrenches gender roles and with them the division in outlook such that, though they may live together for years, the couple remain to one another unknown and unknowable—little more than intimate strangers.[85]

Though by no means an anarchist, the journalist W. T. Stead, whose crusade against prostitution (as we shall see) had severe consequences for Wilde personally, was sympathetic to such critiques. He wrote in his *Review of Reviews* that he was glad to see "Modern Woman" escape the "monogamic prostitution of loveless marriage and the hideous outrage of enforced maternity." He offered up a slogan: "Better lawless love than loveless marriage."[86]

At Home in the House Beautiful

Naturally Oscar Wilde's views on women and family life had their effect in his own home. Wilde advised, "Men must give up the tyranny in married life which was once so dear to them, and which, we are afraid, lingers still, here and there."[87] He was eager that his wife Constance have and pursue her own ideas, her own interests, her own projects and commitments.

Though Constance's politics were generally more moderate than Oscar's, she was in fact much more active. She joined the Women's Liberal Federation; advocated women's suffrage; canvassed for Liberal candidates (including Margaret Sandhurst); delivered speeches on subjects such as "rational dress," international peace, and Home Rule in Ireland; and edited the *Rational Dress Society Gazette*.[88] (The journal defined its aims: "The Rational Dress Society protests against the introduction of any fashion in dress that either deforms the figure, impedes the movements of the body, or in any way tends to injure the health," including "tightly-fitting corsets . . . , high-heeled or narrow-toed boots and shoes . . . , [and] heavily-weighted skirts.")[89] Perhaps most notably, Constance believed that marriage should exist as a contract of limited duration, renewable if desired.[90]

Together Oscar and Constance took an attitude toward their sons quite at odds with the disciplinarian norm. In the Wilde home the children were allowed full access to the house, excepting only Oscar's study.[91] And Oscar, who was anything but the stern and remote Victorian patriarch, gloried in their play, often joining in himself, in addition to mending their toys, building sandcastles at the beach, and teaching them Irish folk songs.[92] His son Vyvyan later recalled, "Most parents in those days were far too solemn and pompous with their children, insisting on a vast amount of usually undeserved respect. My own father was quite different; he had so much of the child in his own nature that he delighted in playing our games. He would go down on all fours on the nursery floor, being in turn a lion, a wolf, a horse, caring nothing for his usually immaculate appearance."[93]

In the end, of course, Wilde's philandering destroyed his family.[94] Moralists, and those with very shallow natures, sometimes assume therefore that he did not love them.[95] Surviving evidence—his letters to Constance, his son's memoirs, the testimony of a French boy who met him in his exile—strongly suggests that he did.[96]

When he heard of his wife's death, Oscar immediately sent a pair of telegrams. One to Robbie Ross: "Constance is dead. Please come tomorrow and stay at my hotel. Am in great grief."[97] The other to her brother, Otho: "Am overwhelmed with grief. It is the most terrible tragedy."[98] The next day he wrote to Carlos Blacker, "It is really awful. I don't know what to do. If we had only met once, and kissed each other. It is too late. How awful life is. . . . I don't dare to be by myself."[99]

The following February Oscar visited Constance's grave and covered it with roses.[100] Reading the name on the stone—"her surname, my name, not mentioned of course"—he broke down sobbing, overwhelmed with the sense of regret, and "the uselessness of all regrets."[101]

The Unwritten Tragedy

That Wilde foresaw the tragedy of his life, and that he regretted what it would do to his wife, is indicated by the theme of his final, ultimately unwritten play.

In 1894 he wrote to the theater manager George Alexander to propose a new drama: "A man of rank and fashion marries a simple sweet country girl—a lady—but simple and ignorant of fashionable life." They live at his country house, and after a while he arranges a party, inviting "a lot of fashionable *fin-de-siècle* women and men." The play opens with him "lecturing his wife on how to behave—not to be prudish, etc.—and not to mind if anyone flirts with her. He says to her, 'I have asked Gerald Lancing who used to admire you so much. Flirt with him as much as you like.'"

At the party, the guests "are horrid to the wife, they think her dowdy and dull." Over the course of the evening, she discovers that her husband is having an affair, yet intercedes to guard the secret from the other woman's husband. As a result of this incident, she decides to abandon her marriage and run away with Gerald. The husband, however, "is rather repentant" and "implores Gerald to use his influence with the wife to make her forgive him." Gerald promises he will try, though "it is a great act of self-sacrifice." When Gerald makes good on this promise and urges the wife to take back her husband, "She refuses with scorn." Gerald feels caught between his duty and his desire. "Do you not see that I am really sacrificing myself?" he asks her, pleading. She retorts: "Why should you sacrifice me? . . . You have no right to hand my life over to anyone else." Moreover: "All this self-sacrifice is wrong, we are meant to live. That is the meaning of life."

The final act is set three months later. It is the day of a duel between Gerald and the husband. Just before the appointed hour, the husband confronts his wife. She is adamant in her love for Gerald, and that "nothing would induce her to go back to her husband." Given the choice, she would rather her husband die, "Because the father of my child must live."

The husband exits the stage, and pistol shots are heard a moment later. Gerald then enters and announces that his opponent did not show for the duel. It seems the husband has shot himself instead.

"What a coward," says Gerald.

"No," she answers, "not at the end. He is dead. We must love one another devotedly now."

The play closes "with Gerald and the wife clinging to each other as if with a mad desire to make love eternal." Wilde was absolutely clear in his intended message: "*I want sheer passion of love to dominate everything,*" he said. "No morbid self-sacrifice. No renunciation."[102]

This sketch was eventually adapted for the stage by Frank Harris, not with great success, as *Mr. and Mrs. Daventry*. Wilde had decided to call it *Love Is Law*, though some sources claim that his original title was *Constance*.[103] The latter may mark the play as an apology, a justification, an homage, or a wish. In any case, it fits the pattern of the other plays by signaling a moral transvaluation: the meaning of "constancy" must seem different at the end of the play than it would at the beginning. The wife in this drama may abandon her husband and commit adultery, but she *is* faithful, after her fashion—if not to her wedding vows, then to the "law" of love; if not to her husband, then to herself.

Chapter 4

A Language of Love

Posing, Speaking, Naming, Queering

The Ordeal

Queensberry Rules

It is not clear when Oscar Wilde had his first sexual encounter with a man. Many think it was with Robbie Ross in 1886; others suggest that it may have been at Oxford.[1] If not at Oxford, then perhaps after, when he shared rooms with the artist Frank Miles.[2] Or, if we like, we can imagine that it might have been in 1882, with Walt Whitman. ("I have the kiss of Walt Whitman still on my lips," Wilde said after visiting the elder poet.)[3] That this is considered an important scholarly question and not mere gossip is itself interesting. Homosexuality (to use our term, not Wilde's) was not simply a matter of taste or personal preference.[4] For Wilde it was a thrilling adventure and a source of inspiration, a subject for artists and philosophers as well as for lovers; whereas for society it was a problem—moral, social, psychological, and legal. The clash between these perspectives lent Wilde's sex life a sense of danger, which he admitted was "half the excitement."[5] It was ultimately to be his undoing.

Oscar Wilde met Lord Alfred Douglas in 1891. Wilde was thirty-seven years old, a famous novelist and poet (not yet a very successful dramatist). "Bosie," as he was known to friends, was not quite twenty-one (and looked much younger), an Oxford undergraduate and aspiring poet. Douglas visited Wilde's Tite Street home ready to worship him. He had read *Dorian Gray* "fourteen times running" and then arranged for a meeting through a mutual friend, the poet Lionel Johnson.[6] Wilde would soon worship Douglas as well, his slender frame, his delicate good looks, his sharp intelligence, his taste, his title, his hedonism, even his faults—his petulant, irresponsible, altogether selfish nature.

Douglas's father, the Marquess of Queensberry, objected to what he viewed as an unwholesome intimacy between Wilde and his son, and he demanded that it end. Their friendship offended Queensberry as much personally as morally. Though estranged from his family, the Marquess nevertheless insisted on his role as patriarchal ruler-protector. It was thus not only paternal concern and moral disapproval that fueled his feud with Wilde but also a sense of personal insult. He took his son's tie to Wilde as an affront to his own authority and ultimately to his masculinity.[7] He found their relationship not only "loathsome and disgusting" but humiliating to himself as well.[8]

Accompanied by a prize-fighting lackey, Queensberry confronted Wilde at his home. "If I catch you and my son together in any public restaurant," he announced, "I will thrash you." To which Wilde replied, "I don't know what the Queensberry rules are, but the Oscar Wilde rule is to shoot at sight."[9] Bosie did in fact begin carrying a revolver, though it only proved embarrassing, going off by mistake at a restaurant and shattering a window.[10]

A few weeks later Queensberry attempted to disrupt the premiere of *The Importance of Being Earnest*, carrying a "grotesque bouquet of vegetables."[11] In all probability, he planned to pelt Wilde with them and deliver a speech denouncing him. The theater received advanced warning, however, and police guarded the entryways.[12] After a few days, Queensberry tried calling at Wilde's club. Wilde was not there, so he left a card at the front desk, the words scribbled on it, "For Oscar Wilde, Posing as a Somdomite [*sic*]."[13] When Wilde received the card, he viewed it as a provocation intended "to insult me before the whole world, and in such a manner that if I retaliated I would be ruined, and if I did not retaliate I would be ruined also."[14] Urged on by Bosie, Wilde decided to prosecute Queensberry for libel. The tactic backfired. Queensberry had hired a private investigator—in fact, a former detective-inspector of the Special Branch dedicated to suppressing the Fenians and anarchists—and stood ready to produce a whole parade of blackmailers, street hustlers, rent boys, and hotel staff to attest to the truth of his accusation.[15] Wilde was forced to withdraw the case, in effect admitting the charge, and the Crown prepared to prosecute. That same evening, April 5, 1895, he was arrested.[16]

Literary Criticism as Cross-Examination

The differences between the trials—one with Oscar as plaintiff, two more as defendant—are perhaps interesting from a legal point of view, but ultimately more important is the total effect, the way themes introduced in the first hearings carried over into the others, even as the locus of argument moved away from the question of libel toward specific allegations of identifiable criminal acts.

The task of Queensberry's counsel, Edward Carson—later a leader of the Ulster Unionists and planner of the Irish Partition—was not primarily to prove that Wilde had *done* anything but to defend the notion that he was "posing" as a sodomite.[17] The emphasis on *image* is the reason—in the first trial, especially—relatively few of the questions put to Wilde concerned either his sexual identity or sexual practices; many more addressed questions of literature and class. Particular attention was given to Wilde's letters to Douglas, *The Picture of Dorian Gray*, and the contents of a college literary magazine, the *Chameleon*.

The letters were of interest partly for what they were—"Isn't that a love letter?" Carson asked; to which Wilde replied, "It is a letter expressive of love"—and partly because they had been the subject of blackmail, a fact that suggested both a shameful secret and an association with disreputable people.[18]

The discussion of *Dorian Gray* was extensive but, for Wilde, familiar. Nearly all the early reviews of the novel had been hostile. The *Athenaeum* called the book "unmanly, sickening, vicious."[19] The *St. James's Gazette* wondered "whether the Treasury or the Vigilance Society will think it worth while to prosecute Mr. Oscar Wilde."[20] The *Scots Observer* conceded that the novel was "ingenious, interesting, full of cleverness, and plainly the work of a man of letters" but nevertheless felt that "its interest is medico-legal," that it was "only fitted for the Criminal Investigation Department" and had been written "for none but outlawed noblemen and perverted telegraph boys."[21] (This last phrase was a reference to the 1889 Cleveland Street scandal, in which the questioning of a fifteen-year-old telegraph messenger, suspected of theft, led to the discovery of a male brothel. Police surveillance identified several prominent people entering the building at 19 Cleveland Street, including two members of Parliament and Lord Arthur Somerset, who soon fled abroad.)²² Wilde had responded to the unfriendly reviews with a series of letters, first denying that "any work of art can be criticised from a moral standpoint," then declaring the novel's moral "extremely obvious" and indeed "too apparent," and finally turning the accusation back against those who made it: "Each man sees his own sin in Dorian Gray. What Dorian Gray's sins are no one knows. He who finds them has brought them."²³ Carson revisited this controversy in the courtroom, even reading aloud from the papers, and had more success than the critics did in trapping the author. Facing persistent questioning about the publication history and the reasons for changes in later editions, Wilde was forced to admit that certain passages from the original *Lippincott's* version might "convey the impression that the sin of Dorian Gray was sodomy."²⁴

However, the most damaging piece of literary evidence was the one with which Wilde had the least to do. The *Chameleon* was an Oxford magazine founded and edited by John Bloxam ("an undergraduate of strange beauty," in Wilde's opinion).²⁵ Wilde contributed a collection of aphorisms under the title "Phrases and Philosophies for the Use of the Young." Douglas submitted his poems "Two Loves" and "I Am Shame." Bloxam anonymously included a story of his own, "The Priest and the Acolyte," which tells of a love affair between a novice priest and a fourteen-year-old boy, ending in a suicide pact.²⁶ Wilde's contribution received relatively little probing in court, but he was questioned at great length about "The Priest and the Acolyte," which he did not even like, much less compose.²⁷ The prosecutor's aim was to establish a continuity between this story, the letters to Lord Alfred Douglas, and *Dorian Gray*: "It is exactly the same idea," Carson said, "exactly the same notion."²⁸

Silence Preserved

The most remarkable moment of any of the trials came when Wilde was asked about Lord Alfred Douglas's writing. His poem "Two Loves" tells of a dream in which the narrator finds himself in a garden. Two figures approach.

The one did joyous seem
And fair and blooming, and a sweet refrain
Came from his lips; he sang of pretty maids
And joyous love of comely girl and boy.

The other child, "that was his comrade," was "sad and sweet" and "sighed with many sighs." Taking pity, the narrator asks the boy, "Tell me why, sad and sighing, thou dost rove / These pleasant realms? . . . / What is thy name?" To which the boy replies, "My name is Love."

But the first boy "Then straight . . . did turn himself to me," and he interrupts, saying:

He lieth, for his name is Shame,
But I am Love. . . .
I am true Love, I fill
The hearts of boy and girl with mutual flame.

The second boy, still "sighing," concedes the point, or seems to: "Have thy will," he says. "I am the Love that dare not speak its name."[29]

Same-sex passion is not specifically identified in the poem, but Carson thought the meaning clear: "Any person can read it and there is no difficulty in seeing in it that the whole object and the whole idea of it is to draw the distinction between what the world calls 'love' and what the world calls 'shame,' one being the love that a man bears towards a woman, the other being the unholy shame that a man ought to have if he ventures to transfer that kind of love and that kind of passion to a man."[30]

Ironically, the poem achieves this clarity by mimicking the social taboo. The very refusal to name the love is itself a way of naming it. According to William Blackstone's *Commentaries on the Laws of England*, "our English law . . . in its very indictments" treats sodomy "as a crime not fit to be named: '*peccatum illud horribile, inter christianos non nominandum.*'"[31] (Literally: "that horrible crime not to be named among Christians.")[32]

The final line of "Two Loves" would become the most famous in all of gay literature, though it may owe its renown less to the quality of the poem than to Wilde's defense of it. In his second trial, Charles Gill, the prosecuting attorney, asked for Wilde's interpretation of "Two Loves": "Is it not clear that the love described relates to natural love and unnatural love?"

"No," Wilde answered with deceptive simplicity, silently rejecting the terms of the question.

But the prosecutor insisted: "What is the 'Love that dare not speak its name'?"

To which Wilde replied, with both candor and courage:

> "The Love that dare not speak its name" in this century is such a great affection of an elder for a younger man as there was between David and Jonathan, such as Plato made the very basis of his philosophy, and such as you find in the sonnets of Michelangelo and Shakespeare. It is that deep, spiritual affection that is as pure as it is perfect. It dictates and pervades great works of art like those of Shakespeare and Michelangelo, and those two letters of mine, such as they are. It is in this century misunderstood, so much misunderstood that it may be described as the "Love that dare not speak its name," and on account of it I am placed where I am now. It is beautiful, it is fine, it is the noblest form of affection. There is nothing unnatural about it. It is intellectual, and it repeatedly exists between an elder and a younger man, when the elder man has his intellect, and the younger has all the joy, hope and glamour of life before him. That it should be so the world does not understand. The world mocks at it and sometimes puts one in the pillory for it.[33]

This short, extemporaneous speech was greeted with a roar of applause from the gallery, prompting the judge to warn, "If there is the slightest manifestation of feeling I shall have the Court cleared. There must be complete silence preserved"—a statement that, under the circumstances, said more than was intended.[34]

Plato Inverted

Wilde's strategy throughout the first trial was one of substitution and transposition. Asked about sex, he speaks instead of art, beauty, philosophy. He consistently moves the conversation away from the physical manifestations of love and desire, and toward the abstract, the intellectual, the ideal. The strategy is one of applied Platonism and points to the irony inherent in the phrase "Platonic love," which originates in the very passages of the *Symposium* dealing with the love between men.

Thomas Wright explains:

> Plato's dialogues lay at the heart of the late nineteenth-century debate about Greek homosexuality. In the *Symposium*, homosexual passion is discussed frankly and with ecstatic enthusiasm at an Athenian drinking party, where the topic of love is examined by various speakers. Socrates offers an ardent and eloquent defense, describing the progression of a human soul from the love of a specific young man to the love of beauty and other abstract virtues. The philosopher ranks the [same-sex] passion far above its heterosexual equivalent in the spiritual hierarchy, depicting the love of women as sensual and degrading. . . . [He particularly] celebrates the *paiderastic* union of an older and a younger man in which wisdom and experience are exchanged for energy, ardor and beauty. . . . [In other dialogues] Socrates tutors Charmides—a young man who captivates him by his boyish grace—in the way of philosophic righteousness.[35]

In his Oxford notebook, Wilde had summed up this process of abstracting from the item to the type, from the immediate to the ideal, and the kind of relationship that might facilitate it. Plato's view, he wrote, encompassed both the "impassioned search after truth, as well as the romantic side of that friendship so necessary for philosophy." We find in our beloved the instance by which we can come to understand the ideal: "from the love of the beautiful object we rise to the ideal *eros*; from Charmides to the *form of the good.*"[36] "Friendship," Wilde later wrote, "could have designed no better warrant for its permanence or its ardours than the Platonic theory, or creed, as we might better call it, that the true world was the world of ideas, and that these ideas took visible form and became incarnate in man."[37]

Foucault reminds us that for the Greeks pederasty was not simply "a fondness for boys" but also a complex set of behaviors and norms: "a courtship practice, a moral reflection, and . . . a philosophical asceticism."[38] For the Greeks, pederasty was constrained and legitimized by an ethics of moderation and self-mastery.[39] Socrates understood "ruling himself" as "being temperate, master of himself, ruling the pleasures and appetites within him." Wilde reverses the formulation: "Only one thing remains infinitely fascinating to me, the mystery of moods. To be master of these moods is exquisite, to be mastered by them more exquisite still."[40]

What these two approaches share is conveyed by Foucault's observation that "the ethics of pleasure is of the same order of reality as the political structure."[41] Where for the Greeks self-control provided the model and justification for authority over others, for Wilde one must free oneself just as one allows others their freedom.[42] "I only demand that freedom which I willingly concede to others," he said.[43]

Social Distinctions

Though it may seem out of place in a court of law, the literary questioning was in fact the aspect of the proceedings to which Wilde was best suited and for which he was most prepared. Just before trial, he had asked Frank Harris to testify to *Dorian Gray*'s moral worth. Harris responded forcefully:

> For God's sake, man, put everything on that plane out of your head. You don't realize what is going to happen to you. It is not going to be a matter of clever talk about your books. They are going to bring a string of witnesses that will put art and literature out of the question. [Your attorney] will throw up his brief. He will carry the case to a certain point; and then, when he sees the avalanche coming, he will back out and leave you in the dock. What you have got to do is cross to France tonight. . . . *I tell you I know.*[44]

Harris did know. That is exactly what happened. As soon as it was clear that the literary questions would be superseded by witnesses testifying that Wilde *was* what he posed as, the libel case collapsed, and the criminal case became inevitable.

Queensberry's lawyers listed thirteen boys with whom Wilde had committed "sodomy and other acts of gross indecency and immorality."[45] For each one, Carson made certain to specify his age and his occupation, then demanded to know if such person was a suitable companion for a gentleman. Wilde, responding with growing impatience, would insist again and again, "I don't care about social positions."[46] For instance:

> "Was he a gentleman's servant out of employment?" . . .
>
> "I had no knowledge of that. . . . I never heard it, nor should I have minded. I don't care two pence about people's social position."
>
> "Even if he was a gentleman's servant out of employment you would become friendly with him?"
>
> "I would become friendly with any human being that I liked and chose to become friendly with."[47]

And:

> "Did you know that one of them was a gentleman's valet and the other was a gentleman's groom?"
>
> "I didn't know it, nor should I have cared."
>
> "Nor should you have cared?"
>
> "No, I don't think two pence for social position; if I like them, I like them. It is a snobbish and vulgar thing to do."
>
> "What enjoyment was it to you, Mr Wilde, to be dining and entertaining grooms and coachmen?"
>
> "The pleasure of being with those who are young, bright, happy, careless, and amusing."[48]

And again:

> "What I would like to ask you is this: What was there in common between you and these young men of this class?"
>
> "Well, I will tell you, Mr Carson, I delight in the society of people much younger than myself. I like those who may be called idle and careless. I recognize no social distinctions at all of any kind. . . ."
>
> "Then do I understand that even a young boy that you would pick up in the street would be a pleasing companion to you?"

"Oh, I would talk to a street Arab [a homeless urchin] if he talked to me, with pleasure."[49]

And so on.

The Only Democratic Thing

Biographer Neil McKenna notes that Wilde's "paean to the joys of youth—and youths—was damaging" but no more damaging than "his views on social distinctions, which struck the jury as something akin to anarchism."[50] In fact, the two attitudes, both subversive—indeed, by Carson's reading, unnatural—were ideologically connected.

John Addington Symonds—a poet and critic, an Oxford Hellenist who used the classics as a means to safely explore homosexuality—thought that same-sex love would undermine the British social hierarchy.[51] He wrote: "The blending of social strata in masculine love seems to me one of the most pronounced, and socially hopeful features. . . . Where it appears, it abolishes class distinctions."[52] Edward Carpenter went still further. He thought that same-sex passion represented a "forward force in human evolution."[53] Carpenter saw such relationships as socially beneficial in that they could produce a sense of responsibility beyond family ties and break down class distinctions, leading ultimately to democracy and peace.[54]

"Love is the only democratic thing," Wilde said to George Ives, the author of several volumes of homoerotic poetry intended as political propaganda.[55] Recording the line in his diary, Ives then commented, "Oscar, you were right there; Love is the only democratic thing. The only bond which really binds the brotherhood of man."[56]

At the end of the first trial, Carson abruptly turned Wilde's social leveling against him by contrasting his elitist ideas about art with his more open attitudes about friendship. The two halves of this duality had already appeared together in Wilde's admiration for the disobedient poor and open disdain for public opinion in "The Soul of Man under Socialism."[57] But in court this seeming contradiction was assigned a more sinister meaning: "As regards literature his standard was a very high one," Carson lectured the jury. "His works could really only be understood by the artists and he was indifferent as to what the ordinary individual thought of them. . . . Gentlemen of the jury, contrast that with the position he takes up as regards these lads."[58] They were not artists but worked as servants or newsboys. And,

> when you confront him with these curious associations of a man of high art, his case is no longer that he's dealing in regions of art, which no one can understand but himself and the artistic, but his case is that he is such a magnanimous, such a noble, such a democratic soul that he draws no social distinctions, and it is equally the same pleasure to him to have a sweeping-boy from the street—if he is only interesting—to lunch with him or to dine with him, as the best educated artists or the greatest *littérateur* in the whole kingdom.[59]

The prosecutor's insinuation was not merely that Wilde was lying—whether about art or about class—but that he used his standing and sophistication to prey on younger, less powerful, unsuspecting boys of the lower classes.

Of course, it is impossible to know how much Carson genuinely believed this and how much it was a cynical rhetorical trick. For to produce the necessary witnesses—men who were, after all, equally guilty of the sexual offenses (plus, in some cases, of blackmail)—it was necessary to grant them a degree of immunity, which meant for narrative purposes casting them as victims rather than accomplices. Carson advised the jury: "Let those who are inclined to condemn these young men for allowing themselves to be dominated, misled, corrupted by Mr Oscar Wilde, remember the relative position of the two parties, and remember that they are men who have been more sinned against than sinning. . . . [In] not one of these cases were these parties upon an equality in any way with Mr Wilde."[60] Wilde then becomes not a lover of boys but a corruptor of the youth; not a mere pederast but a predator.

There is a bitter irony to this line of argument. Had Wilde simply paid these young men for sex, then they would have been prostitutes and that would be that. Had they gone to bed with him and then demanded money not to go to his wife or the press or the authorities, then they would have been blackmailers.[61] Had Wilde been content to hire prostitutes or pay off blackmailers, his guilt may have been unchanged, but the character assigned to him at trial would have seemed very different.[62] Instead he took an interest in these boys, wanted to know them, to hear about their lives, their aspirations, and their ideas. He was generous to them.[63] He took them on trips, bought them suits and silver cigarette cases, paid for dinners in expensive restaurants, gave them champagne. All of this, in Carson's eyes, was so much worse. He denounced Wilde for taking one fellow "out of his proper sphere . . . giving him champagne lunches, taking him to his hotel, treating him in a manner which, of course, . . . in the future [he] could never expect to live up to."[64] As Carson saw it, Wilde did not merely hire young men for sex but also seduced and corrupted them. He did not simply pay them but treated them, spoiled them, gave them ideas above their station. Even his kindness stood as a mark against him.

Pronouncing Judgment

The first trial ended when Wilde withdrew his complaint. The second trial failed to produce a verdict. At the third trial Wilde was convicted.

Though he was guilty of many of the charges, and much else beside, he later held that in some instances "the sins of another were being placed to my account" and that the prosecution's witnesses had been "coached . . . in the absolute transference, deliberate, plotted, and rehearsed, of the actions and doings of someone else on to me." (Textual evidence suggests that the unnamed party was Lord Alfred Douglas.) Had Wilde revealed the ruse, "I could have walked out of Court with my tongue in my cheek, and my hands in my pockets, a free man." But that would have meant "sav[ing] myself at [another's] expense. . . . Such a course of action would have been beneath me. . . . To have secured my acquittal by such means would have been a lifelong torture to me."[65] And so Wilde resigned himself to his fate, accepted it as a matter of principle, a point of honor.

In this resolve, he was not alone. Next to him in the dock stood Alfred Taylor, a good-natured gentleman who excelled at picking up working-class boys and playing matchmaker, setting them up with his older and wealthier friends. Sometimes these friends, including Wilde, would show their gratitude by buying him dinner or making a gift of money. If they were so inclined, Taylor was in no position to refuse. He had spent through his inheritance and was quickly nearing bankruptcy.[66] His role as procurer was exposed in the Queensberry trial, and he had been arrested the same evening as Wilde. Facing an almost certain conviction, he was offered his own freedom if he would testify for the prosecution. He heroically refused. The two men were condemned together.[67]

Announcing the penalty, the judge was unequivocal:

> Oscar Wilde and Alfred Taylor, the crime of which you have been convicted is so bad that one has to put stern restraint upon one's self to prevent one's self from describing, in language which I would rather not use, the sentiments which must rise to the breast of every man of honour who has heard the details of these two terrible trials. . . .
>
> It is no use for me to address you. People who can do these things must be dead to all sense of shame, and one cannot hope to produce any effect upon them. It is the worst case I have ever tried. That you, Taylor, kept a kind of male brothel it is impossible to doubt. And that you, Wilde, have been the centre of a circle of extensive corruption of the most hideous kind among young men, it is equally impossible to doubt.
>
> I shall, under such circumstances, be expected to pass the severest sentence that the law allows. In my judgment it is totally inadequate for such a case as this. The sentence of the Court is that each of you be imprisoned and kept to hard labour for two years.

Cries of "Oh!" and "Shame!" erupted throughout the courtroom.

"And I?" Wilde implored. "May I say nothing, my lord?"

But the judge only gestured to the warders, who took the prisoners away.[68]

Names and Laws

Victorian Babylon

The statute under which Wilde was prosecuted was not primarily concerned with homosexuality but with prostitution. It originated in a campaign by the liberal journalist W. T. Stead, who purchased a thirteen-year-old girl in order to demonstrate the existence of child prostitution in Britain's "Babylon."[69] The outrage that Stead's reporting provoked quickly translated into legislative action. Barely a month after the exposé first ran, in August 1885, Parliament passed "an Act to make further provisions for the Protection of Women and Girls; the suppression of brothels, and other purposes."[70] Among its stipulations, the new law raised the age of consent from thirteen to sixteen, made procurement a crime, and imposed whipping or penal servitude as the penalty for assaulting a child.[71] Prostitution had been understood as a pressing social problem for some time—the Salvation Army's General William Booth estimated that there were thirty thousand prostitutes living in London—but whether it was a problem of economics or morality was roundly debated, and in practice society proved much more eager to rescue young women from sex than from poverty.[72]

Neither Stead's article nor the drafted legislation initially mentioned homosexuality or male prostitution; that was literally an afterthought. Late in the debates, Henry Labouchere, the Liberal-Radical MP representing Northampton, added an amendment reading: "Any male person who, in public or private commits or is a party to the commission of, or procures the commission by any male person, of any act of gross indecency with another male person, shall be guilty of a misdemeanour, and being convicted thereof shall be liable at the discretion of the Court to be imprisoned for any term not exceeding two years, with or without hard labour."[73]

Sodomy and Identity

Before the Labouchere Amendment, the only law specifically proscribing homosexual activity was that against sodomy. First introduced in 1533 by that paragon of sexual morality and domestic virtue Henry VIII, the law prohibited "the detestable and abominable vice of buggery committed with mankind or beast." It pertained equally to acts occurring between two men, a man and a woman, or a man and an animal. The penalty was death.[74] But the rate of prosecution was always uneven, and the last execution for sodomy had taken place in 1830. In 1861 Parliament passed the Offenses Against the Person Act, which removed the threat of death and substituted a sentence of ten years to life.[75]

It was not merely the law that changed. During the later nineteenth century, a more fundamental shift was also underway, one altering the entire understanding of same-sex desire. *Sodomy* had been an act, a sin, a crime, a momentary or habitual deviation; a *sodomite* was simply a man who had been tempted and succumbed, once or a thousand times. *Homosexuality*, in contrast, was a disposition, an orientation, an outlook, an identity, and perhaps also a lifestyle and a worldview. The *homosexual* was a distinct personality, a psychological type. Sodomy was nobody's property, in either sense of the word. It was neither the unique possession of some identifiable group, like a trade secret, nor an inherent quality of an individual's personality, like intelligence or taste. But homosexuality *was*—or was argued to be—both the distinctive attribute of particular individuals and the common feature of a specific population. Sodomy represented a general temptation, not a specific temperament; homosexuality, the reverse.[76]

There had, of course, been same-sex passions before the reign of Victoria—and likewise love affairs, sexual encounters, committed relationships, and even distinct subcultures with their own codes, customs, argot, and established roles.[77] What was new in the late 1800s was the articulated notion that participation in such practices, relationships, or cultures might constitute or reveal an *identity*—that is, at once a deeply personal psychological truth *and* a sense of collectivity, of community, of shared interests and a common outlook. "The homosexual" as a figure was only beginning to enter the public consciousness, the result not merely of multiple, overlapping, and sometimes contradictory discourses but also of complementary but conflicting political programs.

Coming to Terms

The words *homosexual* and *heterosexual* are of expressly political origin.

Karl Ulrichs led a campaign for a more tolerant view of same-sex love after he was fired from the German civil service after his own proclivities were discovered. He was not a scientist, but he searched the medical literature for evidence that same-sex desire was natural, innate, and immutable. Extrapolating from the research on hermaphroditism, Ulrichs believed that same-sex attraction was the result of divergent physiological and psychological development at the embryonic stage, producing a feminine personality inhabiting a male body (a condition called *inversion*).[78] In 1864 he anonymously published two pamphlets on this theory, hoping it might lead to the repeal of Paragraph 143 of the Prussian Penal Code, which assigned five years hard labor as the penalty for "unnatural fornication between people and animals, as well as between persons of the male sex."[79] Over the next fifteen years, he published a dozen volumes on the subject.[80] Ulrichs was clear about the political nature of his project. "I am an insurgent," he declared. "I rebel against the existing situation, because I hold it to be a condition of injustice. I fight for freedom from persecution and insults. I call for the recognition of Urning [i.e., male-male] love. I call for it from public opinion and from the state."[81]

Around the same time, Karl Maria Kertbeny, a physician, was moved to join the cause after one of his patients committed suicide under the threat of blackmail. Kertbeny too wrote anonymous pamphlets, though his argument was very different than that of Ulrichs, maintaining that Paragraph 143 was a violation of human rights derived from the French Declaration of the Rights of Man and Citizen. It was in a letter from Kertbeny to Ulrichs, May 6, 1868, that the words *homosexual* and *heterosexual* were first used. *Homosexual* appeared in print the next year, in one of Kertbeny's pamphlets; *heterosexual* would not debut until 1880 (ironically enough, in a book defending homosexuality).[82]

It took a few decades for the language of *homosexuality* to gain prominence. In the meantime, there was no generally accepted term for same-sex desire or those who experienced it.[83] Probably the most common term was *Urning* or *Uranian*, coined by Ulrichs in 1862, drawing from Plato's *Symposium*. That dialogue imagines two gods of love, the Uranian Eros (heavenly love), the pure and spiritual love between men, and the Pandemian Eros (earthly love), the lustful animal attraction between those of different sexes.[84]

Classicists and Sexologists

As the references to the *Symposium* might suggest, another strategy for understanding and legitimizing same-sex desire was to root it in the classics. To this project Oscar Wilde made a surprisingly early contribution. In 1874 while still a student at Trinity College, Dublin, Wilde spent several weeks helping his tutor, the Dr. John Pentland Mahaffy, revise his study *Social Life in Greece*, among the first volumes in English to address classical pederasty frankly and sympathetically.[85] "As to the epithet *unnatural*," Mahaffey states, "the Greeks would answer that all civilisation was unnatural."[86]

J. A. Symonds picked up this discussion in his 1883 *Studies of the Greek Poets* and then *A Problem in Greek Ethics* later that same year.[87] Taking a historical and sociological approach, he argued that, among the ancients, pederasty was a social convention and ethical practice. In 1891 he pushed the point further with *A Problem in Modern Ethics*, surveying the fields of medicine, psychology, and literature for current ideas on the subject, both favorable and unfavorable.[88] Ultimately he endorsed a kind of cultural relativism and, by implication, tolerance. He concludes, "The problem ought to be left to the physician, the moralist, the educator, and finally to the operation of social opinion"—in other words, to anything besides the law.[89]

The two main approaches to understanding same-sex desire—the classical and the sexological—came together in 1892 when Symonds began collaborating with the physician Havelock Ellis on a study that would become *Sexual Inversion*. Ellis wrote from a scientific and legal perspective, Symonds as a classicist, and together they compiled anonymous sexual case histories.[90] Edward Carpenter helped find people willing to submit their case histories and sent in his own as well.[91]

Ellis wrote to Carpenter that he was drawn to the subject of homosexuality "partly through realising how widespread it is, partly through realising also, how outrageously severe the law is in this country (compared with others) and how easily the law can touch a perfectly beautiful form of inversion. We want to obtain sympathetic recognition for sexual inversion . . . to clear away many vulgar errors—preparing the way if possible for a change in the law."[92] Like Carpenter and his German colleagues, Ellis understood his sexological research politically, as part of a larger liberatory program. His 1890 book *The New Spirit* advocated individual freedom, scientific inquiry, and social planning and expressed sympathy with anarchism.[93] Ten years later, in *The Nineteenth Century: A Dialogue in Utopia*, he echoed Wilde's "Soul of Man under Socialism": "True individuality . . . is impossible until a social state is attained in which the whole of what was alleged the material side of life—that side on which all have common wants—is automatically supplied."[94] Rejecting the dominant theories of his time, Ellis argued against the stereotyped view of gender implicit in Ulrichs's model, and he pointed to the accomplishments of Erasmus, Leonardo da Vinci, Michelangelo, Cellini, and Sappho as evidence against the more popular view that same-sex passion was a form of degeneration.[95]

But *Sexual Inversion* was beset with problems. Symonds died in 1893, and Ellis had to complete the work without him. It appeared in German in 1896 and a year later in English, though—at the insistence of Symonds's family—omitting Symonds's work and his name.[96]

A quarter-century later, Emma Goldman looked back to this body of work and considered how the literature on "sex psychology" had shaped her thinking about homosexuality. She recalled that at the time of Wilde's arrest, her "only familiarity with homosexuals was limited to a few women whom I got to know in jail." But seeing that Wilde's case represented "an act of horrible injustice and repulsive hypocrisy," and reasoning that "as an anarchist, my place has always been alongside the persecuted," Goldman, among others, "stood up in defense of Oscar Wilde." It was only later that she "found out about the works of Havelock Ellis, Krafft-Ebing, Carpenter, and many others," which gave her thinking on the issue a more scientific basis and drove home "full awareness for the first time of the crime perpetrated at the time upon Oscar Wilde and people like him." Psychological theory invested the legal case with a new significance. Goldman came to see it not only as the persecution of a single individual but also as emblematic of the oppression of a whole group of people. "From that point on, I stood up both in my speeches and my writings for those whose sexual feelings and needs are differently oriented."[97]

The Cause

This new understanding was particularly liberating for those who had hitherto lived with crippling shame, and some became intoxicated with the new sense of possibility. Pointing to "Greek ideals"—"the cold rectitude of Socrates, or the sublime idealism of Plato"—the "evolutionary anarchist" George Ives wrote a short essay in the *Humanitarian* defending sexual freedom on utilitarian grounds while praising love in all its forms, elevating it to an eternal, universal principle.[98]

> Without light all things must die, and without love all souls must die....
> It has many forms as speech takes many languages....
> It knows not rank or wealth.
> It knows not form or fane.
> It knows not sex, or race, or progeny, but where it dwells is sacred.
> It knows not Time, or change, or fear; it was, it is to all eternity; it knows no grave, no ending, no one world.
> Where Love is, all is well.[99]

This essay was soon attacked in the *Review of Reviews* as a "dissertation in praise of unnatural vice," "seeking for a new heaven and a new earth" by looking "for its ideal . . . to Sodom and Gomorrah."[100] Wilde wrote to congratulate Ives on being attacked by "the prurient and the impotent" and later compared the essay's effect to that of a bomb.[101]

Wilde had previously suggested that Ives "establish a Pagan Monastery, possibly on some small rocky island in the Mediterranean."[102] Instead, in August 1893, Ives founded the Order of the Chaeronea, a secret society devoted to the liberation of Urnings, which Ives referred to simply as "The Cause." The Order's "Rules of Purpose" identify it as "A Religion, A Theory of Life, and Ideal of Duty," specifying: "We demand justice for all manner of people who are wronged and imperiled by individuals or multitudes or the laws."[103] The group had approximately 250 members.[104]

Ives confided to his diary on October 26, 1893, "Oscar Wilde's influence will be considerable, I think," and some of Wilde's aphorisms were quoted in the Order's literature.[105] Wilde was already known for offering money and advice to Urnings who found themselves in trouble, either with the law or by blackmail. Douglas, who early benefited from this guidance, spoke admiringly of "what he has done for the 'new culture' . . . the people he has pulled out of the fire and 'seen through' things not only with money, but by sticking to them when other people wouldn't speak to them."[106]

Yet in practical matters, Ives found Wilde irresolute and directionless: "He seems to have no purpose, I am all purpose."[107] He later wrote of Wilde and Douglas together, "Their ideals of life are so different from mine and, though I appreciate their brilliancy and charm, we can never I fear work together for public ends."[108] Whatever his reservations, however, Ives stuck by Wilde in the end and offered to open his home to Wilde when he was released from prison.[109]

Nameless Love

Though the theory of inversion, the language of homosexuality, and the notion of a sexual identity gradually achieved a wide acceptance, the movement itself was not united in its outlook. Some objected to the scientific (and thus medical) approach, worrying that it tended to pathologize their desires. Many also felt themselves to be fully masculine, not feminine souls in male bodies, thus rejecting the theories of inversion.[110] Indeed, some argued that their sexuality, by excluding the feminine aspect altogether, made them *more* masculine than straight men.[111]

Giving voice to this dissenting tendency was *Der Eigene*. Founded by the anarchist Adolph Brand in 1896, largely in reaction of Wilde's imprisonment, it became the first long-running gay periodical.[112] In theory, *Der Eigene* rejected a strict gender binary and emphasized cultural factors in shaping sexual behavior. In practice, the magazine celebrated a homoerotic masculinity, with relationships described in terms of "chivalric love" and "the love of friends"; it sometimes slid into vulgar misogyny.[113]

Another representative of this alternative politics was John Henry Mackay, the first English-language translator of Max Stirner's *The Ego and*

His Own.[114] Mackay was an individualist anarchist, a pacifist, and a fierce critic of Christianity.[115] He refused all medical, legal, and moralistic terms, speaking instead of "the nameless love of a man for a youth of his own sex," and protesting, "This love is misunderstood and despised, persecuted and misinterpreted as nothing else in the world!"[116]

Mackay was a longtime friend of the American individualist anarchist Benjamin Tucker, and the two men translated and published one another's work. Tucker found Mackay's attraction to adolescent boys distasteful but refused to let it interfere with their friendship, and—despite, or maybe because of, their differences—Tucker sought out his friend's views on sexual politics.[117] Likely owing to Mackay's influence, Tucker read Carpenter, Ellis, and other sexologists but did not adopt their terminology or the accompanying conception of a homosexual identity. He couched his politics instead in terms of individualism, of rights and desires, and of the ability to find fulfillment by freely associating as equals, looking forward to a time "when the love relations between these independent individuals shall be as varied as are individual inclinations and attractions."[118]

The question this dissenting tendency poses—one that is still with us, likely an irreconcilable ambivalence at the center of queer politics—is whether the project of liberation is best advanced by establishing and legitimating a new identity or rather through an *escape* from all identities.[119] The advantage of identity is that it can provide a sense of belonging and a basis for solidarity. By the same token, however, it also marks out a limit to belonging and supplies a rationale for exclusion, which implies also a limit to the freedom enjoyed by those within the identity group. There is always the worry that identities may degenerate into stereotypes, that appearances might be mistaken for essences, that cultural cues come to be treated as natural laws.[120] "The danger" in identity, as Wilde said of metaphysics, "is that men are often turning *nomina* into *numina*"—that is, names into gods.[121]

Wilde's view of liberation was expansive, and he looked to the broadening rather than narrowing of experience. Though in practice he lost all interest in sex with women, in principle he favored "the possibility of passionate friendship between any two human beings" and "the liberation of the sexual emotions over the greatest possible area."[122] When Frank Harris commented that advocating same-sex love was simply "proposing to use the left hand instead of the right," Wilde declared himself for "the seizure of enjoyment boldly with both hands."[123]

An Exceptional Type

Nevertheless, Wilde contributed in multiple ways to the creation of a gay identity and the figure of "the homosexual." The accusation of "posing" as a sodomite necessarily implied that there was something that sodomites *are like*. At trial, that image was to some degree produced as a kind of negative, beginning with assumptions about the character of a healthy, moral, respectable, non-sodomitical English gentleman, and then showing where Wilde diverged from the type in his attitudes, manner, and behavior. During this same period, responding to growing anxieties about class, race, gender, and the future of the empire, a new *heterosexual* identity was also being formulated. Centering on family life—characterized by strict gender roles, patriarchal domesticity, and the productive function of sexual intercourse— heterosexuality was less a matter of desire than a set of moral imperatives and, as such, a political tool for distinguishing the respectable commercial classes from (as they saw it) the decadent and debauched aristocracy (on the one hand) and the sensuous and undisciplined lower classes and primitive and promiscuous colonial subjects (on the other). Like homosexuality, heterosexuality was largely a negative construction, defined mainly in opposition to the concept of degeneracy.[124]

The specific details of the homosexual profile were unwittingly to be supplied by Wilde himself. "The image of the queer cohered at the moment when the leisured, effeminate, aesthetic dandy was discovered in same-sex practices, underwritten by money, with lower-class boys," the scholar Alan Sinfield writes.[125] "As a consequence, the entire, vaguely disconcerting nexus of effeminacy, leisured idleness, immorality, luxury, insouciance, decadence and aestheticism, which Wilde was perceived as instantiating, was transformed into a brilliantly precise image." The work of the trial was to brand Wilde as a particular type of person. To do that work, it had to fabricate the type using elements already circulating in the culture. "The parts were there already, and were being combined, diversely, by various people. But at this point, a distinctive possibility cohered, far more clearly, and for far more people, than hitherto."[126] Therefore, the historian Neil Miller concludes, "'the love that dare not speak its name' was given a name, a voice, a face. . . . In that sense, the downfall of Wilde may [have] been as significant as all the case histories and classifications of the sexologists."[127] This image, once established, provided the elements for the stereotyped understanding of male homosexuality for the century to come.

The Wilde scandal—not so much his crimes and the judicial proceedings as the talk accompanying them: the exploitative journalism, the dire sermons, and even the appeals for tolerance—set in the public mind a certain image of the homosexual, drawn from Wilde's individual characteristics.[128] Wilde became the type for the gay man—a model for emulation, a profile for suspicion.

The Secret of the Sonnets

As the new "homosexual" identity was being formed but before it crystallized into a type, its adherents sought out predecessors, forerunners, ancestors. They claimed the inheritance of a long tradition, creating for themselves a history, constructing a unity out of scattered fragments. Wilde participated in this historical myth-making, though he also warned of its dangers and limitations.

"The Portrait of Mr. W. H." is a strange and beautiful story containing within it a kind of romance, a theory about Shakespeare's sonnets, an essay regarding same-sex passion as a factor in the development of culture, and a caution concerning the quest for certainty and the desire for any too-definite a definition.

The story begins with a conversation between an unnamed narrator and his friend Erskine, concerning forgeries. The discussion leads Erskine to tell of his long-ago friendship with Cyril Graham, who believed that "he had at last discovered the true secret of Shakespeare's sonnets," namely that the "Mr. W. H." to whom they are dedicated was a boy-actor named Willie Hughes. "It is of course evident that there must have been in Shakespeare's company some wonderful boy-actor of great beauty, to whom he intrusted the presentation of his noble heroines."[129]

The homoerotic element of the theory, and the story, is scarcely concealed: "Yes; who else but he could have been the master-mistress of

Shakespeare's passion, the lord of his love to whom he was bound in vassal-age, the delicate minion of pleasure, the rose of the whole world, the herald of the spring decked in the proud livery of youth, the lovely boy whom it was sweet music to hear, and whose beauty was the very raiment of Shake-speare's heart, as it was the keystone of his dramatic power?"[130]

The boy-actor theory is elaborated at some length in the course of Wilde's tale, "working purely by internal evidence." "Internal" here has a dual meaning, referring both to the clues present in the text of the sonnets and to the subjective feelings of the reader. Explicitly, and crucially, the theory depends "not so much on demonstrable proof or formal evidence, but on a kind of spiritual and artistic sense."[131]

Erskine, however, is unsure of Graham's thesis, since "Willie Hughes" did not appear among the actors listed in the 1623 First Folio. He makes Graham promise that they must find some definite proof of Hughes's existence before they make the theory public. For weeks the two men search church registries and similar records, without success. At last, and quite by chance, Graham comes into possession of a portrait of a young man "of quite extraordinary personal beauty, though evidently somewhat effeminate," wearing Elizabethan dress and posed by a copy of Shakespeare's *Sonnets*. He is identified in the portrait as "Master Will. Hews."[132]

But the painting is a forgery, as Erskine soon discovers. Graham then kills himself, leaving his friend a letter, insisting "that he believed absolutely in Willie Hughes . . . and that in order to show me how firm and flawless his faith in the whole theory was, he was going to offer his life as a sacrifice to the secret of the Sonnets." Erskine now dismisses the whole idea as nonsense—"a perfectly unsound theory from beginning to end"—and laments Graham's suicide as a tragic folly. The narrator, how-ever, hearing this tale, is enchanted and convinced: "It is the only perfect key to Shakespeare's Sonnets. . . . I believe in Willie Hughes." He resolves to embark on his own search for conclusive proof. The story digresses for many pages to explore further details: the interference of the "dark woman" who separates the Bard from his young muse, the artistic pact that exists between playwrights and actors, and the long list of notable geniuses inspired by their intimate friendships with other men—Michelangelo, Montaigne, Ben Jonson, Winckelmann, and Pico della Mirandola, among them.[133]

The sonnets, the narrator tells us, reveal "more . . . than the mere delight of a dramatist in one who helps him to achieve his end." There is also "a subtle element of pleasure, if not passion," and, further still, "the soul, as well as the language of neo-Platonism." In Shakespeare's day, the *Symposium* was beginning "to exercise a strange influence over men, and to colour their words and thoughts, and manner of living." With its "subtle suggestion of sex in soul, in the curious analogies it draws between intellectual enthusiasm and the physical passion of love, in its dream of the incarnation of the Idea in a beautiful living form," it captured the poetic imagination. As a result, "the spirit of the Renaissance, which already touched Hellenism at so many points, . . . sought to elevate friendship to the high dignity of the artistic ideal, to make it a vital factor in the new culture, and a mode of self-conscious intellectual development."[134]

All of this the narrator includes in a letter, considering it proof of the Willie Hughes theory, and he mails it to Erskine. As soon as he does, however, he finds that he "had given away my capacity for belief" and suffered less a crisis of faith than a perfect "indifferen[ce]." Lacking now the enthusiasm that propelled his research, he finds the theory ridiculous and absurd. "Suddenly, I said to myself: 'I have been dreaming, and all my life for these two months has been unreal. There was no such person as Willie Hughes.'"[135] He goes to Erskine to make his apologies, only to discover that his letter has had its intended effect. Erskine is renewed in his devoted belief in the sonnets theory. The two men argue and part.

They do not speak for two years, until Erskine writes to declare his intention to make himself a martyr to the theory of the sonnets: "as Cyril Graham had given his life for this theory, he himself had determined to give his own life also to the same cause." The narrator rushes to intervene but arrives too late. Erskine is already dead. But it turns out the suicide was itself a kind of forgery. "Poor Erskine did not commit suicide," the attending doctor explains. "He died of consumption."[136]

Erskine leaves the portrait of Willie Hughes to his friend as a legacy, and in the story's very last lines the narrator admits that "sometimes, when I look at it, I think there is really a great deal to be said for the Willie Hughes theory of Shakespeare's Sonnets."[137]

A Genealogy

What Wilde offers in "Mr. W. H." is, in James Campbell's memorable phrase, "a homoerotic genealogy," and the argument of the story is that same-sex love is "the secret engine that drives cultural progress."[138] The relationships in the story, unlike heterosexual couplings, do not consist of bodies capable of producing children but of minds producing ideas. This more spiritual type of creativity is purely imaginative and entirely male.[139]

This great secret, however—at the heart of Shakespeare's sonnets, and by extension his drama, and likely the Renaissance and possibly all of civilization—is not exactly true.[140] The portrait is a forgery; Willie Hughes is a myth. Various characters exhaust themselves trying to prove the theory or discover the boy. But the idea cannot be proved; the central figure is not there to be discovered. What does that imply for Wilde's homoerotic genealogy, for gay history, for queer identity?

One reading, proposed by Alan Sinfield, is that "the idea of a queer identity is ill-founded. . . . 'Mr W. H.' enacts not the discreet presentation of an existing queer identity, but the elusiveness of the quest for such an identity."[141] Of the three principal characters, it is only the narrator who survives, and he seems to survive precisely because of his uncertain and ambivalent attitude about the sonnets theory. It may also be significant that he remains nameless.[142] By this interpretation, the story is a warning against the search for a name and the fabrication of an image. Graham tries to compel belief by creating just such an image. He simultaneously attempts to exteriorize his sense of identity, his sense of himself—to invest it in this outside object. *Dorian Gray* suggests that this sort of transference is always a kind of suicide. But it is not the act of *creation* that is the error. Shakespeare's sonnets are beautiful, as is the forged portrait. In fact, the story begins with a defense of beautiful forgeries as "the result of an artistic desire for perfect representation" and "an attempt to realise one's own personality on some imaginative plane out of reach of the trammeling accidents and limitations of real life."[143] The mistake lies in thinking that such imaginings can ever *prove* anything. Shakespeare and the *Symposium* may have their uses, but we must not "degrade the classics into authorities."[144]

The narrator's ambivalence, especially at the end, offers us a way forward. In the course of the story, he accepts the theory, then rejects it, and finally puts the forgery on display in his home, remaining mute about its origins. He aestheticizes it: he treats it as a beautiful object, not as a piece of evidence. Likewise, he considers that "there is really a great deal to be said" for Graham's theory, but what there is to be said, he does not say—or he does, but (again) by aestheticizing it, by enclosing it in this story. His attitude at the end is one of aesthetic appreciation but also of critical detachment. He *admires* the painting, the sonnets, the theory—but he does not *believe* them.

This solution is consistent with Wilde's own critical theory, that "no artist desires to prove anything," "that Lying, the telling of beautiful untrue things, is the proper aim of Art," and that "the highest criticism is that which reveals in the work of Art what the artist had not put there."[145] By encoding his ideas about sexuality, identity, and history in a story rather than an essay—that is, in a work of art, in a beautiful lie—Wilde makes such questions the subject of interpretation rather than proof, of appreciation rather than belief.[146]

By the most radical reading, then, Wilde is not especially problematizing queer identities, but *all* identities. The story of "Mr. W. H." reminds us that every tradition is an invention as well as an inheritance, and it is partly an invention of its heirs. Our communities are always imagined as well as inhabited. It may even be that social construction and self-creation coincide, and depend on one another, just as socialism and individualism do.

Imitating Art

There is one final irony to "The Portrait of Mr. W. H."

After reading the story, Wilde's lover, the American playwright Clyde Fitch, wrote to convey his admiration. He had picked up the magazine "just [to] look at it," but the story had engaged him—"I could not leave it"—and he read it straight through in one sitting. Fitch expressed his enthusiasm for the tale and its author, without reservation or restraint:

Oh! Oscar!
The story is *great*—and—fine!
I believe in Willie Hughes: I don't care if the whole thing is out of

your amazing brain. I don't care for the laughter, I only know I am convinced, and I *will*,
I *will* believe in Willie H.

He closed: "Invent me a language of love. *You* could do it."[147]

Wilde's story both posits a homoerotic genealogy and undermines any basis for belief. But Wilde himself was soon added to its lineage and arguably became the central figure in its canon. In the epic illustrated poem *The Mirror of Love*, Alan Moore retraces Wilde's homophile history—Greece, the Renaissance, and Shakespeare's love for Mr. W. H.—and then takes the story further: the sexologists, Wilde's downfall, Nazi death camps, the Mattachine Society, Stonewall.[148]

Moore does not recount this history for fun. There is joy and beauty in his work, but there is also the consciousness of danger. Moore was writing, for one thing, in the midst of the AIDS crisis. And more specifically, *The Mirror of Love* was first published in a collection called *AARGH!* (the acronym standing for Artists Against Rampant Government Homophobia). He had produced, with all deliberation, not only a history but also an artistic protest against repression and discrimination—most directly, against the efforts of Margaret Thatcher's government to suppress homosexuality, even as an abstract idea.[149]

A century after his trials, Wilde's prosecution remained politically important. When British justice made Wilde a martyr, it also made him an icon.

Aftermath

The Triumph of the Philistines

When Wilde was arrested, George Ives contemplated suicide.[150] Three weeks later, on April 25, 1895, he wrote in his diary, "There is nothing to be done yet, though it may do good in the future—I have been so grieved about it, but the greater movement will go on, though individuals fall."[151]

The trials were a disaster, and the consequences reached far beyond Wilde personally.[152] After the Reverend Stewart Headlam posted Wilde's bail, a mob menaced the Anglican priest outside his home.[153] Another crowd gathered in front of the offices of Wilde's publisher, the Bodley Head (nicknamed the "Sodley Bed"), breaking its windows with rocks. Two of its popular authors—William Watson and Alice Meynell—demanded the firm dissociate from Wilde, and thus his name was deleted from its catalog.[154] The Theatre Royal closed *An Ideal Husband*. The play then opened at the Criterion but without the author's name. The St. James's Theatre likewise removed his name from *Earnest*, which in any case soon closed to be replaced by the *Triumph of the Philistines*.[155] Across the Atlantic, too, performances of Wilde's plays were abruptly canceled, and his books were removed from American libraries.[156]

A silence blanketed the culture like a thick fog, even affecting people with no connection to the legal proceedings. Aubrey Beardsley, who had illustrated *Salomé*, was fired from his position as art editor for the *Yellow Book*.[157] Two publishers refused to consider the work of the Irish nationalist, libertarian socialist, and philosophical hedonist Grant Allen.[158] Carpenter's publisher, Fisher Unwin, withdrew *Towards Democracy* and canceled *Love's Coming of Age*, even though the type had already been set. Carpenter commented: "The Wilde Trial had done its work; and silence must henceforth reign on sex-subjects."[159]

The atmosphere of repression, though generalized, also supplied a pretext for more narrowly political ends. When a young man in Liverpool bought a copy of *Sexual Inversion*, his parents notified the police. The man who sold it, George Bedborough, was charged with distributing "a certain lewd, wicked, bawdy, scandalous libel" and attempting to "debauch and corrupt the morals of British citizens."[160] Bedborough was not an ordinary bookseller, however. He was an atheist, an anarchist, and an advocate of free love.[161] He was the secretary of the Legitimation League and editor of its journal, the *Adult* (for which Louise Michel sometimes wrote).[162] The Legitimation League had been founded to advocate for the rights of illegitimate children, but its mission soon expanded to include sexual liberation more generally, advocating the abolition of marriage laws and campaigning for the release of Edith Lanchester, who was institutionalized after entering into a free union with an Irish factory worker. Its members included Lillian Harman, Mona Caird, and numerous anarchists—which was likely the true reason for the authorities' attentions.[163] The detective in the case, John Sweeney, said he hoped to "kill a growing evil in the shape of a vigorous campaign of free love and Anarchism, and at the same time discover the means by which the country was being flooded with books of the 'Psychology' type."[164]

A committee, the Free Press Defense Committee, was organized to assist Bedborough. It included Frank Harris, Edward Carpenter, Edith Lanchester, Grant Allen, Henry Seymour, George Bernard Shaw, and the Social Democratic Federation's H. M. Hyndman. Detective Sweeney called it "a nice little gang of Secularists, Socialists, Anarchists, Free Lovers and others anxious to obtain a little cheap notoriety by defending Ellis' book on principle." Ultimately Bedborough reached a deal with the prosecutor: he would resign from the Legitimation League, and the charges against him would be dropped. But bookshops still refused to carry the *Adult*, and *Sexual Inversion* was practically if not legally banned. The Legitimation League was fatally defeated and dissolved soon after.[165]

For those who lived through it, the effects of this period were deeply felt and long-lasting. "To me, the shock and stupour were slow to pass away," Charles Ricketts confessed. "Something happened from which I have never quite recovered, a mistrust of the British conscience, a mistrust of modern civilization."[166]

Défense d'Oscar Wilde

A hundred years after the trials, in June 1995, at the ceremony initiating

Wilde to Westminster Abbey's Poet's Corner, Seamus Heaney suggested that Wilde's "reckless tactic" of prosecuting Queensberry "prefigured the non-violent politics of the century ahead" in that "he provoked the violence of the system and suffered it in order to expose it."[167] Though Heaney surely gave too much credit to Wilde's strategy, this elegy does point to an important result of the affair. The arrest of Oscar Wilde initiated a new period of persecution and fear, but ultimately, Havelock Ellis thought, the trials "generally contributed to give definiteness and self-consciousness to the manifestations of homosexuality, and . . . have aroused inverts to take up a definite attitude."[168] George Ives compared Wilde to a flower that, when "stamped" on, "scattered the seed, and the wind took it up upon its wings and spread it over miles of land; and so that flower was multiplied."[169]

"The era closed with Wilde's mauve nineties fading into grey," Alan Moore would later write, "and yet contained the seeds of something proud, humane: From Germany, before the century's end, came the first protests against laws on sodomy. Emancipation had begun."[170]

Die Neue Zeit, a journal of the Second International, defended Wilde immediately, if ambivalently, running two articles by Eduard Bernstein in April and May 1895. In the first, Bernstein reverses the logic of the Queensberry case and argues that because Wilde's "*pose* is pederastic" and "anyone familiar with his writings knew what Wilde was," it was not he who stood exposed by the proceedings but "the pharisees of the press and the hypocritical public."[171] In the second essay, Bernstein urges "the German social-democratic movement" to "discard judgments [of homosexuality] based on more or less arbitrary moral concepts in favour of a point of view deriving from scientific experience." Citing the anthropological and historical evidence of cultural variations in sexual norms, with the usual reference to the Greeks, he then points to the specifically patriarchal origins of the prohibition against homosexuality. Echoing Mahaffy, he responds to the idea that such practices are "unnatural" with the observation that, strictly speaking, "our entire cultural existence . . . is a constant offence against nature," and, by the standard of nature, "the worst sexual excess would be no more objectionable than, say, writing a letter." He concludes that "there is no argument which can justify the criminal punishment of male love." Yet Bernstein also takes issue with the psychologists' approach to the matter, warning that the tendency to "exaggerat[e] pathological explanations" in effect "accept[s] the standpoint of the reactionary criminal laws, which even the drafters defend by reference to existent popular prejudice."[172] Ultimately Bernstein does not defend homosexuality (and still less Wilde personally) so much as he discredits any basis for judgment or stigma.

A more direct defense appeared the following year. In a pamphlet titled *Sappho and Socrates*, the physician Magnus Hirschfeld wrote: "Oscar Wilde, this genius of a writer, who loves Lord Alfred Douglas with a passionate love, has been put into prison in Wandsworth. And this because of a passion which he shares with Socrates, Michelangelo, and Shakespeare."[173] Hirschfeld, whose motto was "Through Knowledge to Justice," was also active in the suffrage movement, legitimation reform, support for unwed mothers, and the promotion of sexual education, especially about venereal disease.[174] He began corresponding with Robbie Ross in 1896, and a few months later, in May 1897, founded the Scientific-Humanitarian Committee with the aim of repealing Paragraph 175 of the Imperial Penal Code, which outlawed male homosexuality in the greater German territory.[175] In 1898 the committee—with the vocal support of August Bebel, a Social Democratic leader—delivered to the Reichstag a petition containing two thousand names calling for the law to be revoked.[176] (It was not.)[177]

Also among Wilde's earliest champions were the anarchists. *Freedom* ran an editorial during the second and third trials, denouncing the prosecution as unjust and hypocritical. It also published a moral defense of homosexuality, written by Edward Carpenter.[178] In May 1895 Paul Adam defended Wilde in *La Revue Blanche*, arguing that homosexuality did less harm than adultery.[179] That summer, Octave Mirbeau, who disliked Wilde personally but felt that he had the right to follow his own natural inclinations, came to his defense in two articles for *Le Journal*.[180] Henri Bauër wrote a lead article in *L'Echo de Paris*, condemning the hypocrisy of English society, the viciousness of the law, the severity of Wilde's sentence, and the Marquess of Queensberry personally. Hugues Rebell wrote in the *Mercure de France* a "Défense d'Oscar Wilde," in which he compared Pentonville Prison, where Wilde was then kept, with the Bastille, the fortress-prison famously attacked during the Revolution. Rebell wrote: "With what joy should I see Pentonville in flames! And not only in Wilde's behalf, but in behalf of all of us pagan artists and writers who are by rights honorary prisoners."[181]

Stuart Merrill, who had corrected the manuscript of *Salomé*, wrote of Wilde's plight in *La Plume*: "Is it not time . . . for the writers of France and England to react with a resounding protest against the bourgeois hypocrisy which once again threatens our two countries? Are we not cowards in the face of Tartuffe's handkerchief and Mrs. Grundy's fan?"[182] Merrill tried circulating a petition among the French intelligentsia, calling for Wilde's release, but hardly anyone would sign it.[183] In England, George Ives helped Frank Harris draft a similar petition, with the same results.[184]

Translations of Mirbeau's articles appeared in Benjamin Tucker's *Liberty*, and Tucker himself argued that same-sex desire was more prevalent than generally assumed. (Unusual for the militantly atheistic Tucker, he even found a kind word for Reverend Headlam.) C. L. James wrote of Wilde's case in *Lucifer, the Light-Bearer*, arguing that homosexuality was at most a minor vice, not a crime or a disease, and pointing to ancient Greece for support, as usual. *Lucifer* also reprinted Wilde's work during and after the trials, and Lillian Harman (who had once been imprisoned for illegal cohabitation) wrote to decry the censorship then ascendant.[185]

Perhaps most notable, simply by reason of the source, was the editorial appearing in the June 18, 1895, edition of the *Torch* ("A Revolutionary Journal of Anarchist Communism"), a magazine produced by Olivia and Helen Rossetti, the teenage daughters of art critic William Michael Rossetti. (In addition to the girls' own contributions, the *Torch* published writing by Malatesta, Zola, Mirbeau, and Michel.)[186] In Wilde's defense, the journal argued that because the case involved "neither violation nor even seduction," and since the witnesses had "reached the age of discretion" and "prostituted themselves before they made Wilde's acquaintance," there was no "harm done to society" and therefore also no "right of society to claim redress, *i.e.* to punish." Indeed, the piece asserted, "If there was an indecency at all in this case, then it was displayed by the prosecutors. . . [and] the repugnant behavior of the Marquess of Queensbury [*sic*]."[187]

For Oscar Wilde, the young editors expressed only admiration: "his attitude in the dock under the terrible circumstances was a very distinguished one. He did not say one bitter word against the miserable wretches who gave evidence against him. He admitted all that he possibly could. At the end of the trial he gave his tormentors a last and striking lesson in decency. It was when the Solicitor General asked him whether he thought Taylor's conduct proper. Wilde's reply: 'I have not to judge other people's actions' contained a lesson which unhappily jurymen and judges did not profit by."[188]

Queering Anarchism

Wilde's conviction profoundly shaped the thought of anarchists in the years and decades that followed.

Before 1895, the sexual politics of American anarchists centered squarely on the question of marriage—opposition to the legal institution, advocacy of free love between equal partners. This view supplied the basis for their understanding of Wilde as another victim of meddling puritanism. As Charlotte Wilson expressed: "It is an intolerable impertinence that Church or State or society in any official form should venture to interfere with lovers." The principle of sexual freedom had already been well established in the critique of marriage and was readily applied to the question of homosexuality.[189] In this sense, historian Terence Kissack argues, the "anarchist politics of homosexuality grew out of a rejection of marriage," and it was the Wilde trials in particular that prompted this development.[190] The Wilde case "made homosexuality a political issue for the anarchists in a way it had not previously been," and, significantly, the anarchists' response "constitute[d] the first articulation of a politics of homosexuality in the United States."[191]

As a victim of persecution and hypocrisy, Wilde had the anarchists' sympathy. But beyond that, the cruelty of his treatment and the nature of his offense prompted many to reexamine their own prejudiced attitudes and prudish morality. For instance, when Alexander Berkman first arrived in prison, he denied even the possibility of homosexuality. "I don't think there can be such intimacy between those of the same sex," he said. "The very thought of the unnatural practice revolts and disgusts me. . . . These things are not credible, indeed, I don't believe they are possible. And even if they were, no human being would be capable of such iniquity."[192] But his feelings on the subject gradually softened, especially after hearing another prisoner speak "with profound sympathy of the brilliant English man-of-letters, whom the world of cant and stupidity has driven to prison and to death because his sex life did not conform to the accepted standards."[193] By the time he left prison, Berkman's attitude had entirely turned. When his friend

Felipe expressed a desire to kiss him, Berkman felt an "unaccountable sense of joy glow[ing] in my heart," and he replied, "I feel just as you do."[194]

Tragedy and Regret

Wilde, for his part, while he languished in prison, embarked on a reassessment of his own, concerning the mode of life that had led him to that place. Over the course of a long period of reflection, he wrote to his lover, Lord Alfred Douglas, considering his mistakes, expressing his regrets, and resolving to change his character and his life. Posthumously published under the title "De Profundis" (From the Depths), the confessional epistolary essay represents Wilde's most direct statement of his philosophy of life and contains some of his most powerful writing.

"I blame myself terribly," Wilde admits—though the source of his remorse was not what the judges and the moralists might have wished.[195] "I don't regret for a single moment having lived for pleasure. I did it to the full, as one should do everything that one does to the full."[196] Instead, he explains, "I blame myself for the entire ethical degradation I allowed you to bring on me. The basis of character is will-power, and my will-power became absolutely subject to yours."[197] Douglas, scarcely seeing what he was doing, had laid siege to Wilde's autonomy; and Wilde, equally unaware, had surrendered it a piece at a time. "I had made a gigantic psychological error," he realized, too late, "[in thinking that] my giving up to you in small things meant nothing."[198] "I forgot that every little action of the common day makes or unmakes character."[199] The habit of indulgence, of submission to Douglas's whims, "had become insensibly a real part of my nature."[200] The result, Wilde reflects, was tragic: "I ceased to be Lord over myself. I was no longer the Captain of my Soul, and did not know it. I allowed you to dominate me, and your father to frighten me. I ended in horrible disgrace."[201]

Looking back on this experience and examining his own errors, Wilde goes on in his letter to consider the ethics of character, the importance of sorrow and humility, and (developing a theme from "The Soul of Man under Socialism") the example set by Christ. From these elements, he sketches for himself the shape of "a new life, a *Vita Nuova*"—though in truth "no new life at all, but simply the continuance, by means of development, and evolution, of my former life."[202] He resolves: "I must be far more of an individualist than I ever was. I must get far more out of myself than I ever got, and ask far less of the world than I ever asked. Indeed my ruin came, not from too great individualism of life, but from too little." Wilde's flaw, as he saw it, lay not in his self-assertion but in his failure to assert himself fully, not in his antinomianism but in his recourse to hypocrisy, not in his criminal rebellion but in his seeking refuge in the law: "The one disgraceful, unpardonable, and to all time contemptible action of my life was my allowing myself to be forced into appealing to Society for help and protection against your father. . . . Of course once I had put into motion the forces of Society, Society turned to me and said, 'Have you been living all this time in defiance of my laws, and do you now appeal to those laws for protection? You shall have these laws exercised to the full. You shall abide by what you have appealed to.' The result is I am in gaol."[203]

The anarchist Thomas Bell, who as Frank Harris's secretary had occasion to meet and talk with Wilde toward the end of the famous author's life, believed that Wilde's tragedy was not that he was exposed as a homosexual or even that he was sent to prison. Wilde's suffering, terrible as it undoubtedly was, is not what makes his story tragic. For tragedy, in its real rather than sentimental form, is not simply misfortune. In tragedy the hero is defeated not by forces much greater than himself but precisely by the weaker elements of his own nature. The tragedy was Wilde's failure to face Queensberry's accusation defiantly, instead reacting "like a damned deacon caught in lechery," attacking those who accused him, and "seeking, apparently, to put Queensberry in jail by bold perjury, pretending indignation." The fatal moment did not occur when Wilde received Queensberry's card or even when the judge read out his sentence. It was the moment when "Oscar Wilde, the rebel, appeared in court to protest that he was a respectable citizen, whose respectability was not to be attacked." Had he "boldly acknowledged the truth of the accusation and asserted his right to live according to his nature," he would not have avoided the stigma of scandal and might still have gone to prison, but "he could have retained his own self-respect intact." Bell argues that Wilde's politics bring a special significance to this story: "it is not merely that Wilde was an Anarchist; it is that the tragedy of his life *cannot be understood without understanding that*."[204]

Chapter 5

Refuse to Be Broken by Force

Prison Writing and Anti-Prison Writing

A Criminal with a Noble Face

During his American tour of 1882, Oscar Wilde visited Lincoln, Nebraska, and lectured on the doctrines of the Aesthetic movement. Afterward his hosts took him on a tour of their city's most impressive public building—the local jail. He later wrote to a friend about the prisoners: "Poor sad types of humanity in hideous striped dresses making bricks in the sun, and all mean-looking, which consoled me, for I should hate to see a criminal with a noble face." Wilde visited the "little whitewashed cells, so tragically tidy, but with books in them. In one I found a translation of Dante, and a Shelley. Strange and beautiful it seemed to me that the sorrow of a single Florentine in exile should, hundreds of years afterwards, lighten the sorrow of some common prisoner in a modern gaol."[1]

Without realizing it, Oscar Wilde had glimpsed his future.

The Poet as Prisoner

Entering Prison, Becoming a Prisoner

When he was first arrested, Wilde was taken to Holloway Prison to await trial. Compared to what came later, his stay there was relatively comfortable. Being merely a suspect and not yet a convict, he was allowed to wear his own clothes, have visitors, send and receive letters, and even order food from restaurants.[2]

After his trials, he was sent to Pentonville—this time as a convict.[3] He would have felt the change in his status immediately.

The standard admission procedure ran as follows: The new inmate's personal details were recorded, including his height and weight. His possessions were taken, his clothing stripped, his hair shorn. A bath was mandatory. Then a doctor performed a cursory medical exam; he declared Wilde "fit for light labour." A uniform was issued and a number assigned in place of a name. At last the guards read out the prison rules—a list so long that it took most of an hour to recite.[4]

For Wilde, the former dandy, this proved "a fiendish nightmare; more horrible than anything I had ever dreamt of." He later recalled, "They made me undress before them and get into some filthy water they called a bath and dry myself with a damp, brown rag and put on this livery of shame."[5]

Later the process was repeated when he transferred to Reading Gaol. A guard recalled: "When he arrived, his hair was long and curly, and it was ordered to be cut at once. . . . 'Must it be cut[?]' he cried piteously to me. 'You don't know what it means to me,' and the tears rolled down his cheeks."[6]

The major features of this process are typical of the initiation into prison, as well as into mental hospitals, the military, and other species of what Erving Goffman has termed *total institutions*. As Goffman explains, "The recruit comes into the establishment with a conception of himself made possible by certain stable social arrangements in his home world. Upon entrance, he is immediately stripped of the support provided by these arrangements. In the accurate language of some of our oldest total institutions, he begins a series of abasements, degradations, humiliations, and profanations of self. His self is systematically, if often unintentionally, mortified."[7]

The admission procedure stood as an encapsulated representation of the work the penitentiary was meant to enact upon the raw material of its captives: to strip them of everything that distinguished their previous lives, their former selves; to remove from them all the signs, contacts, and influences of their social milieu; to cleanse them of their sinful habits and their vicious traits; to clothe them with the uniform of the institution, restrict their behavior with rules, and subject them to doctrines preached by its clergy; to instill new habits according to the virtues praised by society; in short, to impose discipline, to save their souls by force, to remake their characters in the image of the perfectly ordered institution, to *rehabilitate* them, reform them, reorder their character, make them ideal Victorian subjects, well suited to family and factory, loyal to Church and Crown. Perfect order meant perfect virtue and perfect obedience.

Each Dreadful Day

In 1887, when Sir Edmond Du Cane was appointed the chair of the Prison Commission, he set out to establish standard, punitive conditions for all inmates. His slogan ran, "hard labour, hard fare, and a hard bed."[8] Under the new system, every action was ruled and rationalized, every moment set out in detail according to an inflexible plan.

The day at Pentonville Prison began with a sharp bell at five thirty in the morning.[9] The prisoners would rise, wash with cold water, and clean their cells. During winter months, Wilde complained, "one has to get up long before daybreak and in the dark-cold cell begin one's work by the flaring gas-jet."[10]

An inspection of the cells would follow, during which the prisoner was required to display his few possessions according to a rigorous formula. The procedure was always a misery for Wilde: "I had to keep everything in my cell in its exact place . . . and if I neglected this even in the slightest, I was punished. . . . I often started up in my sleep to feel if each thing was where the regulations would have it, and not an inch either to the right or to the left."[11]

Only after the inspection would the inmate be allowed to empty the lavatory bucket—his "slops."

Thin cocoa and stale bread would then be served for breakfast.

At seven thirty, if the weather was suitable, the prisoners would be permitted forty-five minutes of exercise in the yard, silently walking in a circle.

At nine thirty, it was required that they attend chapel. One warder described a typical sermon:

> The Chaplain was addressing his shorn and grey-garbed flock, telling them how wicked they all were, and how thankful they should all be that they lived in a Christian country where a paternal Government was as anxious for the welfare of their souls as for the safe-keeping of their miserable bodies; that society did not wish to punish them, although they had erred and sinned against society; that they were undergoing a process of purification; that their prison was their purgatory, from which they could emerge as pure and spotless as though they had never sinned at all; that if they did so society would meet and welcome them with open arms; that they were the prodigal sons of the community, and that the community, against which they had previously sinned, was fattening calves to feast them, if they would but undertake to return to the fold and become good citizens.[12]

To Wilde, the moralizing was intolerable. He confided to a guard: "I long to rise in my place, and cry out, and tell the poor, disinherited wretches around me that it is not so; to tell them that they are society's victims, and that society has nothing to offer them but starvation in the streets, or starvation and cruelty in prison!"[13]

After chapel the inmates would return to their cells, where they would remain for the rest of the day.

Under the "Separate System" established by the Prison Act of 1865, most prisoners spent sixteen hours a day alone in their cells, and when they were together—during exercise or at chapel—any communication, even eye contact, would be severely punished. There was nothing with which to occupy oneself but tedious labor, the Bible, and perhaps a single volume from the prison library.

At noon they ate dinner—"composed of a tin of coarse Indian meal stirabout"—in their cells, alone.[14]

At five thirty they received "a piece of dry bread and a tin of water" for supper, which they also ate in their cells, still alone.[15]

At eight o'clock in the evening, the lights went out.

But the horrors did not cease during the night. Sleeplessness had been deliberately claimed as a punitive instrument. Wilde explained: "The object of the plank bed is to produce insomnia . . . and it invariably succeeds. . . . Every prisoner who has been on a plank bed suffers from insomnia."[16]

Uncomfortable and cold, sleeping uneasily, each prisoner would stay in bed until the morning bell—when the cycle would begin again.

As much as possible, each day was made exactly like the last. The result was a kind of mental stasis. As Wilde described it in "De Profundis," "With us time itself does not progress. It revolves. It seems to circle round one centre of pain. The paralysing immobility of a life, every circumstance of which is regulated after an unchangeable pattern, so that we eat and drink and walk and lie down and pray, or kneel at least for prayer, according to the inflexible laws of an iron formula: this immobile quality . . . makes each dreadful day, in the very minutest detail like its brother. . . . And in the sphere of thought, no less than in the sphere of time, motion is no more."[17]

Hard Labor

The order that the prison sought to create was one of perfect uniformity and endless repetition. In "The Ballad of Reading Gaol," Wilde recounts in some detail the stultifying routine. He mentions the cleaning of the cells:

> We rubbed the doors, and scrubbed the floors,
> And cleaned the shining rails:
> And, rank by rank, we soaped the plank,
> And clattered with the pails.

He describes the miserable hour of exercise:

> Silently we went round and round
> The slippery asphalte yard;
> Silently we went round and round,
> And no man spoke a word.

And he recalls the grueling physical labor:

> We tore the tarry rope to shreds
>   With blunt and bleeding nails. . .
> We sewed the sacks, we broke the stones,
>   We turned the dusty drill. . .
>   And sweated on the mill.[18]

Work occupied a central place in the ideology of the penitentiary—both as a means to reformation and as an end in itself. Du Cane frankly advocated "hard, dull, useless, uninteresting monotonous labour . . . for its penal effect," complemented by "employment which plays its part as a moral reformatory agent."[19]

Reproducing, in miniature, an idealized model of the outside society, Du Cane instituted a system of stages and classes, stratifying the inmate population and ordering each individual's prison career according to a uniform, rational plan, a progression that conceptually linked greater discipline and increased comfort. As he explained it, "Promotion into each of these classes is followed by certain privileges," which were "necessarily very limited but still . . . much sought after." Everything from the type of work assigned, the amount and quality of food provided, and access to amenities such as mail, visitors, books, or a mattress was governed by this system.

Being only "fit for light labour," Wilde was first assigned the sewing of mailbags.[20] More often, however, he was given the job of picking oakum—that is, using his fingers to separate the fibers of old rope. This rope, which had been retired from use aboard ships, was typically an inch or so thick and hard with tar. The work was thus difficult and dirty; it left one's hands sticky with filth—and often bleeding as well. The finished product was a pile of thin thread, which could then be spun into new rope or used as caulk in the walls of ships. Economically it was near-worthless, fetching about a penny a pound.[21]

The most famous and most dreaded prison task was the futile walking on the treadwheel. The treadwheel worked as an endless staircase, a forced march to nowhere. On it, prisoners would each day climb between 6,000 feet (at York) and 19,400 feet (at the New Bailey).[22] Experiments were made in using the wheel to grind flour or for some other productive purpose. Usually, however, the labor was pointless.

Other unlucky convicts spent their days turning a crank to pump water—or, again, in most cases, to pump nothing at all.[23] The prisoners exhausted themselves solely to avoid punishment, to earn privileges, and to learn virtue. Du Cane wrote, "Day by day, week by week, and year by year, [the prisoner] can count and record the progress he is making towards an advance in class, in accumulation of money, and towards conditional release; and he is made perfectly to see and feel that his fate is in his own hands, and that he has something more to work and to hope for than the mere avoidance of punishment."[24]

By rationalizing the system of rewards, it was hoped, the prison could instill in its inmates the habits of self-regulation and self-restraint, as well as a general tendency toward living a well-planned and neatly ordered life.

Prison Philosophy

The philosophy of the penitentiary was an imperfect blend of Quaker self-reflection and utilitarian rationing.[25] The institution was designed not only to shape the behavior of the prisoners but also to modify their characters, to instill virtue, and even to impose a specific worldview. As such the prison came to embody a sort of idealized version of the values of society at large, combining a scrupulous concern for the interior world of the individual prisoner with an obsessive attention to planning, regimentation, and institutional control. The prison concentrated and perfected the moral system implicit in the ideology of class society. It served as an institutional embodiment of the Protestant Ethic.[26]

Inherent to the theory of the penitentiary was a particular view of the causes, and therefore the correction, of crime. It was not poverty that caused crime, but vice—idleness, indiscipline, drunkenness, profligacy, and so on. These faults, in turn, were not seen as the *consequences* of poverty but as its *causes*. (The prisoner Edward Johnson complained, "The rich send poor people to prison," to which his missionary visitor, Sarah Martin, replied: "What made you poor? Was it not drunkenness and wickedness?")[27] The solution to crime, therefore, was to improve the moral character of the inmates, meaning to produce individuals suitable to the society—in particular, to the emerging order of industrial capitalism. Prisoners were to be instilled with the habits of self-control, hard work, patience, reverence, and obedience. How better to do this than by a system of degrading austerity, forced labor, intense boredom, mandatory worship, minute regulations, and harsh penalties?

The result of these edifying lessons, however, was not often what had been intended. Many prisoners saw in their punishments a justification for their crimes. As Kropotkin observed: "[The prisoner] accustoms himself to hate—cordially to hate—all those 'respectable' people who so wickedly kill his best feelings in him. . . . Prison education will make him consider society as an enemy."[28] Writing in secret from an American prison at the beginning of 1896, Alexander Berkman echoed Kropotkin's words: "The prisoner . . . looks upon the State as his direct punisher, and his hate turns to the law and its representatives, whom he holds responsible for his misfortune; he nurtures in his heart his wrath, and wild thoughts of revenge fill his mind; ultimately he becomes the enemy of society as a whole."[29]

For Wilde, this attitude was readily comprehensible and perhaps an inevitable consequence of the prison system itself and the resentment it produced. As he remarked to an interviewer in 1894, the year before his arrest: "What a perfect fiasco is our system of penal administration! . . . To punish a man for wrong-doing, with a view to his reformation, is the most lamentable mistake it is possible to commit. . . . If he has any soul at all, such procedure is calculated to make him ten times worse than he was before. . . . It is a sign of a noble nature to refuse to be broken by force."[30]

Wilde's Criminology

Wilde argued against every element of the Victorian penal theory. He found the source of crime not in the bad character of the individual criminal but in the social system that made crime necessary: "Starvation, and not sin, is the parent of modern crime. . . . [Criminals] are merely what ordinary respectable, commonplace people would be if they had not got enough to eat."[31] As early as 1890, Wilde had understood inequality as the cause of crime. Citing Chuang Tzu, he wrote: "The accumulation of wealth is to him the origin of evil. It makes the strong violent, and the weak dishonest. It creates the petty thief, and puts him in a bamboo cage. It creates the big thief, and sets him on a throne of white jade."[32]

A year later, in "The Soul of Man under Socialism," Wilde expanded this analysis to incorporate the role of the state. He suggested, with his characteristic sense of paradox, that crime results in part from the very institutions presented as its remedy—authority, law, and punishment: "A community is infinitely more brutalised by the habitual employment of punishment than it is by the occasional occurrence of crime. It obviously follows that the more punishment is inflicted the more crime is produced. . . . The less punishment, the less crime."[33] Wilde's thought here was in line with that of other anarchists. Kropotkin also concluded that "prison does not prevent anti-social acts from taking place. It increases their numbers."[34] And Tolstoy argued, "The activity of governments with their cruel forms of punishment . . . contributes more to the barbarizing of the people than to their culture, and hence rather to the multiplication than to the diminution of such criminals."[35]

By Wilde's theory, society produces crime, first by depriving masses of its citizens of the essential elements of life, and then through the "brutalis[ing]" influence of official violence. If the causes of crime are economic and political, the solutions must be as well. Therefore, he proposes, economically, the elimination of capitalism and the introduction of socialism: "When private property is abolished there will be no necessity for crime, no demand for it; it will cease to exist."[36] Politically, he insists, "The State must give up all idea of government. . . . With authority, punishment will pass away. . . . [And] when there is no punishment at all, crime will either cease to exist, or, if it occurs, will be treated by physicians as a very distressing form of dementia, to be cured by care and kindness."[37]

Wilde advocates not the production of individuals suited to the present society but the creation of a new society, suitable for the individuals who live in it. The solution to crime is not confinement but freedom.

Transfer and Decline

On July 4, 1895, Wilde was moved from Pentonville Prison to Wandsworth, where he suffered constantly from hunger and dysentery.[38] The chaplain wrote the Home Office: "He is now quite crushed and broken. . . . In fact some of our most experienced officers openly say that they don't think he will be able to go through the two years."[39] Yet the prison doctor suspected him of faking and refused to release him from his duties. Wilde told Frank Harris:

> One Sunday morning after a very bad night I could not get out of bed. The warder came in and I told him I was ill. . . .
>
> Half an hour later the doctor came and looked in the door. He never came near me; he simply called out: "Get up; no malingering; you're all right. You'll be punished if you don't get up," and he went away.[40]

Though ill, Wilde was thus forced to attend chapel. During services, he fainted and fell, injuring his ear when his head struck the ground. As a result, he spent nearly half of his time at Wandsworth in the infirmary.[41]

After his fall, Wilde was visited by his friend R. S. Kennedy, who asked extensively about his treatment there. The nature of the discussion worried the guard, who then wrote a report to the governor: "In the course of conversation [the visitor] informed the prisoner that it was thought something could be done, by means of the *Daily Chronicle*, to call attention to his case, meaning to me to infer that a correspondence should be started in this paper." Wilde, however, demurred: "The prisoner expressed himself as not being in favour of this course, and the prisoner seemed very averse to any publicity of this kind."[42]

Still, the authorities had reason to worry. Even before his collapse, reports on Wilde's poor health had already received attention in the newspapers. After visiting Wilde at Wandsworth, Robert Sherard had complained to the *Chronicle* that the poet was "suffering greatly from sheer want of nourishment."[43] Similar reports appeared in French newspapers, and members of Parliament—especially the Liberal Richard Haldane and the Conservative Ernest Flowers—were beginning to make inquiries on Wilde's behalf.[44]

The Home Office ordered a special exam by two doctors from Broadmoor Criminal Lunatic Asylum, David Nicolson and Richard Brayne. They met with and examined Wilde, and they issued a report on October 29, 1895, to the effect that there were "no indications of disease or derangement" and that the "tokens of mental depression" were more or less what was to be expected "due to the natural and not unhealthy operation of circumstances." In short, "taking imprisonment for what it is and what it is intended to be, its operation upon the mind of prisoner Oscar Wilde has not been such as to give rise to anxiety or alarm."

Nevertheless, the doctors offered several recommendations for changes in his treatment. First, "it would be well . . . to select a suitable prison in the country or away from London to which he should be transferred." Furthermore, they urged "the continuation of such minor relaxations of the full rigour and discipline of prison life as have already been sanctioned." And they suggested additional privileges, including "a cell larger than the usual size," some limited "association with other prisoners," "variation of employment" (specifically bookbinding), "a freer range of books . . . and a larger supply," "outdoor exercise *with some garden work,*" and "additional food."[45]

No Shape or Form

About three weeks later, Wilde was transferred to Reading, which did not, at first, represent much of an improvement. Reading Gaol had been constructed in conscious imitation of Pentonville. Separate confinement, silent exercise, oakum picking, and mandatory chapel were all part of the regime there as well.

Oscar Wilde's cell, number C.3.3, was spare and small: just thirteen feet by seven feet, and ten feet high. Its floors were red and black tile, and its walls were whitewashed brick. The room had two high, south-facing windows, allowing in just a little sunlight. Additional light was provided by gas jets set behind thick glass. The doors were made of heavy wood, with iron studs and a small glass spy hole, which allowed the guards to peer in.[46] One warder remembered watching the poet pacing—"pacing his cell—one, two, three. Three steps when he has to turn. Three steps and turn again."[47]

Wilde would later struggle to describe such surroundings, to convey the effect they have on one so confined: "The difficulty is that the objects in prison have no shape or form. . . . A cell again may be described *psychologically,* with reference to its effect on the soul: in itself it can only be described as 'whitewashed' or 'dimly-lit.' It has no shape, no contents. It does not exist from the point of view of form or colour. . . . [T]he horror of prison is that everything is so simple and commonplace in itself, and so degrading, and hideous, and revolting in its effect."[48]

Prison clothes were no better. On entering Pentonville, Wilde handed over the clothes he had worn to court—including a frock coat, a silk hat, and a pair of patent leather boots.[49] In their place he received a jacket, waistcoat, and trousers made of thick, stiff brown cloth and marked "with crooked arrows"; a striped cotton shirt; woolen underwear and socks; and old, patched, ill-fitting boots.[50] The uniforms came in two sizes only: men and boys.[51]

One guard remembered, "[Wilde] was dreadfully distressed because he could not polish his shoes or brush his hair. 'If I could but feel clean,' he said, 'I should not feel so utterly miserable. These awful bristles'—touching his chin—'are horrid.'"[52]

Prison represented an assault not only on Wilde's presentation of himself, or even just on his self-image, but on his entire philosophy of life. Prison stood both as an aesthetic (or anti-aesthetic) assault on the senses and as a sensual (or anti-sensual) assault against aesthetics. Everything in prison was deliberatively made as ugly as possible—the cells, the clothes, the food, the inmates.

Yet, as another guard recalled of Wilde: "Not even the hideous prison garb . . . could altogether hide the air of distinction and ever-present intellectual force."[53]

Library Privileges

The governor at Reading, Lieutenant Colonel Jacob Isaacson, was known for the frequency and severity of his punishments. Even minor mistakes were punished harshly, and Isaacson made a special project of, in his own words, "knocking the nonsense out of Wilde."[54]

"The governor loves to punish," Wilde told his friends, "and he punishes by taking my books from me."[55] These books, which had traveled with him from Pentonville, were a privilege granted him thanks to the intervention of Richard Haldane. Haldane had known Wilde socially and was "haunted by the idea of what this highly sensitive man was probably suffering under ordinary prison treatment."[56] So the Liberal legislator visited Wilde on June 12, 1895, and promised to "try to get for him books and pen and ink."[57] Wilde was not only allowed *more* books but also *better* ones. He was given special leave to request additional titles; subject to the approval of the authorities, these could be sent by his friends and added to the prison library.[58] Wilde's books, it seems, were sacrosanct. Thanks to the agitation of Wilde's friends, Isaacson was transferred to a new position.

The new governor, Major James Nelson, proved more friendly by far. Throughout the prison, the instances of punishment decreased dramatically—from 700 punishment reports per year to 360.[59] Of Nelson, Wilde wrote, "Though he cannot alter the rules of the prison system, he has altered the spirit in which they used to be carried out under his predecessor. . . . Indeed he has quite altered the whole tone of the prison life."[60]

It was not long before Wilde's work was changed, from oakum-picking and crank-turning to library work and gardening. As his warder recalled, "The only task Wilde was put to was to act as 'schoolmaster's orderly,' which was in the nature of a great privilege, for it meant that he could take charge of the books and go round with them to other prisoners, besides having the pick of the literature for himself. Strange as it may seem considering his literary bent, he failed to accomplish even this task satisfactorily."[61] Whatever his faults as a library worker, indifference was surely not among them. Wilde loved books, and he took a sincere interest in the intellectual development of his fellow prisoners. He extended, in a way, his own special privileges to the others held alongside him. In one of his requests for books, he noted: "The Library here contains no example of Thackeray's or Dickens's novels. I feel sure that a complete set of their works would be as great a boon to many amongst the other prisoners as it certainly would be to myself." Likewise, after he procured a copy of *Treasure Island*, he was pleased to learn that it was "in great request and much appreciated" by the other inmates. There even survives a note he left for one of his prison friends: "Have a very good Sunday . . . reading Goethe's *Faust*, a very great work of art."[62]

In addition to his new work assignment, Wilde was also allowed to keep a score of books in his cell and to leave the light on as late as he wished. One guard explained: "on account of his former greatness a small concession was made him, and he was allowed to read and write as much as he liked. . . . Had this boon not been granted him he would, I am confident, have pined away and died."[63]

The Prisoner's Plea

Of course, there were limits to what political influence could win. Wilde's friends could help safeguard his health, they could provide him special privileges and send him books, but they could not give him what he wanted most—his freedom.

On July 2, 1896, while Isaacson was still in charge and before the granting of the fullest privileges, Oscar Wilde used the standard form to petition the home secretary for release, arguing (with reference to himself in the third person, as required by bureaucratic procedure) that "the terrible offenses of which he was rightly found guilty . . . are forms of sexual madness . . . diseases to be cured by a physician, rather than crimes to be punished by a judge." He cited some of the recent psychological literature to this effect and then argued that his incarceration could only make matters worse, causing "this insanity, that displayed itself in monstrous sexual perversion before" to "extend to the entire nature and intellect." Citing his "terror of madness," as well as concerns over his failing hearing and eyesight, Wilde asked that he be let out of prison.

The tone of this letter is utterly abject, with Wilde repeatedly confessing his "sexual perversity," "erotomania," and "vice" and expressing his regret, repentance, and self-loathing. But there comes, in this unlikely place, an extension of the critique of punishment that began in "The Soul of Man under Socialism." In among the desperate pleading—and we should remember that the poet is begging for his life—we find this: "Dreadful as are the results of the prison system—a system so terrible that it hardens their hearts whose hearts it does not break, and brutalises those who have to carry it out no less than those who have to submit to it—yet at least amongst its aims is not the desire to wreck the human reason. Though it may not seek to make men better, yet it does not desire to drive them mad." This passage borrows a line from "The Soul of Man under Socialism" and anticipates others from "The Ballad of Reading Gaol" and his post-prison letters to the

Daily Chronicle, thus showing the continuity, as well as the development, of Wilde's thought on these questions.

Wilde's petition also employs a clever rhetorical trick. He insists, somewhat against the evidence, that however cruel the prison may be, *at least* it does not intentionally produce insanity. But by so flatly stating the assumption, and by surrounding it with pronouncements of his fears to the contrary, Wilde also draws that very claim into question. The presumed humanity of those with power serves as a sort of challenge: Surely the authorities do not mean to drive us mad! Or do they?

Yet an appeal to his jailers was perhaps not the wisest place to decry the institution they oversaw and call into question its very purposes. Wilde's plea was dutifully forwarded by the governor, together with a report from the prison doctor saying, in brief, that the petitioner was gaining weight and showed no signs of mental illness. In fact, using the logic of the catch-22, the doctor argues, "from the lucid way in which he quotes authorities and gives his own ideas of insanity, [the petition itself is] clear evidence of his present sanity."[64]

The Home Office sent a committee of doctors to Reading to verify Wilde's condition, and on July 27, 1896, the chairman of the Prison Commission, Evelyn Ruggles-Brise, issued secret instructions concerning Wilde's treatment: "With reference to the Petition of Oscar Wilde, dated 20th instant, the Secretary of State has decided that this prisoner should be provided with foolscap paper, ink and pen, for use in his leisure moments in his cell." Furthermore, "The Prison rules limiting the issue of books to two per week may be relaxed in the case of this prisoner, and you will use your discretion as to allowing to the prisoner sufficient books to occupy his mind." Lastly, the prison doctor was authorized to consult with an outside specialist should the problems with Wilde's ear warrant it. Several conditions attached to these privileges, chiefly that Wilde not use the paper for communicating with people outside the prison, and that such accommodations "not interfere with the ordinary labour required of the prisoner in fulfillment of his sentence."[65] Wilde was not released, but he was given additional books and paper. And he received daily medical attention for his ear and spectacles for his eyes. Still, he had hoped for more.

A few months later, on November 10, 1896, Wilde tried again, writing a second petition. The tone of this letter is quite different. It is much less plaintive, though not quite defiant. He begins by remonstrating with the home secretary for failing to send a reply to his earlier letter, and, though he notes the improved conditions, he insists that "these alleviations, for which the petitioner is naturally grateful, count for but little in relieving the terrible mental stress and anguish that the silence and solitude of prison-life intensify daily."[66]

Wilde does not, in this letter, make a show of his remorse, but only mentions that he has been imprisoned "for offenses which are in other countries of Europe more rightly recognized as tragic forms of madness." He repeats—with infinitely more dignity and even with some sense of indignation—the argument that prison only makes things worse:

> While one may bear up against the monotonous hardships and relentless discipline of an English prison: endure with apathy the unceasing shame and the daily degradation: and grow callous even to that hideous grotesqueness of life that robs sorrow of all its dignity, and takes from pain its power of purification: still, the complete isolation from everything that is humane and humanising plunges one deeper and deeper into the very mire of madness, and the horrible silence, to which one is, as it were, eternally condemned, concentrates the mind on all that one longs to loathe, and creates those insane moods from which one desires to be free, creates them and makes them permanent.

He asks again to be let out and promises that he will seek medical treatment if he is.

And then, as the coup de grâce, Wilde offers a surprisingly general critique of the institution that holds him: "Prison is but an ill physician: and the modern modes of punishment create what they should cure, and, when they have on their side Time with its long light of dreary days, they desecrate and destroy whatever good, or desire even of good, there may be in a man."[67]

Oscar Wilde, at last, sounds again like himself. But his most powerful argument is the one least suited to his immediate purposes. For Wilde's petition to have its desired effect, it had to claim that his was a special case. It did so, seemingly, with references to his deteriorating health and the suggestion that stultifying isolation is somewhat worse for a man of letters. But

Wilde cannot resist stating the general case: that the prisons are cruel, that the laws are wrong, and that the system of punishment only succeeds in destroying whatever is best in both warder and inmate. What begins as a confession ends as an indictment.[68]

Taken literally, Wilde's argument would constitute a plea not just for his own freedom but also for that of all those similarly confined. As he remarked to one of his guards, "Sir, if this is the way Queen Victoria treats her convicts, she doesn't deserve to have any."[69]

The Prisoner as Poet

One of the Criminal Classes

Oscar Wilde was let out of prison on May 19, 1897, but his punishment did not end with his release. Late that night, he left England for good. Wilde was freed—but he was freed to a life of sickness, poverty, and anonymous exile.[70] He died in France in 1900, less than four years after leaving Reading Gaol. He was forty-six years old.

But, as much as he lost, Wilde also gained something from his prison experience. In prison he earned a kind of self-knowledge, the kind that only comes from tragedy. He learned to view suffering as he had always viewed pleasure, as a mode of beauty and a means of self-realization. And he came to understand sympathy, not as mere sentimentality but as a species of imagination that enlarges the individual personality and through which we share in the lives of others.

He learned his lessons in sympathy in large part from his fellow inmates.[71] One day at exercise, while the prisoners marched in their cheerless circle, Wilde suddenly heard a voice. One of the other men in the line whispered, "Oscar Wilde, I pity you because you must be suffering more than we are." Without looking to see whom he addressed, the poet replied, "No, my friend, we are all suffering equally."

Unfortunately, the brief exchange did not go unnoticed. A watchful guard shouted, "C.3.3 and C.4.8, step out of line! You're going to be brought up before the warden." Both men would be punished, but the one who initiated the conversation would be punished more severely. Yet each one insisted it was he who first spoke, and both accepted the harsher penalty—three days in a dark cell, with a bread-and-water diet.[72]

This sort of solidarity marked Wilde deeply, and the sense of connection with his fellow inmates proved most genuine.[73] He kept in touch with several of them after his release, and one came to visit him in France.[74] He also sought to aid them personally, writing small notes of encouragement, trying to set them up with work, and sending money when he could.[75] Wilde himself was bankrupt and living chiefly on the generosity of his friends. But that, as he saw it, only increased his responsibilities. As he wrote to Reginald Turner: "Now Robbie . . . is very severe on me for having sent some money to four chaps released last week. He says I can't afford it. But, dear Reggie, I must look after my prison-friends, if my good friends, like you, look after me."[76]

Oscar Wilde had sympathized with criminals throughout his literary career—from his defense of Thomas Griffiths Wainewright in "Pen, Pencil, and Poison" to his memorial for Charles Thomas Wooldridge in "The Ballad of Reading Gaol." But it was not until he was sent to prison that he became, at last, fully one of their number. As he wrote to Major Nelson after his release: "Of course I side with the prisoners: I was one, and I belong to their class now."[77]

An Intention to Reform

Prison had changed Wilde, and he knew it. He could not return to singing the praise of beauty and pleasure. Nor could he re-create the success of his comedies, mocking society with his paradoxes while forcing respectable audiences to laugh at their own cherished hypocrisies. Moreover, Wilde had to expand his philosophy to include what he had endured, to make use of sorrow as well as joy. He wrote from prison of his new outlook:

> The laws under which I am convicted are wrong and unjust laws, and the system under which I have suffered a wrong and unjust system. But, somehow, I have got to make both of these things just and right to me. . . . I have got to make everything that has happened to me good for me. The plank-bed, the loathsome food, the hard ropes shredded into oakum till one's finger-tips grow dull with pain, the menial offices with which every day begins and finishes, the harsh orders that routine seems to necessitate, the dreadful dress that makes sorrow grotesque to look at, the silence, the solitude, the shame—each and all of these things I have to transform into a spiritual experience. There is not a single degradation of the body which I must not try and make into a spiritualising of the soul. . . . The important thing, the thing that lies before me, the thing that I have

to do, or be for the brief remainder of my days one maimed, marred, and incomplete, is to absorb into my nature all that has been done to me, to make it part of me, to accept it without complaint, fear, or reluctance.[78]

This was, in effect, the reformatory ideal of the penitentiary turned inside out. Wilde *would* change. He would seek out or create a vantage point from which prison would be good for him—not by the standards of society but by his own measure. He would turn his disgrace into a triumph.[79] And the prison would not reform *him*; he would reform *it*: "It is not the prisoners who need reformation. It is the prisons."[80]

Wilde expressed this intention in a note that still survives. It is jotted on a small scrap of envelope, the front of which is marked "Private" and addressed to Major Nelson, the governor of Reading Gaol. On the back Wilde has written: "I hope to write about prison-life and to try and change it for others, but it is too terrible and ugly to make a work of art of. I have suffered too much in it to write [a] play about it."[81] This is the perspective from which we must understand Wilde's post-prison writing, especially his greatest poem, "The Ballad of Reading Gaol."

Some Cruelties of Prison Life

Not counting "De Profundis," which was not published until after his death, Wilde's attack on the penitentiary comprised three written works: "The Ballad of Reading Gaol" and two long letters to the *Daily Chronicle*. Together these represent the entirety of his literary output between imprisonment and death.[82]

The first letter in the *Chronicle* appeared on May 28, 1897, just a few days after his release. To call the piece a letter is actually somewhat misleading. It is more of a polemic, running to nineteen paragraphs and approximately eleven hundred words. (The second letter is about half as long.) Under the heading "The Case of Warder Martin, Some Cruelties of Prison Life," Wilde addresses two incidents that had troubled him toward the end of his confinement.

A guard at Reading, Thomas Martin, had been removed from his post for the grave offense of giving biscuits (cookies) to some children who had been imprisoned for poaching rabbits.[83] The *Chronicle* had been following the case with some attention, running letters from Martin as well as news reports concerning the case.[84] The incident had also led to questions in Parliament, posed to the home secretary.[85]

In his letter, Wilde begins by saying that he had seen the children in question: "They were quite small children, the youngest—the one to whom the warder gave the biscuits—being a tiny little chap, for whom they had evidently been unable to find clothes small enough to fit." He also, soon after, tells of another "small boy," placed in "the dimly lit cell right opposite my own" at Reading. "I heard him at breakfast-time crying, and calling to be let out. His cry was for his parents. From time to time I could hear the deep voice of the warder on duty telling him to keep quiet."[86]

The feelings of these children, Wilde thinks, are easy enough to understand: "The child consequently, being taken away from its parents by people whom it has never seen, and of whom it knows nothing, and finding itself in a lonely and unfamiliar cell, waited on by strange faces, and ordered about and punished by the representatives of a system it cannot understand, becomes an immediate prey to the first and most prominent emotion produced by modern prison life—the emotion of terror."[87] "This terror," he continues in the next paragraph, "seizes the grown man also." It is "intensified beyond power of expression by the solitary cellular system of our prisons."[88] Though Wilde returns, again and again, to the plight of the children, he uses their suffering to critique the entire prison system. The specific complaints he makes are more general than particular. They address, in fact, some of the main characteristics of prison life: hunger, bad food and sanitation, insanity.

Insanity becomes the second major theme of the essay, as Wilde proceeds to draw attention to "the large number of men who become insane or weak-minded" owing to the isolation. He relates the story of a man named Prince, number A.2.11: "About three months ago I noticed amongst the prisoners who took exercise with me a young man who seemed to me to be silly or half-witted. . . . [At] exercise he always seemed hysterical, and used to walk round crying or laughing." Rather than recognizing his condition as an illness to be treated with compassion, prison officials could only view it as willful disobedience: "Of course he was continually punished. . . . I saw that he was becoming insane, and was being treated as if he was shamming."[89]

The case followed its inevitable trajectory. Prince's condition made him incapable of following the prison rules, so he misbehaved and was punished. Of course, his condition worsened, leading to harsher punishment. Eventually he was flogged with a birch rod. Wilde describes hearing "the most horrible and revolting shrieks, or rather howls, for at first I thought some animal like a bull or a cow was being unskillfully slaughtered outside the prison walls. I soon realised, however, that the howls proceeded from the basement of the prison, and I knew that some wretched man was being flogged."[90] Prince received twenty-four lashes.

Wilde ends the piece, almost oddly, with praise for "the present Governor of Reading . . . a man of gentle and humane character greatly liked and respected by all the prisoners." The state of the prison is *not*, Wilde insists, the fault of Major Nelson: "His hands are tied."[91]

So, where does the fault lie? This Wilde makes clear early on, in the second paragraph of his letter: "Ordinary cruelty," he argues, is not the product of individual sadism but instead "the result in our days of stereotyped systems, of hard-and-fast rules, and of stupidity. Wherever there is centralisation there is stupidity. What is inhuman in modern life is officialism. Authority is as destructive to those who exercise it as it is to those on whom it is exercised. . . . Responsibility is shifted on to the disciplinary regulations. It is supposed that because a thing is the rule it is right."[92]

When Wilde writes of Prince, he testifies from observation. But he also, without acknowledgment, writes of his own experience. During his time in prison, Wilde feared for his sanity, and he too was suspected of faking. Wilde tells his own story by telling that of another. This becomes a motif—in fact, a strategy—for his post-prison work.[93] He expresses his own sorrow by expressing sympathy for others. Their pain *is* his pain. As he wrote in "De Profundis": "*Whatever happens to another happens to oneself.*"[94] So Wilde defends himself by defending his fellow prisoners. He offers his sympathy, and thus he silently demands sympathy from the reader. In this hidden autobiography, poetic imagination, moral sympathy, and political solidarity converge.

The Prison Guard's Dilemma

Wilde saw the demoralizing effect of the prison system on prisoner and guard alike—the stifling of all kind or gentle impulses, the depression of all mental or imaginative energy, the deadening of all sensitivity, and the denial of all compassion or sympathy.

In the *Chronicle*, Wilde relayed a further story of Thomas Martin's unlawful generosity: "Some days before my release, Martin was going the rounds at half-past seven with one of the senior warders." They came upon a new inmate who, "suffering from violent diarrhoea," "asked the senior warder to allow him to empty the slops," noting "the horrible odour of the cell and the possibility of illness again in the night." But it was after five thirty, the last time prisoners were scheduled to leave the cells. And so the senior officer refused. Martin, however, took pity and emptied the bucket himself. "A warder emptying a prisoner's slops is of course against the rules, but Martin did this act of kindness to the man out of the simple humanity of his nature."[95]

Martin's simple acts of humanity were no small thing. He was not dismissed merely over the question of whether children should be given cookies or whether guards might empty an inmate's chamber pot. At bottom, the issue was whether any institution could require cruelty or any rule forbid what most people would regard as basic human decency.

Martin's kindness seemed so wonderful to Wilde *because* it represented disobedience. With kindness manifest in an illegal act, individual and defiant, it was grand and even Christ-like. Were such actions to be legalized, all their poetic beauty would disappear. Once authorized, they would become just elements of the prison routine—better than some others but not to be singled out as symbolic of deep compassion. But the institution could not incorporate Martin's perspective any more than he could adjust himself to the unfeeling demands of the prison environment.

Martin's disobedience and his punishment illustrate a fundamental, irreconcilable conflict between the morality of the individual and the morality of the institution. The good of the institution lies in order and discipline: every action must be planned, regulated, and rule-bound. But for Thomas Martin, the good lay in kindness and sympathy; his greatest actions—those that were most his own, and those for which we admire him—were spontaneous, unpracticed, and defiant.

Martin's transgressions of prison rules may have been minor, but they were not trivial. His offenses represented his real virtues.

A Hidden Autobiography

Though Wilde had always opposed society's hypocrisies, in the case of the warder Thomas Martin he also had personal reasons for intervening. There survive, in the Oscar Wilde collection at UCLA's Clark Library, a handful of notes that Wilde and Martin exchanged surreptitiously at Reading. One note was passed back and forth, making a sort of dialogue. It reads:

> My Dear Friend,
> What have I to write about except that if you had been an officer in Reading Prison a year ago my life would have been much happier. Everyone tells me I am looking better—and happier.
>   That is because I have a good friend who gives me the *Chronicle*, and *promises* me ginger biscuits!
>   Oscar

At the bottom is Martin's reply: "Your [*sic*] ungrateful. I done more than promise."[96]

Another note to Martin directly foreshadows the letter to the *Chronicle*:

> Please find out for me the name of a.2.11.
>   also: the names of the children who are in for the rabbits, and the amount of their fine.
>   Can I pay this and get them out? If so I will get them out tomorrow. Pleas [*sic*] dear friend do this for me. I must get them out.
>   Think what a thing for me it would be to be able to help three little children. I would be delighted beyond words: if I can do this by paying the fine tell the children that they are to be released tomorrow by a friend, and ask them to be happy and not to tell anyone.[97]

Martin was fired, in effect, for his kindness—a kindness that Wilde had himself received and that he knew to be all too rare. Wilde must have felt not only intense gratitude toward Martin but also some responsibility for his predicament. In another note, Wilde had promised, "Of course I vow not for worlds [to] get such a friend as you are into *any danger*."[98]

But more startling, the elements of these notes—the children, the biscuits, Martin himself, the violation of the rules, even the mention of the *Chronicle*—allow us to read Wilde's later epistle not only as an altruistic intervention on behalf of justice but again as a form of disguised autobiography. For Wilde here is not only pleading Martin's case or that of the poor children—or, later, that of Prince. He is also pleading his own case, recounting his own story, and doing so in a form that will allow him to avoid accusations of self-pity.

These children become in Wilde's treatment the stand-ins for the entire inmate population, an identification highlighted by the utter pity that the adult prisoners felt for their young colleagues. "There is not a single man in Reading Gaol that would not gladly have done the three children's punishment for them."[99]

With this contrast between the sympathy of the prisoners and the indifference and cruelty of the prison system, Wilde effects a reversal of the moral theory of incarceration—especially the notion of "contamination."[100] He wrote in the *Chronicle*:

> [A] great deal has been talked and written lately about the contaminating influence of prison on young children. What is said is quite true. A child is utterly contaminated by prison life. But the contaminating influence is not that of the prisoners. It is that of the whole prison system—of the governor, the chaplain, the warders, the lonely cell, the isolation, the revolting food, the rules of the Prison Commissioners, the mode of discipline, as it is termed, of the life. . . . [T]he only really humanising influence in prison is the influence of the prisoners. . . . [T]he bad influence on children is not, and could never be, that of the prisoners, but is, and will always remain, that of the prison system itself.[101]

Wilde's letter became a news item, earning articles not only in the *Chronicle* but in the *Catholic Times* and *Le Soir* as well.[102] In February 1898 the letter was reprinted as a pamphlet by Murdoch and Company, under

the title *Children in Prison and Other Cruelties of Prison Life.* It included a
note from the publisher, explaining that it was intended "as evidence that
the prison system is opposed to all that is kind and helpful. Herein is shown
a process that is dehumanizing, not only to the prisoners, but to every one
connected with it."[103] This is a point that Wilde made repeatedly and more
forcefully: first in "The Soul of Man under Socialism" (1891), then in his
petition to the home secretary (1896), and finally in the *Chronicle* (1897):
"Authority is as destructive to those who exercise it as it is to those on whom
it is exercised."[104]

A Prison Poem

"The Ballad of Reading Gaol" likewise argues that the laws are useless, and
that punishment is worse than useless: "Every Law / That men hath made
for Man /. . . straws the wheat and saves the chaff."[105] On one level this
means that the law punishes the best people and spares the truly wicked;
on another it means that the law's operations kill what is best in its victims
and save what is worthless. This second meaning is reiterated a few lines
later:

> The vilest deeds like poison weeds,
>   Bloom well in prison-air;
> It is only what is good in Man
>   That wastes and withers there.[106]

The poem, Wilde's one major literary achievement after his release,
tells the story of an unnamed soldier who kills his wife and is sentenced
to hang. It follows his journey from the exercise yard, to death row, to the
gallows, and then digresses for seventeen verses to articulate a thorough
indictment of the prison system, revisiting many of the points raised in the
Chronicle:

> For they starve the little frightened child
>   Till it weeps both night and day:
> And they scourge the weak, and flog the fool,

> And gibe the old and grey,
> And some grow mad, and all grow bad,
> And none a word may say.[107]

Only at the end does the poem return to the soldier, with a brief meditation on the unmarked grave.

"The Ballad of Reading Gaol" was inspired by the execution of Charles Thomas Wooldridge, who was hanged at Reading while Wilde was there.[108] The soldier's wife, Laura Ellen Wooldridge, had left him for another man, and Charles, overcome with jealousy, had killed her with a razor on March 29, 1896. He was executed on July 7 that same year.[109]

One of the Reading guards recalled, "Wilde, of course, never saw the murderer after his condemnation, but he heard the bell tolling for the execution, and it made a terrible impression on his mind. . . . Wilde told me that those moments when the bell rang out, and his imagination conjured up the execution scene, were the most awful of a time rich in horrors."[110] Thus the subject of the poem—Wooldridge's crime and subsequent execution—was in some respect determined by proximity. But, as the focus of a political pamphlet, it was also a smart choice. Already Wooldridge had become a figure of public sympathy and agitation. A petition for clemency received one thousand signatures from people in the surrounding towns, but the authorities refused mercy on the grounds that the murder was premeditated.[111]

Anti-Prison Propaganda

Wilde intended "Reading Gaol" as a kind of political intervention. As he wrote to Robbie Ross, as a result "[it] suffers under the difficulty of a divided aim in style. Some is realistic, some is romantic: some poetry, some propaganda."[112] Replying to editorial suggestions from Ross, he admitted, "You are quite right in saying that the poem should end at 'outcasts always mourn,' but the propaganda, which I desire to make, begins there."[113]

Clearly Wilde's priorities had shifted. Early in his career he had argued against sacrificing the aesthetic purity of art for any political or moral purpose. In "The Decay of Lying" he had criticized Charles Reade for his "foolish attempt . . . to draw public attention to the state of our convict prisons," lamenting the image of a true artist "raging and roaring over the abuses of contemporary life like a common pamphleteer."[114] Yet here is Wilde doing the same thing. The poem's subject likewise marked a departure. As Wilde mentioned in a letter to Laurence Housman, "I am occupied in finishing a poem, terribly realistic for me, and drawn from actual experience, a sort of denial of my own philosophy of art in many ways."[115]

Wilde's adoption of the ballad form—"a new style for me, full of actuality and life in its directness of message and meaning"—may have helped signal the political intentions behind its composition, given the ballad's association with Irish protest songs.[116] But it also certainly indicated his intended audience.[117] Unlike the decadent poetry of his youth, Wilde was not writing here for other artists and intellectuals but for the wider public. Hence, he considered having the poem printed in the *Chronicle* or in *Reynolds*—the first because it was always "reckless in art"; the second because "it circulates among the lower orders, and the criminal classes, and so ensures me my right audience for sympathy."[118]

And so Oscar Wilde ended his career with a piece of self-conscious propaganda, though he insisted that "there is more in the poem than a pamphlet on prison-reform."[119] Indeed, "The Ballad of Reading Gaol" is without rival Wilde's best poem, far superior—aesthetically—to any of his purely aestheticist works.

The poem was a commercial success as well. With the first printing as a book, in February 1898, 800 copies sold out in a few days. The second printing, of 1,000, was gone within a month. All told, the book was in its sixth printing, for a total of 5,099 copies, by May. Two thousand more were printed the following year.[120] Moreover, "The Ballad" was promptly translated, with French and Spanish versions appearing in 1898, and German, Italian, Greek, Russian, and Yiddish following within a few years.[121] In 1925 an illustrated edition appeared, featuring beautiful woodcuts by Frans Masereel, an artist with pronounced anarchist sympathies. Perhaps the most remarkable of these illustrations is the frontispiece, which shows a man in prison, his hands bound, a locked door behind him. Covering his face is a square labeled "C33"—Wilde's prison number.[122]

The anarchist Benjamin Tucker decided to delay publication of two other pamphlets in order to bring out an American edition of "Reading Gaol." He saw in the poem not only a critique of the prison system but also an argument against hierarchical society. Where Wilde's earlier political writing had conveyed the hopeful prospects of humanity under socialism, Tucker writes, "In this poem we get a terrific portrayal of the soul of man under Archism."[123]

For decades after his death, Wilde's work served as a kind of scripture for those advocating prison reform—or, in the case of the anarchists, abolition. Edward Carpenter used a section from "The Ballad of Reading Gaol" as the epigraph to *Prisons, Police, and Punishment*. Later in the book he discusses Wilde's first letter to the *Chronicle* at some length.[124] Alexander Berkman likewise takes a passage from "Reading Gaol" as the epigraph for *Prison Memoirs of an Anarchist*. He then uses lines from the poem as chapter headings, for instance: "And by All Forgot, We Rot and Rot" (part 2, chapter 31) and "How Men Their Brothers Maim" (part 2, chapter 38).[125] In January 1917, the cover of Berkman's magazine the *Blast* featured an excerpt of the poem laid over an illustration by Robert Miner, depicting a lynch mob.[126] Marie Ganz read the poem aloud to the other inmates in the Queens County Jail and recalled them listening "intently to every word until they burst into tears."[127] Ben Reitman's poem "Vengeance"—written while he was in prison for distributing information about birth control—makes several overt references to "Reading Gaol" and appeared in *Mother Earth* anonymously (attributed only to "Cell 424").[128] When Reitman was released, he delivered a speech in which he declared, directly echoing Wilde, that "Jail, Judges, [and] Governments . . . are all miserable failures."[129] Emma Goldman twice quoted "Reading Gaol" in "Prisons: A Social Crime and Failure."[130] Decades later, the anthology *Forces of Law and Order (Selected Articles from the Anarchist Journal "Freedom")* again quoted Wilde in an epigraph, this time from "The Soul of Man under Socialism": "Wherever there is a man who exercises authority, there is a man who resists authority."[131]

The Prison Reform Bill

Building on the success of his ballad, Wilde composed a second letter to the *Chronicle*, which appeared on March 24, 1898, under the heading "Don't Read This If You Want to Be Happy Today."

In this piece, Wilde's political aims are at their most explicit. He begins, "Sir,—I understand that the Home Secretary's Prison Reform Bill is to be read this week. . . . I hope that you will allow me, as one who has had long personal experience of life in an English gaol, to point out what reforms in our present stupid and barbarous system are urgently necessary."[132] His first argument dismisses the agenda of the bill under consideration: "The chief reform proposed is an increase in the number of inspectors. . . . Such a reform as this is entirely useless. . . . The visitors arrive not to help the prisoners, but to see that the rules are carried out. Their object in coming is to ensure the enforcement of a foolish and inhuman code." In fact, Wilde suggests, such inspections actually make things worse: "A prisoner who has been allowed the smallest privilege dreads the arrival of the inspectors. And on the day of any prison inspection the prison officials are more than usually brutal to the prisoners . . . to show the splendid discipline they maintain."

Wilde argues, as an alternative to better (that is, stricter) adherence to the rules, that reforms should concern themselves with "the needs of the body and the needs of the mind of each unfortunate prisoner." The authorities may have described the prison regime in terms of "hard labour, hard fare, and a hard bed."[133] However, Wilde lists the "three permanent punishments authorized by law in English prisons" as: "1. Hunger 2. Insomnia 3. Disease." He proceeds through each subject with some detail: the "revolting" quality and "insufficient" quantity of the food, its result being "incessant diarrhoea"; the "sanitary arrangements" consisting of a "small tin vessel" that the prisoner may empty only at set intervals; "the foul air of the prison cells"; the plank bed.[134]

He then turns his attention to the needs of the mind. In his petition to the home secretary, he had tactfully advanced the proposition that the prison "does not desire to drive [the inmates] mad."[135] Here he forthrightly states the opposite: "The present system seems almost to have for its aim the wrecking and the destruction of the mental faculties. The production of insanity is, if not its object, certainly its result." It is on this point that Wilde's rhetoric achieves its greatest force: "Deprived of books, of all human intercourse, isolated from every humane and humanising influence, condemned to eternal silence, robbed of all intercourse with the external world, treated like an unintelligent animal, brutalized below the level of any of the brute creation, the wretched man who is confined in an English prison can hardly escape becoming insane."[136]

The remedies Wilde proposes are commonsense to the point of being banal: "The food supplied to prisoners should be adequate and wholesome." "Every prisoner should be allowed to have access to the lavatories when necessary, and to empty his slops when necessary." "Every prisoner should have an adequate supply of good books . . . whatever books they want." "A prisoner should be allowed to see his friends once a month." "Every prisoner should be allowed to write and receive a letter at least once a month." "The habit of mutilating and expurgating prisoners' letters should be stopped." "Prison doctors . . . [should be] compelled to take some interest in the health and sanitary condition of the people under their charge."[137]

Wilde's advocacy seems to have had some effect. "Reading Gaol" was twice quoted in the course of parliamentary debate. MP John Redmond read out an entire stanza, and the radical Irish MP T. P. O'Connor confidently asserted, "Everybody in this House has read the startling and striking poem, written by a prisoner recently released, entitled 'The Ballad of Reading Gaol.'"[138] Christopher Millard later reported:

> The Commissioners appointed to inquire into the question of Prison Reform in the years 1897 and 1898 spent three days considering the suggestions made in Wilde's letters, with what good results may very briefly be stated as follows:—At the end of the first month's imprisonment a prisoner is allowed to write a letter or to receive a visit, and to read a book, instead of waiting three months as formerly; the sanitary arrangements have been improved; the food weighed out each day is somewhat less scanty and more varied; [and] the plank bed is insisted on for the first fourteen days only, instead of a month.[139]

Furthermore, the law abolished the treadwheel, crank, and other pointless labor and replaced it with useful work and technical instruction—though the picking of oakum was reserved as a punishment. The regime of silence and cell confinement was relaxed somewhat, the reliance on corporal punishment reduced, and the system of early release liberalized.[140]

Wilde himself was jubilant in this victory: "Yes: I think that, aided by some splendid personalities like [Michael] Davitt and John Burns, I have been able to deal a heavy and fatal blow at the monstrous prison-system of English justice. There is to be no more starvation, nor sleeplessness, nor endless silence, nor eternal solitude, nor brutal floggings. The system is exposed, and, so, doomed."[141]

This assessment was, of course, entirely too optimistic. Nearly a century later, Peter Southerton described the conditions at Reading Gaol in the 1980s, saying that "the quality of life had improved little. . . . [O]vercrowding meant spending most of every twenty-four hours locked up, not alone but with one or, more often, two other people and a full slop bucket, wearing clothes which soon became dirty and smelly, looking forward to the statutory minimum of an hour's exercise a day if it didn't rain and hoping that a few hours' work, however menial or unconstructive, might be available to ease the boredom."[142]

Rethinking Reform

The history of the prison system is, more than anything else, a cautionary tale concerning the dangers of reform. The penitentiary was itself the child of reformers; proposed as a humane alternative to corporal punishment and public humiliation, it was to work gently, quietly, on the prisoner's conscience, rather than brutally, publicly, on his flesh.[143] But since its inception, its progress—if it can be called progress—has been marked by a long series of tragic experiments, each undertaken with the best intentions.[144]

How do we attend to the pressing needs of those who live under such a system without inadvertently reinforcing that system with legitimizing improvements? It was for just such reasons that, early in his career, Wilde had dismissed the whole notion of reform and any concern with practicality: "For what is a practical scheme? A practical scheme is either a scheme that is already in existence, or a scheme that could be carried out under existing conditions. But it is exactly the existing conditions that one objects to; and any scheme that could accept these conditions is wrong and foolish."[145]

Yet after prison, in the *Chronicle*, he argues most explicitly in favor of reform.

The change is easily explained. The experience of prison had shown him what the loss of freedom did to a person. He had come to know from bitter experience how wrong he had been when he had written that "even in prison, a man can be quite free. His soul can be free."[146] He had felt the impact of confinement on his imagination; he had seen its devastating effects on his fellow prisoners.

In his early work, Wilde had wanted to assert the power of the artistic imagination over sordid reality. But in his romanticization of prison and his idealization of freedom, he seems to have forgotten his own maxim: "Those who see any difference between soul and body have neither."[147] If we can "cure the soul by means of the senses, and the senses by means of the soul," then it stands to reason that one could also starve the soul by means of the senses, and kill the senses by means of the soul.[148] And prison—with its thoroughgoing lack of sensual pleasure, mental stimulation, and emotional connection—punishes both the physical and the spiritual, leaving "soul and body marred."[149]

Realizing this, Wilde determined to push for reforms, imperfect though they might be, while with the same breath acknowledging the inadequacy of *any* possible improvements and emphasizing at each opportunity the corruption inherent in the institution itself.

"Of course," he argues in his first letter to the *Chronicle*, "no child under fourteen years of age should be sent to prison at all. It is an absurdity, and, like many absurdities, of absolutely tragic results. *If, however, they are to be sent to prison* . . . [their days should be spent] in a workshop or schoolroom." "They should sleep in a dormitory." "They should be allowed exercise for at least three hours a day." They should be fed "tea and bread-and-butter and soup." He thus begins with an assertion of the "absurdity" of the entire practice and then, without backtracking, offers practical reforms that could at least ameliorate some of its worst effects and that *could* be enacted under the present system. "A resolution of the House of Commons could settle the treatment of children in half an hour."[150]

In his second letter, Wilde again "tried to indicate . . . a few of the reforms necessary to our English prison system. They are simple, practical, and humane." Yes, and entirely inadequate: "They are, of course, only a beginning. But it is time that a beginning should be made."[151]

Wilde's experience in prison convinced him of the urgent need for change, but it did nothing to move him away from his most radical positions. Instead he developed his radical politics toward a more comprehensive view, one that offered a layered critique of the penal institution—arguing against specific conditions and practices while also denouncing the structures of authority that created such conditions, the standards of morality that sought to justify them, and the degrading effect they had on everyone concerned.[152]

The Prison Revolt of Morality

With this in mind, it is important that Wilde placed the blame on the *prison system* rather than on its particular functionaries. Clearly he had no wish to libel those guards and administrators, like Martin and Nelson, who had been kind to him.[153] Moreover, he did not want to imply that the faults of the prison could be remedied simply by hiring new staff. He knew from his own experience that a change in leadership could improve conditions, but the same experience showed him how little effect a humane administrator could permissibly achieve. As he wrote of Major Nelson: "The system is, of course, beyond his reach as far as altering its rules is concerned."[154]

Likewise, in "Reading Gaol," when he describes those officials closest to the prisoners—the warders—Wilde emphasizes the imperatives suppressing any sense of human compassion. For a warder, Wilde saw, must learn to silence his sympathy and disguise his humanity. He "must set a lock upon his lips, / And make his face a mask."[155] The prison did everything that it could to grind all sense of mercy and fellow-feeling out of those who entered its gates—whether prisoner, guard, governor, chaplain, or doctor. The unyielding regimentation, the humiliation, the brutality, and the lack of human contact all combined to silence any feelings of pity or tenderness: "The most terrible thing about it is not that it breaks one's heart . . . but that it turns one's heart to stone." To "hard labour, hard fare and hard bed," then, we can add hard hearts. "To those who are in prison, tears are a part of every day's experience. A day in prison on which one does not weep is a day on which one's heart is hard, not a day on which one's heart is happy."[156]

Wilde refused, as a kind of resistance, to become unfeeling or indifferent. He would sooner accept suffering than apathy. He determined not to turn away from misery and pain; to do so would have been to renounce the full experience of life. He would instead embrace it as he had previously embraced pleasure and joy—to its fullest, without hesitation or restraint. Wilde refused to let his heart grow hard; he would allow it to be broken instead: "hearts are made to be broken."[157]

In this sorrow, in this brokenheartedness, Wilde found a kind of salvation. "[W]hat chills and kills" the prisoners, he says, even more than "lean Hunger and green Thirst," is their bitter apathy, the feeling "that every stone one lifts by day / Becomes one's heart by night." Sorrow, then, comes almost as a mercy; for "God's eternal Laws are kind / And break the heart of stone." And it is through suffering that one may learn to love: "How else but through a broken heart / May Lord Christ enter in?"[158]

This sounds at first like the very aim of the penitentiary—the reform of the inmates, the saving of their souls. But Wilde repeatedly contrasts divine sympathy with human law. Jesus is on the side of the prisoners, not that of the chaplain or the hangman. Christ is reclaimed on behalf of the oppressed, and the moral conventions of Victorian respectability are perfectly reversed. The criminals are vindicated, their judges condemned.

In "The Ballad of Reading Gaol," Wilde accomplishes this reversal through a series of sympathetic identifications. The prisoners sympathize with the murderer; the readers sympathize with the prisoners. More, the poem *identifies* the prisoners with the murderer, the reader with the narrator, the innocent with the guilty.[159]

The prisoners understand that, like the hanged man, they are not blameless: "Had each got his due, / They should have died instead." Their attitude is contrasted with that of the chaplain, who is blinded by his own righteousness. And so, on the eve of the execution, the prisoners—"the fool, the fraud, the knave"—keep an "endless vigil." Some men "weep / Who never yet have wept," and some men "knelt to pray / Who never prayed before." But after the soldier is hanged, "The Chaplain would not kneel to pray / By his dishonoured grave" and refused to mark it with the sign of "that blessed Cross / That Christ for sinners gave." Thus, the convicted criminals call upon God while the pious clergyman, without any sense of the irony, refuses to extend grace to "one of those / Whom Christ came down to save" and will not mark the grave of one condemned man with the sign of another.[160] Like the "philanthropic people" Lord Henry Wotton condemns in *Dorian Gray*, the minister "lose[s] all sense of humanity," for much the same reason—*precisely because he believes himself good.*[161]

The prisoners, on the other hand, know how "to feel another's guilt" and weep with pity and regret "for the blood we had not spilt." Hence each prisoner takes on the guilt of the murderer, but the murderer takes the punishment for all—if not as one innocent of sin, then at least as one no more guilty than the rest. ("For each man kills the thing he loves, / Yet each man does not die.")[162] Sympathy erases the distinctions between innocence and guilt. And isn't that, after all, a kind of forgiveness?

One surprising result of this sympathetic identification is that capital punishment, which drives the plot of the ballad, is not singled out for special criticism. Death is not presented as a separate, unique category of penalty but as another barbarous aspect of the whole system of punishment—statistically exceptional, but typical in its cruelty. The other prisoners are not so different from the murderer, and their punishment contains traces of his. Thus Wilde describes confinement as a kind of death and compares the prison cell to a "numbered tomb."[163] He may have drawn this comparison because, during his long days in gaol, alone and ill, he felt that death would come as a relief. His thoughts often turned to suicide. Or it may be that, feeling the depressing effects of isolation on his imagination and his mental faculties, he believed that something had died within him already. But Wilde also understood the implicit claim to one's life inherent in any system of authority and the threat of violence implicit in every exercise thereof. As he wrote in "De Profundis": "All trials are trials for one's life, just as all sentences are sentences of death."[164]

The hanged man therefore stands in for the other prisoners at every point. His crime is their crime; his punishment is their punishment. He is a murderer by his deeds; they are murderers in their hearts. He takes the penalty for them all, but they suffer while he is punished. The first-person narration, all the while, draws the reader in and encourages us to identify with the unnamed prisoner who addresses us. The poem calls on our sympathy and, more subtly, demands we take sides. Are we like the prisoners, sinful but compassionate, or are we like the chaplain and those other representatives of the penal system, self-righteous and cruel?

Wilde develops this perspective in part by turning away from questions of justice and law. The fifth, and most polemical, section of the ballad begins:

> I know not whether Laws be right,
>> Or whether Laws be wrong;
> All that we know who lie in gaol
>> Is that the wall is strong;
> And that each day is like a year,
>> A year whose days are long.[165]

The relevant issue is not one of right or wrong but of the actual suffering that results from the law. Moral judgments, it seems, are individual and uncertain, while the experience of suffering is collective and sure: It is *I* who *knows not* "whether Laws be right," but it is *we* "who lie in gaol" and *do know* what it means to languish there.

Wilde thus places the discussion of punishment on different ground, moving it away from guilt or innocence, away from right and wrong, and to the question of suffering and sympathy for suffering. The guilt of Wooldridge, or of the other prisoners, is suddenly irrelevant compared to their shared experience of sorrow. And the justice of the laws that convicted them is unimportant compared to the cruelty of the punishments imposed on them.[166]

Chapter 6

The Eternal Rebel

Outcast and Icon, in Exile and Utopia

Last Days

Oscar Wilde died, exiled and impoverished, in Paris on November 30, 1900.

"His will had been broken," André Gide later recalled. "Nothing remained in his shattered life but a mouldy ruin, painful to contemplate, of his former self."[1]

This image of Wilde at the end—desperate, friendless, alcoholic, exhausted—is largely the result of his biographers' need to fit messy reality into neat narrative forms. But the truth, as Wilde once observed, is "rarely pure and never simple."[2] There is a real tragedy to Wilde's story, but he was not the broken, useless man that both the moralists and the martyr worshippers imagine. In assuming that he was, both camps are really telling the same story: the rebel must be punished—in one version, to show that rebellion is wrong; in the other, to show that the punishment is wrong. Whether they view him as a saint or a heretic, they each conspire to see Wilde destroyed. Disciples, more even than tyrants, require a proper crucifixion. A martyr who remains stubbornly alive is of no use to anyone.

Society condemned Wilde, imprisoned him, bankrupted him, separated him from his children, pressed him toward madness, and, through medical neglect, finally killed the exhausted poet.[3] Yet, despite everything, it did not defeat him.

In his study of Wilde's "unrepentant years" after prison, biographer Nicholas Frankel writes: "Until his final illness in the autumn of 1900, he delighted in the pleasures of conversation, sex, companionship, and alcohol, unafraid at the prospect of courting the disapproval of others. . . . He seized pleasure whenever and wherever he could find it, especially among the bohemian denizens of the bars, cafés, and boulevards of Paris, and his young lovers were numerous by his own reckoning."[4] Lord Alfred Douglas said

as much, attesting to Wilde's "extraordinarily buoyant and happy temperament, . . . splendid sense of humour, and . . . unrivalled faculty for enjoyment
of the moment," even in the years of his exile.[5] Robbie Ross too thought that
though "Wilde suffered at times from extreme poverty and intensely from
social ostracism," nevertheless "his temperament was essentially a happy one,
and I think his good spirits and enjoyment of life far outweighed any bitter
recollections or realisations of an equivocal and tragic position."[6]

By losing his status, his name, his wealth, Oscar Wilde was at the same
time released from the social conventions, the personal attachments, and the
expectations that had constrained him. Exile and anonymity proved to be a
kind of escape.[7]

And so Wilde was annoyed by those who wished that he would reform.[8]
"I believe they would like me to edit prayers for those at sea," he wrote, "or
to recant the gospel of the joy of life in a penny tract."[9] His refusal to repent
was practically a political principle: "A patriot put in prison for loving his
country loves his country, and a poet in prison for loving boys loves boys."[10]

Wilde came to view his hardships, his punishments, and even his
own admitted faults simply as a part of his story—episodes in an unfold-
ing drama, lending his life the element of tragedy. Sorrow, as he wrote in
"De Profundis," was "the other half of the garden" of life—darker, more
bitter, but with "its secrets for me also."[11] It was a side he had to learn to
accept. But that was in itself no reason to avoid the sunnier, more joyful half.
The challenge, as always, was to embrace the whole.[12] His early triumph
and glory were not annihilated or even contradicted by his later downfall
and disgrace but were in a way *completed* by them, just as his tragedy only
had meaning because of his former greatness. The depth of his tragedy is
in fact the measure of his greatness, and true victory lay in the ability "to
make everything that has happened to me good for me . . . , to absorb into
my nature all that has been done to me, to make it part of me, to accept it
without complaint, fear or reluctance," to embrace with Chuang Tzu's peace
and Nietzsche's will the insight that "whatever is realised is right."[13] In this,
Wilde was resolute, believing that in "moments of submission and acceptance" he might find "whatever beauty of life still remains to me." Humility
might become dignity, disgrace transcended, defeat overcome. "I can, at any
rate, merely proceed on the lines of my own development, and by accepting
all that has happened to me make myself worthy of it."[14]

Perhaps Wilde's attitude is best relayed through one of his heretical parables, which he told repeatedly toward the end of his life. In this story, the resurrected Jesus returns to Nazareth and meets again the people he had known there, each one profoundly changed. The leper he miraculously healed is now a drunkard living for pleasure: "I was a leper; Thou hast healed me. Why should I lead another life?" The blind man, given sight, is now driven by lust: "I was blind; Thou hast healed me. What should I do otherwise with my sight?" Christ sees a woman "whose face and garments were painted, and whose feet were shod with pearls." He chastises her, "The road which you follow . . . is that of sin; wherefore follow it?" But she replies, laughing, "Thou hast pardoned me all my sins." At last, Jesus finds a young man weeping at the edge of the city. "My friend," he asks, "wherefore weepest thou?" "I was dead and Thou hast raised me up; what should I do otherwise with my life?"[15]

As Wilde told Anna de Bremont, "I have lived—yes—I have lived. . . . I have lived all there was to live. Life held to my lips a full flavoured cup, and I drank it to the dregs—the bitter and the sweet. I found the sweet bitter, and the bitter, sweet—yes, I have lived."[16]

A Good Blaze

Long after his death, Wilde remained a controversial and even a polarizing figure.

The posthumous publication of "De Profundis" elicited protests from the clergy, in part because the publisher, Methuen, also supplied religious texts. The Canon of Westminster, Reverend H. C. Beeching, denounced the book from the pulpit, calling it "a doctrine of devils." When he later learned that the publisher was releasing a second edition, he wrote a letter urging against it. Methuen responded, "It is quite clear that the spirit of the Spanish Inquisition is not yet defunct." To which Beeching replied, "I am not sure . . . that the Spanish Inquisition would not have been well occupied in burning OW. He would have made a good blaze."[17]

Two years later, the *Methodist Review* declared itself "tolerant of mere theories, however pernicious, immoral, or destructive" but condemned Wilde for displaying "the reckless daring to practice what he preaches."

Describing him as the "chief prophet, apostle, and teacher" of "the aesthetes, these anarchists against the moral law," the journal thus expressly identified aestheticism, anarchism, and homosexuality, all embodied in Wilde. "Wilde lived his principles to the full, and so he became the consummate flower of aestheticism," the essay explained, and thus he also earned society's wrath. Society, maintaining an "effective machinery . . . for its own protection . . . does not discriminate between aesthetes and anarchists."[18]

The stigma attached to Wilde, and the silence surrounding his crimes, penetrated into artistic circles as well. Coulson Kernahan wanted to dedicate a book to Wilde after his death, but the publisher forbade it.[19] Years later he was visited by another of Wilde's friends who, upon seeing a signed portrait of the poet, soberly advised: "If I were you, I should put that thing out of sight, and, if you happen at any time to hear his name mentioned, I should keep the fact that he had been a friend of yours to yourself."[20]

The effects lingered for decades. In 1954, when a plaque was added to Wilde's Tite Street residence, it was almost immediately vandalized.[21] And as recently as 2010, the computer company Apple censored Tom Bouden's all-male comics adaptation of *The Importance of Being Earnest*, blacking out a scene in which two partly nude men share a kiss.[22]

Censoring *Salomé*

Perhaps the most suppressed of Wilde's works is his Symbolist tragedy *Salomé*, which reimagines the events leading to the death of John the Baptist. The play was first produced in Paris in 1896, at the anarchist-run Théâtre de l'Oeuvre—but it was not produced in England until 1931. At the time of its writing the Lord Chamberlain, who was responsible for the licensing of plays, rejected it under a Cromwellian law against the portrayal of religious figures on the stage.[23] It was refused again in 1910.[24] A Russian production starring Ida Rubinstein was similarly suppressed at the insistence of the Holy Synod.[25]

Even the Paris production, which was staged while Wilde remained in prison, took steps to avoid official sanction, omitting a homosexual subplot by casting a woman in the role of the page who is passionately in love with a young soldier. Despite a deliberate lack of publicity (intended to avoid the attentions of the authorities), the opening night sold out.[26] When Wilde learned of the event, he wrote to Robbie Ross: "Please write to Stuart Merrill in Paris, or Robert Sherard, to say how gratified I was at the performance of my play: and have my thanks conveyed to Lugné-Poe"—the director, who also played Herod. "[I]t is something that at a time of disgrace and shame I should be still regarded as an artist."[27]

Yet in England attitudes toward Wilde and his play remained hardened even after his death. During the First World War, *Salomé* endured a renewed controversy when the far-right member of Parliament Noel Pemberton Billing—with the assistance and support of Lord Alfred Douglas—denounced a private performance, alleging it to be part of an international homosexual/Jewish conspiracy to promote decadence and "debauchery," weaken the nation's moral character, blackmail prominent figures in government and business, and lose the war.[28] (The play's producer, Jack Grein—a Jew, a socialist, and a supporter of women's suffrage—was no doubt already thrice guilty in Billing's view.)[29] The actress playing Salomé, Maud Allan, sued Billing for libel after his paper the *Vigilante* (formerly the *Imperialist*) accused her of leading a "Cult of the Clitoris." Along with open conspiracy-mongering and sexual innuendo (including accusations against the presiding judge), much of the trial turned on questions concerning the play's obscenity.

Douglas, now a devout Catholic and defensive heterosexual, called *Salomé* "an exhibition of perverted sexual passion excited in a young girl" and demonstrated his characteristic lack of perspective in his denunciation of Wilde: "I think he had a diabolical influence on everyone he met. I think he is the greatest force for evil that has appeared in Europe during the last 350 years. . . . He was a man whose whole object in life was to attack and sneer at virtue, and to undermine it in every way by every possible means, sexually and otherwise. . . . I do not think he ever wrote a thing in his life that had not an evil intention."[30]

Allan's suit, like Wilde's, failed. Her career never recovered, and the Lord Chamberlain determined that *Salomé* would continue to be proscribed.[31] Robbie Ross accused the authorities of "kicking Oscar's corpse to make up for the failure of the 5th Army."[32] The verdict renewed official repression against homosexuals, pacifists, the cultural avant-garde, and the

Left more broadly. It also emboldened the extreme Right, whose politics became increasingly anti-Semitic, and then fascist, in the years following.[33]

Grave Controversies

Ironically, France—a country Wilde always considered as a refuge from English philistinism—proved barely more hospitable to his memory.[34]

In 1912 the monument at Wilde's tomb—a massive nude "flying demon-angel" carved by the anarchist Jacob Epstein, modeled on Assyrian and Egyptian imagery and inspired by Wilde's poem "The Sphinx"—was outlawed by Préfet de Police Louis Lépine. The limestone sculpture was covered with a tarp and a gendarme posted at the Père Lachaise Cemetery to prevent public viewing.[35] Wilde's chief defenders were anarchists, especially those associated with *Action d'Art*. The magazine, which had been founded by the individualist anarchist André Colomer, published a petition defending the freedom of art and the dignity of the nude form and demanding that the monument be uncovered.[36] Illustrated with a large photograph of the exposed sculpture, their petition declared: "With the monument to Oscar Wilde it is the very principle of liberty for Art that is threatened. . . . Thinkers, artists, and writers owe it to themselves to protect their rights and, beyond their rights, their ideal of liberty."[37]

For two years, the cemetery was the site of numerous protests against the obfuscation of the monument. But the authorities won, for a while. When the statue was unveiled, it included a bronze butterfly covering the genitalia. Epstein, outraged, refused to attend the debut. However, the butterfly was soon stolen. (One legend suggests that it was removed by the occultist Aleister Crowley, who then wore it as a codpiece.)[38] The statue was thus nude until 1961, when vandals broke off the genitals altogether.

By the end of the century, Wilde's tomb had become a kind of shrine, continuously visited by his admirers, queer pilgrims in particular. It became a minor ritual to kiss the stone, and the monument was always covered with lipstick traces.[39] However, the practice of kissing the sphinx eventually began to erode the limestone. Wilde's worshippers were in danger of killing the thing that they loved. In 2010, the monument was carefully cleaned and surrounded with glass. Intrepid admirers still manage to surmount the barrier and kiss the sculpture, while others throw flowers, letters, and similar offerings over the crystalline wall.[40]

The Eternal Rebel

It is fitting that Wilde, as undoubtedly the most famous victim of Victorian prudery, became a gay icon. "The Outcast of one age," Edward Carpenter wrote, likely with Wilde in mind, "is the Hero of another."[41] And, accordingly, the anarchist iconography of Wilde has depicted him as a hero, a rebel, and a saint, not just as a piteous victim. Hakim Bey, for example, has produced a mixed-media montage centered on the image of Wilde (with St. Patrick above and a rattlesnake below), labeled "Oscar Wilde[,] Saint & Martyr."[42] Clifford Harper featured Wilde's portrait on one in his series of anarchist postage stamps.[43] Early in this century, the militant queer liberation group Bash Back featured a photo of Wilde on a flier announcing a demonstration. A bandanna covers the lower half of his face, giving us an image of Wilde as a black-bloc streetfighter.[44]

But Wilde's significance for anarchism reaches beyond the purely symbolic. Along with Kropotkin, Goldman, Berkman, Reitman, Masereel, Woodcock, Alan Moore, and others already discussed, a wide array of other anarchists and near-anarchists similarly saw Wilde as an influence or cast him as a forerunner, including Jean Grave, Herbert Read, Paul Goodman, Malcolm McLaren, and CrimethInc.[45]

Alfred Jarry attended the first night of *Salomé* and later incorporated some of its themes into his novel *Messaline*, itself illustrated by Aubrey Beardsley.[46] A century later the band Chumbawamba included this paraphrase of the story in the liner notes to one of its albums: "Salomé was a dancer who performed a dance so well that the King granted her whatever wish she pleased. To his surprise she demanded the head of John the Baptist on a plate. He provided it. Where are today's entertainers?" The song, titled "Salomé (Let's Twist Again)," continues the theme: "Oh Salomé waits. She says, 'Bring me all the heads of all the heads of state.'" Elsewhere the notes quote Wilde about disobedience being "the original virtue."[47] John William Lloyd quotes "The Soul of Man under Socialism" and reprises many of Wilde's views in his utopian novel *The Dwellers in the Vale Sunrise*.[48] Rose

Florence Freeman wrote a poem titled "Oscar Wilde" for the *Free Spirit*, describing the liberating effect of Wilde's work on her own sexual morality.[49] John Cowper Powys called "The Soul of Man under Socialism" "perhaps the wisest and most eloquent revolutionary tract ever written."[50] And when Aldous Huxley joined the Balliol Fabian Group, he told Rajane Palme Dutt, who recruited him, that he didn't want to be "an economic type of Socialist" but that he supported the movement for the same reasons as did Oscar Wilde.[51]

In 1905 Peter Kropotkin wrote Robbie Ross to ask for a picture of Wilde's mother, Speranza, for "a lady friend of ours in Germany—Madame Landauer,—a poet who is publishing a book on Oscar Wilde's poetry (of which both herself and her husband are great admirers)."[52] "Madame Landauer" is better known as Hedwig Lachmann, who later translated *Salomé*. Her husband was the anarchist-pacifist Gustav Landauer, and together they also translated "The Soul of Man under Socialism," *The Picture of Dorian Gray*, "The Critic as Artist," "The Decay of Lying," and Wilde's letters to the *Daily Chronicle* concerning the state of British prisons.[53]

The effect of Wilde's thinking on Landauer's is evident both in the latter's private correspondence and in his public pronouncements. On November 24, 1918, shortly before he was appointed commissioner of enlightenment and public instruction for the short-lived Bavarian Soviet Republic, Landauer wrote to his daughter Gudula: "That socialism is the basis on which individuals can develop freely . . . is absolutely right; but that is no new idea. It has been remarkably laid out, for example, in Oscar Wilde's 'The Soul of Man under Socialism.'"[54]

Addressing the Council of Intellectual Workers during the Munich uprising that same year, Landauer emphasized the role of the artist, and the poet in particular, as "the eternal rebel"—to such a degree that "in times of revolution . . . he is the first to press again for conservation, both of what has been newly achieved, and of that which eternally remains." This spirit of rebellion, Landauer argued, is an essential element of progress: "Philistines and wizened systematicians dream the unutterably dreary dream of introducing a patent socialism which, with its established mechanisms and methods will, they say, once and for all do away with and . . . render impossible all injustice and social wrongs." This understanding of revolution, Landauer believed, was mistaken. "What we need in truth," he said, clearly echoing

Wilde, "is a constant process of renewal, the willingness to be jolted out of our complacency. . . . [W]e need spring, delusion, intoxication and madness, we need—again and again and again—revolution, we need the poet."[55]

Pursuing Utopia

Especially in times of crisis, imagination is crucial. If we cannot imagine a better world, we surely cannot achieve one. Even John Zerzan, the Old Major of the anarchy-as-apocalypse or apocalypse-as-anarchy set, has recently made this point. Dismayed at the turn toward nihilism and the surrender of all hope, he wrote: "[As] the global system now shows itself to be failing at every level, shows itself to have no answers at all, there stands every chance of qualitatively surpassing the Movement of the '60s. But not, needless to say, if we renounce any hope of overcoming." He ends his plea by quoting Wilde: "We are all in the gutter but some of us are looking at the stars."[56]

The stars do not only dazzle, they also guide us. We cannot reach them, but they provide direction: Nature, Wilde wrote from prison, "will hang the night with stars so that I may walk abroad in the darkness without stumbling."[57] Alan Moore draws on this pair of images in his novel *Jerusalem*, suggesting that when one finds oneself "enmired" in the suffering of the world as it is, one "has got to have a star up there above him so as he can navigate, and what that star is, it's some manner of ideal what you can't reach but what shows you the way."[58]

It is much the same with utopia. "Utopia is on the horizon," Eduardo Galeano wrote. "I take two steps towards it, and it retracts two steps. I walk two steps and the horizon moves two steps further back. However much I walk, I never reach her." But that, he said, was her singular importance. "What then is utopia for?" he asked. "It is for this: for walking."[59]

Wilde too saw the value of utopia, that it draws us toward it, that it keeps us moving. In "The Soul of Man under Socialism," he wrote: "A map of the world that does not include Utopia is not worth even glancing at, for it leaves out the one country at which Humanity is always landing. And when it lands there, it looks out, and seeing a better country, sets sail." That is the nature of progress: we are always achieving it and always seeking better. "Progress is the realisation of Utopias."[60]

Flores Magón agreed, "[T]he progress of humanity is indebted to the dreamers and the utopians. This thing called civilization: what is it if not the result of utopian efforts? The visionaries, the poets, the dreamers, the utopians, so disdained by 'serious' people . . . , nevertheless, have been the engines of all movements forward, the prophets who have pointed the blind masses towards luminous paths leading to glorious summits."[61]

Wilde's politics, though utopian, are not perfectionist. Or rather they *are* perfectionist but in the paradoxical sense articulated by William Godwin: "Man is perfectible" in that he is "susceptible of perpetual improvement"—but he is *not* "capable of being brought to perfection." In fact, the latter "stands in express opposition to" the former: "If we could arrive at perfection, there could be an end to our improvement."[62] Wilde went further. He thought moral perfection an *impediment* and saw the eternal value of *imperfection*, of sin, of discord, as the seed of development, "an essential element of progress."[63]

Wilde's politics are utopian in that he looks beyond the confines of the possible. He views impossibility as no objection. At times, he suggests that it is no obstacle. He readily admits that his vision cannot be realized, yet he goes right on expecting to see it fulfilled. In all his work, Wilde urges us not to know our proper place, to push against our limits, to pursue the unrealistic, the fantastic, the ideal.

We must always keep utopia in view, yet we must remain mindful of the distance before us—not as one traveling a day to some fixed point but as an adventurer reaching a summit and, looking ahead, facing a horizon that recedes even as it expands.

A Vision

Let us return, therefore, at last, to Wilde's vision in "The Soul of Man under Socialism." It is a vision of a world in which there is no poverty, no hunger, no crime, no prisons. It is a world of personal freedom and social equality. It is a world where work is pleasurable and its products are beautiful—where work is indistinguishable from art, which is in turn inseparable from life. It is a utopia, but it does not present itself as a final destination. It is one of a series of consecutive utopias, in which the critical spirit (which is also the creative spirit) remains alive, and progress is continuous—not merely progress in the political sense, and still less in the technological sense, but progress in terms of human knowledge and humane values, progress in science, philosophy, and art. It is, most of all, a world populated by individuals, individuals free to "develop what is wonderful, and fascinating, and delightful" in themselves.[64]

Wilde's philosophy offers many lessons for anarchism, lessons that we have yet to learn. He saw that imagination is a better guide than doctrine and that new values are as important as new economics. He understood that criticism is the force that moves us forward and therefore insisted that nothing be exempt from it. Yet he was careful to avoid all varieties of moralism. Instead he mocked the conventions of his time, recognizing that laughter is more fatal than argument. Thus he engaged the public, even appealed to it, but without pandering.[65] And finally, he knew that freedom requires one to trust one's desires, and he believed that utopia is where our hopes finally reside.

This idea is laid out most clearly in "The Soul of Man under Socialism," but one can also see aspects of it in "De Profundis" and "The Ballad of Reading Gaol." It is present in Wilde's critical essays and some of his letters, it is there in the fairy tales, just below the surface of *Dorian Gray*, and in the verbal sparring of the society plays. What unites all of Wilde's work, as much as a love of beauty and a dream of freedom, is the hostility toward puritans, philistines, and moralists. Individualism, Wilde saw, makes its demands— but they are demands that arise from within, not demands imposed from without.[66] Wilde's aim was not to make individuals more suited to society— whether that be the society of Victorian London or that of the anarchist utopia—but to make society more suited to the individuals who inhabit it. If we are to pursue perfection, it must remain a perfection *of individuals*, with "as many perfections as there are imperfect men."[67]

Wilde saw that we can only evaluate a social system by the lives that people actually lead under it—the freedom of their actions, the pleasures they enjoy, their experience and appreciation of beauty—and also by their "souls," by which he meant their unique personalities, their creative capacity, their compassion and their depth of character.[68] Society can only be judged from the standpoint of the individual. But Wilde also saw that individual freedom—to some degree, individuality itself—depends upon a healthy and functioning society.[69] And so he understood that my freedom is tied to yours, and that individual freedom depends on collective liberation.[70]

Wilde championed an individualism that was generous and sympathetic rather than selfish and mean.[71] One expansive in its vision and more concerned with the beauty of one's soul than with crass materialism: "The true perfection of man lies, not in what man has, but in what man is."[72] His individualism was not bourgeois but bohemian, gregarious and sociable, an individualism most at home in the midst of a cocktail party. For a free individual is free precisely in relation to others—that is, *in society*.

The very purpose of socialism is that it would make such individualism possible.[73] In fact, one might say, that is the very purpose of society, and society must be judged by that standard. That is true of the society in which we live, and it is true of the society we wish to make.

I do not know that we can achieve the world that Wilde imagined in "The Soul of Man under Socialism." I do not know that it is even, precisely, the world that we would want to achieve. I do know, however, that his vision stands as a reminder of our half-forgotten ideals, that it invites us to consider, dares us to imagine, the world that we do want, and that it may inspire us to fight for it, to build it—and the lives we want within it—together.

Acknowledgments

I was a long time writing this book. It occupied a dozen years of my life, or a bit more, with numerous gaps and digressions, and equally many periods of intense concentration. In the course of a prolonged and sometimes difficult intellectual endeavor such as this, one incurs innumerable debts. My thinking and my writing have benefited from the generosity of a great many people, not only those who directly assisted me with funds, advice, and editing, but also those who provided friendly conversation, words of encouragement, and forgiveness for my long absences. I owe my thanks, and sometimes my apologies, to all those who, whether they recognized it our not, contributed in some manner to the process of bringing this book into reality. Some of these were friends, some fellow scholars, some practically strangers. It would not be possible for me to list them all here. At times, this book has taken over my life, and I have put everything into it—which means that every kindness done to me, every idea shared with me, has had some effect, subtle or pronounced, on what this book has become.

However, there are a few individuals and institutions whose assistance was essential, and without whom the book might not have been written at all. I am grateful to the Ludwig Vogelstein Foundation and the Institute for Anarchist Studies for funding my research on Wilde; and to the librarians at the Kate Sharpley Library and the staff of the Clark Library at UCLA, for accommodating my special visits and offering expert advice. I also owe thanks to Jerusha McCormack, for advice and encouragement in the earliest stages of the project; to Daniel Buck, for his early and lasting interest in Wilde and his encouragement of me in this project; and to Adam Warner, for his generous hospitality during my research trip to London. My long-suffering parents, Robert and Dolores Williams, deserve particular recognition for their careful review of my near-final manuscript. And I am especially thankful to Emily-Jane Dawson, Gabriel Ryder, and Kevin Van Meter for their support and encouragement at several stages of this process, improving both the book and its author in many ways. More than once their enthusiasm sustained my own.

Endnotes

Introduction: The Soul of Man under ... Anarchism?

1.   Oscar Wilde, "The Soul of Man under Socialism," in *Collins Complete Works of Oscar Wilde* (Glasgow: HarperCollins, 2003), 1197.

2.   Stuart Merrill, "Oscar Wilde," in *Oscar Wilde: Interviews and Recollections*, vol. 2, ed. E. H. Mikhail (New York: Barnes and Noble Books, 1979), 466.

3.   The title is from Wilde's play, *Lady Windermere's Fan*. Oscar Wilde, *Lady Windermere's Fan*, in *Collins Complete Works of Oscar Wilde*, 424.

4.   Quoted in Roy Morris Jr., *Declaring His Genius: Oscar Wilde in North America* (Cambridge, Mass.: Harvard University Press, 2013), 18. Elsewhere he elaborated: "The truth about the life of a man is not what he does, but the legend which he creates around himself. I have never paraded the streets of London with a lily in my hand; for any caretaker or coachman could do the same. That legend merely indicates the impression I have made on the masses, and it indicates the nature of my temperament better than what I have (actually) done. ... Legends should never be destroyed. It is they which help us catch a glimpse of the genuine life of man." Quoted in Jacques Daurelle, "An English Poet in Paris," in *Oscar Wilde: Interviews and Recollections*, ed. E. H. Mikhail, vol. 1 (New York: Barnes & Noble, 1979), 171.

5.   Quoted in Richard Ellman, *Oscar Wilde* (New York: Alfred A. Knopf, 1988), 301.

6.   Quoted in Morris, *Declaring His Genius*, 5.

7.   Though the brief summary presented here could be taken from any of several sources, the standard biography remains Richard Ellmann's *Oscar Wilde*.

8.   See Karl Beckson, ed., *Oscar Wilde: The Critical Heritage* (New York: Barnes & Noble, 1970), 33–58.

9.   David Goodway situates anarchism in a broader tradition of "Left-Libertarian Thought," while Chris Dixon describes contemporary anarchism as one tendency within a general "anti-authoritarian current." David Goodway, *Anarchist Seeds beneath the Snow: Left-Libertarian Thought and British Writers from William Morris to Colin Ward* (Oakland: PM Press, 2012); Chris Dixon, *Another Politics: Talking across Today's Transformative Movements* (Oakland: University of California Press, 2014), 3–5.

10.   Goodway offers something of a sense for the web of influences that existed in the libertarian tradition of the British Left—near anarchism, both influencing and influenced by it, but often departing from it on crucial points. He writes: "[Edward] Carpenter was acknowledged by [Herbert] Read as a major influence and Wilde and [Aldous] Huxley read him with approbation. ... [William] Morris's impact is pervasive, with Wilde

an early admirer, but with Read, as an advocate of industrialism and the machine, having an uneasy, though increasingly close, relationship to his outlook. Wilde and [John] Powys shared a common debt to Taoism and Chuang Tzu (as well as to Walter Pater) and Powys in turn was much influenced by Wilde. Morris and Carpenter were on excellent terms, Morris staying at Millthorpe, and Carpenter expressing 'great admiration and friendship' for the other man." Goodway, *Anarchist Seeds beneath the Snow*, 11.

11.   George Woodcock, *Anarchism: A History of Libertarian Ideas and Movements* (Cleveland: Meridian Books, 1962), 439. For an account of the emergence of anarchism as a distinct tendency, coming out of the split in the First International, see Robert Graham, *"We Do Not Fear Anarchy, We Invoke It": The First International and the Origins of the Anarchist Movement* (Oakland: AK Press, 2015).

12.   Quoted in George Woodcock and Ivan Avakumovic, *Peter Kropotkin: From Prince to Rebel* (Montreal: Black Rose Books, 1990), 208–9. Paragraph breaks added for clarity.

13.   Wilde, "Soul of Man under Socialism," 1178.

14.   Wilde, "Soul of Man under Socialism," 1192, 1193, 1181.

15.   Wilde, "Soul of Man under Socialism," 1175. Walter Crane, who illustrated Wilde's book *The Happy Prince*, later recalled: "The essential difference between anarchist and socialist ideas and aims was not then very well understood or generally recognized, especially as both schools could join in their protests and denunciations of the existing economic order." Walter Crane, *An Artist's Reminiscences* (New York: Macmillan, 1907), 259. I have written elsewhere about Crane's likely influence on Wilde's essay. See Kristian Williams, "The Roots of Wilde's Socialist *Soul*: Ibsen and Shaw, or Morris and Crane," *Oscholars*, Spring 2010, oscholars.com.

16.   See E. P. Thompson, *William Morris: Romantic to Revolutionary* (Oakland: PM Press, 2011), 564–72.

17.   Goodway, *Anarchist Seeds beneath the Snow*, 76–77. Wilde had previously written, in "The Truth of Masks" (1885), "Monarchy, Anarchy, and Republicanism may contend for the government of nations; but a theatre should be in the power of a cultured despot. There may be division of labour, but there must be no division of mind." Oscar Wilde, "The Truth of Masks," in *Collins Complete Works of Oscar Wilde*, 1172.

When his collection of critical essays, *Intentions*, was to be released in a French edition, Wilde suggested removing "The Truth of Masks" ("je ne l'aime plus") and replacing it with "The Soul of Man under Socialism." Oscar Wilde to Jules Cantel [Summer 1891], in *The Complete Letters of Oscar Wilde*, ed. Merlin Holland and Rupert Hart-Davis (New York: Henry Holt, 2000), 487.

18.   Oscar Wilde, "Libertatis Sacra Fames," in *Collins Complete Works of Oscar Wilde*, 858.

19.   Oscar Wilde, "Sonnet to Liberty," in *Collins Complete Works of Oscar Wilde*, 859.

20.   "Oscar Wilde: An Interview with the Apostle of Aestheticism (*San Francisco Examiner*, March 27, 1882)," in *Oscar Wilde in America: The Interviews*, ed. Matthew Hofer and Gary Scharnhorst (Urbana: University of Illinois Press, 2010), 102–3.

21.   Wilde, "Soul of Man under Socialism," 1182.

22.   Wilde, "Soul of Man under Socialism," 1176.

23.   Wilde, "Soul of Man under Socialism," 1188.

24.   Wilde, "Soul of Man under Socialism," 1184.

25.   Percival W. H. Almy, "New Views of Mr. Oscar Wilde," in *Oscar Wilde: Interviews and Recollections*, vol. 1, 232.

26.   Almy, "New Views," 229, 233. A similar view is expounded in *Earnest* but ironically subverted: "I do not approve of anything that tampers with natural ignorance. Ignorance is like a delicate exotic fruit; touch it and the bloom is gone. The whole theory of modern education is radically unsound. Fortunately in England, at any rate, education produces no effect whatsoever. If it did, it would prove a serious danger to the upper classes, and probably lead to acts of violence in Grosvenor Square." Oscar Wilde, *The Importance of Being Earnest*, in *Collins Complete Works of Oscar Wilde*, 368. Did Percival Almy end his quote too soon and miss the joke?

27.   Almy, "New Views," 231–32. Compare with Wilde, "Soul of Man Under Socialism," 1179–81 (on Christ), 1182 (on punishment), and 1180 (on law-breaking).

28.   Almy, "New Views," 231–32.

29.   See Oscar Wilde, "The House Beautiful," in *Collins Complete Works of Oscar Wilde*, 913–25, though here too Wilde insists that beautiful things should be *used*: "Whatever you have that is beautiful if for use, then you should use it, or part with it to someone who will" (921).

30.   Wilde, "Soul of Man under Socialism," 1178.

31.   Wilde, "Soul of Man under Socialism," 1183. George Woodcock later proposed a similar idea: "Instead of the government of men, anarchists base society on the administration of things. It is on the economic plane alone, in the necessary production of goods consumed by men and in the provision of necessary social service, that they see the need for organization, not from above but on a voluntary and co-operative basis, among the individuals whose work actually produces the necessities of a civilised life." George Woodcock, *Anarchy or Chaos* (Willimantic, Conn.: Lysander Spooner, 1992), 22.

32.   Wilde, "Soul of Man under Socialism," 1177.

33.   Oscar Wilde to Lord Alfred Douglas [August 13, 1894], in *Complete Letters of Oscar Wilde*, 602. Emphasis in original.

34.   George Woodcock, *The Paradox of Oscar Wilde* (New York: Macmillan, 1950), 160.

35.   "Books to Be Had through Mother Earth," advertisement, *Mother Earth*, June 1906, 62–64, reprinted in *Mother Earth Bulletin*, series 1, vol. 1, *1906–7* (New York: Greenwich Reprint Corporation, 1968).

36.   Woodcock, *Anarchism*, 448; Oscar Wilde, *The Soul of Man under Socialism* (London: Porcupine Press, 1948).

37.   Robert Graham, ed., *Anarchism: A Documentary History of Libertarian Ideas*, vol. 1, *From Anarchy to Anarchism (300 CE to 1939)* (Montreal: Black Rose Books, 2017), 212–15.

38.   Quoted in Emer O'Sullivan, *The Fall of the House of Wilde: Oscar Wilde and His Family* (New York: Bloomsbury Press, 2016), 186.

39.   James Hulse's *Revolutionists in London: A Study of Five Unorthodox Socialists* (Oxford: Clarendon Press, 1970) profiles "five unorthodox socialists" living in the city at the end of the nineteenth century—Stepniak, Kropotkin, Bernstein, Morris, and Shaw.

Excepting Bernstein, all these were friends of Wilde's, and Bernstein was the first to write in protest of his prosecution.

40. Goodway, *Anarchist Seeds beneath the Snow*, 78.

41. Oscar Wilde to May Morris [mid-April 1889], in *The Complete Letters of Oscar Wilde*, 396.

42. George Bernard Shaw, "My Memories of Oscar Wilde," in Frank Harris, *Oscar Wilde* (n.p.: Michigan State University Press, 1959), 331; Goodway, *Anarchist Seeds beneath the Snow*, 74.

43. Wilde to May Morris [mid-April 1889], 396. Emphasis in original.

44. The central text, of course, is Peter Kropotkin, *Mutual Aid: A Factor of Evolution* (London: William Heinemann, 1902). The first of the articles that would eventually be collected into *Mutual Aid* appeared in the September 1890 issue of the *Nineteenth Century*, alongside the second part of Wilde's dialogue "The Critic as Artist." Oscar Wilde, *Oscar Wilde's Oxford Notebooks: A Portrait of Mind in the Making*, ed. Philip E. Smith II and Michael S. Helfand (New York: Oxford University Press, 1989), 236n164.

45. Philip E. Smith II and Michael S. Helfand, "The Context of the Text," in *Oscar Wilde's Oxford Notebooks*, 77, 81–22.

46. Oscar Wilde, "De Profundis," in *Collins Complete Works of Oscar Wilde*, 1038.

47. As a young nobleman, Kropotkin found himself wondering, "What right had I to these higher joys [of scientific investigation] when all round me was nothing but misery and struggle for a mouldy bit of bread; when whatsoever I should spend to enable one to live in that world of higher emotions must needs be taken from the very mouths of those who grow the wheat and had not bread for their children?" Quoted in George Woodcock and Ivan Avakumovic, *Peter Kropotkin: From Prince to Rebel* (Montreal: Black Rose Books, 1990), 94.

48. Wilde, "De Profundis," 1038.

49. Peter Faulkner, "William Morris and Oscar Wilde," *Journal of William Morris Studies* 14, no. 4 Summer (2002): 33.

50. Oscar Wilde, "The Critic as Artist," in *Collins Complete Works of Oscar Wilde*, 1129.

51. I am thinking here specifically of the portrayal of the manager of the theater where Dorian Gray meets Sibyl Vane: a "fat Jew" with "an oily, tremulous smile," "fat jeweled hands," and "a sort of pompous humility." Oscar Wilde, *The Picture of Dorian Gray*, in *Collins Complete Works of Oscar Wilde*, 68.

Wilde's later friendship with Ferdinand Esterhazy, the villain of the Dreyfus affair, might also give one pause, though it seems to have been more a matter of curiosity than affinity. "Esterhazy is considerably more interesting than Dreyfus who is innocent," Wilde wrote. "It's always a mistake to be innocent. To be a criminal takes imagination and courage." Quoted in Ellmann, *Oscar Wilde*, 563–64. For details of Wilde's association with Esterhazy, including his fortuitous contribution to winning Dreyfus's freedom, see Nicholas Frankel, *Oscar Wilde: The Unrepentant Years* (Cambridge, Mass.: Harvard University Press, 2017), 217–31.

52. Ellmann, *Oscar Wilde*, 542–43. On his American tour Wilde visited Jefferson Davis and later stated: "His fall, after such an able and gallant pleading of his own cause, must necessarily arouse sympathy, no matter what might be the merits of the plea. The

head may approve the success of the winner, but the heart is sure to be with the fallen." However, and inconsistently, he was also to add: "The cause of the South in the Civil War was to my mind much like that of Ireland today. It was a struggle for autonomy, self-government for a people." He repeated this point in a second interview: "We in Ireland are fighting for the principle of autonomy against empire, for independence against centralization, for the principles for which the South fought." Quoted in "Oscar Wilde: Arrival of the Great Aesthete (*Atlanta Constitution*, July 5, 1882)," in *Oscar Wilde in America*, 157, 159–60.

53. Oscar Wilde, "Rise of Historical Criticism," in *Collins Complete Works of Oscar Wilde*, 1216.

54. Wilde, *Picture of Dorian Gray*, 131.

55. Oscar Wilde, "Love Song," in *Collins Complete Works of Oscar Wilde*, 756–57.

56. Quoted in "A Talk with Wilde (*Philadelphia Press*, January 17, 1882)," in *Oscar Wilde in America*, 29.

57. Quoted in "The Apostle of Art (*Chicago Inter-Ocean*, February 11, 1882)," in *Oscar Wilde in America*, 60.

58. Wilde, "Soul of Man under Socialism," 1174–75.

59. Wilde, "Soul of Man under Socialism," 1179.

60. Wilde, "Soul of Man under Socialism," 1181.

61. Wilde, "Soul of Man under Socialism," 1181.

62. Wilde, "Soul of Man under Socialism," 1194.

63. Wilde, "Soul of Man under Socialism," 1197.

64. Oscar Wilde, "Poetical Socialists," in *Selected Journalism*, ed. Anya Clayworth (Oxford: Oxford University Press, 2004), 34–35.

Chapter 1: The Dynamite Policy

1. Percival W. H. Almy, "New Views of Mr. Oscar Wilde," in *Oscar Wilde: Interviews and Recollections*, vol. 1, ed. E. H. Mikhail (New York: Barnes & Noble, 1979), 232.

2. John Quail, *The Slow-Burning Fuse* (London: Paladin, 1978), 169.

3. David Sweetman, *Explosive Acts: Toulouse-Lautrec, Oscar Wilde, Félix Fénéon and the Art and Anarchy of the Fin de Siècle* (New York: Simon & Schuster, 1999), 374–75.

4. An anarchist historian and historian of anarchism, George Woodcock, writes: "At no time was a policy of terrorism adopted by anarchists in general. The terrorists . . . were mostly lonely men driven by a curious blend of austere idealism and apocalyptic passion, the black aspect of the same passion that turned other anarchists, like Peter Kropotkin and Louise Michel, into secular saints." George Woodcock, *Anarchism: A History of Libertarian Ideas and Movements* (Cleveland: Meridian Books, 1962), 16.

5. Quoted in Quail, *Slow-Burning Fuse*, 97.

6. Albert Camus, *The Rebel: An Essay on Man in Revolt* (New York: Vintage Books, 1991), 164–65.

7. Alex Butterworth, *The World That Never Was: A True Story of Dreamers, Schemers, Anarchists and Secret Agents* (London: Vintage Books, 2011), 164.

8.   Quoted in Peter Marshall, *Demanding the Impossible: A History of Anarchism* (Oakland: PM Press, 2010), 174.

9.   Quoted in Marshall, *Demanding the Impossible*, 633. Some certainly had the courage of their convictions. After she was shot delivering a speech, Louise Michel rose to the defense of her assailant as a man driven to desperation by the existing social system. Butterworth, *World that Never Was*, 231.

10.   Quail, *Slow-Burning Fuse*, 126, 134.

11.   Quoted in Quail, *Slow-Burning Fuse*, 195.

12.   David Goodway, *Anarchist Seeds beneath the Snow: Left-Libertarian Thought and British Writers from William Morris to Colin Ward* (Oakland: PM Press, 2012), 79.

13.   Quoted in Marshall, *Demanding the Impossible*, 438.

14.   Oscar Wilde, *Vera, or The Nihilists*, in *Collins Complete Works of Oscar Wilde* (Glasgow: HarperCollins, 2003), 715–18.

15.   Wilde, *Vera*, 720.

16.   Elizabeth Carolyn Miller, "Reconsidering Wilde's *Vera, or the Nihilists*," in *Wilde Discoveries: Traditions, Histories, Archives*, ed. Joseph Bristow (Toronto: University of Toronto Press, 2013), 65. On the substitution of Russian for British imperialism, see 73.

17.   Richard Ellmann, *Oscar Wilde* (New York: Alfred A. Knopf, 1988), 121–22; Roy Morris Jr., *Declaring His Genius: Oscar Wilde in North America* (Cambridge, Mass.: Harvard University Press, 2013), 20.

18.   Butterworth, *World That Never Was*, 126; Yves Ternon, "Russian Terrorism, 1878–1908," in *The History of Terrorism from Antiquity to Al Qaeda*, ed. Gérard Chaliand and Arnaud Blin (Berkeley: University of California Press, 2007), 143–44.

19.   Quoted in Michael Burleigh, *Blood and Rage: A Cultural History of Terrorism* (New York: Harper Perennial, 2009), 44. Zasulich later became uncertain about terrorism, reflecting, "In order to carry out terrorist acts all one's energies must be expended, and a particular frame of mind almost always results: either one of great vanity or one in which life has lost all its attractiveness." Quoted in Burleigh, *Blood and Rage*, 46.

20.   See, for example, Goodway, *Anarchist Seeds beneath the Snow*, 67.

21.   Wilde, *Vera*, 705.

22.   Karl Beckson, *London in the 1890s: A Cultural History* (New York: W. W. Norton, 1992), 18; David Weir, *Anarchy and Culture: The Aesthetic Politics of Modernism* (Amherst: University of Massachusetts Press, 1997), 72. The rhetorical slippage proved contagious: in Russia toward the end of the century, combat units of the Socialist Revolutionary Party sometimes referred to themselves as "anarchists," using the word as a synonym for "militants." Butterworth, *World That Never Was*, 375.

23.   Wilde, *Vera*, 689; Paul Bew, *Ireland: The Politics of Enmity* (Oxford: Oxford University Press, 2007), 323.

24.   Oscar Wilde to Marie Prescott, [July 1883?], in *The Complete Letters of Oscar Wilde*, ed. Merlin Holland and Rupert Hart-Davis (New York: Henry Holt, 2000), 214.

25.   Elizabeth Carolyn Miller, for instance, argued that in choosing suicide over murder Vera abandons revolution in favor of reform and chooses individual heroism over collective action. Miller, "Reconsidering Wilde's *Vera*," in *Wilde Discoveries*, 78.

26.   Wilde, *Vera*, 715.

27.   This suggestion came from a member of the audience during the question-and-answer portion of Miller's lecture at the 2009 "Wilde Archive" symposium. Elizabeth Carolyn Miller, "Reconsidering Wilde's *Vera, or the Nihilists*," presented at "The Wilde Archive," May 2009, Clark Library, University of California, Los Angeles.

28.   Quoted in Butterworth, *World That Never Was*, 127.

29.   Camus, *Rebel*, 169–70.

30.   Camus, *Rebel*, 171.

31.   Camus, *Rebel*, 164, 166.

32.   Camus, *Rebel*, 154–55.

33.   Quoted in Burleigh, *Blood and Rage*, 37.

34.   Søren Kierkegaard, *Purity of Heart Is to Will One Thing; Spiritual Preparation for the Office of Confession*, trans. Douglas V. Steere (New York: Harper, 1948).

35.   On Vasulich: Ternon, "Russian Terrorism," 133; on Bakunin: Woodcock, *Anarchism*, 172.

36.   Sergey Nechayev, *The Revolutionary Catechism* (1869), https://www.marxists. org/subject/anarchism/nechayev/catechism.htm.

37.   Paul Avrich and Karen Avrich, *Sasha and Emma: The Anarchist Odyssey of Alexander Berkman and Emma Goldman* (Cambridge, Mass.: Belknap Press, 2012), 35.

38.   Alexander Berkman, *Prison Memoirs of an Anarchist* (New York: New York Review of Books, 1999), 11. Berkman's lover, Emma Goldman, saw matters differently. While Berkman disapproved of "useless things" like flowers, when the money could be used for the Cause, Goldman argued: "I did not believe that a Cause which stood for a beautiful ideal, for anarchism, for release and freedom from conventions and prejudice, should demand the denial of life and joy. I insisted that our Cause should not expect me to behave like a nun and that the movement should not be turned into a cloister. If it meant that, I did not want it." Quoted in Avrich and Avrich, *Sasha and Emma*, 37.

39.   Berkman, *Prison Memoirs of an Anarchist*, 11.

40.   Avrich and Avrich, *Sasha and Emma*, 75.

41.   Butterworth, *World That Never Was*, 63; Ternon, "Russian Terorism," 139; Burleigh, *Blood and Rage*, 38. Nechaev died in prison after years in solitary confinement. To his credit, he refused to the last to exchange information on the underground movement for leniency in his own treatment. Butterworth, *World That Never Was*, 148.

42.   Ellmann, *Oscar Wilde*, 122; quote from Wilde, *Vera*, 686.

43.   Wilde to Marie Prescott [July 1883?], in *Complete Letters of Oscar Wilde*, 214.

44.   Ellmann, *Oscar Wilde*, 124.

45.   "Oscar Wilde Returns," in *Oscar Wilde: Interviews and Recollections*, vol. 1, 115–16.

46.   James W. Hulse, *Revolutionists in London: A Study of Five Unorthodox Socialists* (Oxford: Clarendon Press, 1970), 7–9; Ellmann, *Oscar Wilde*, 122.

47.   Quoted in Hulse, *Revolutionists in London*, 46.

48.   Quoted in Marshall, *Demanding the Impossible*, 284.

49.   Oscar Wilde, *The Picture of Dorian Gray*, in *Collins Complete Works of Oscar Wilde*, 39. Camus summarizes Nechaev's contribution to the philosophy of revolution: "If the revolution is the only positive value, it has a right to claim everything. . . . Henceforth, violence will be directed against one and all, in the service of an abstract idea. . . . [T]he

revolution, in itself, was more important than the people it wanted to save." Camus, *Rebel*, 161–62.

50.   Wilde, *Vera*, 714.

51.   Oscar Wilde, "The Soul of Man under Socialism," in *Collins Complete Works of Oscar Wilde*, 1196.

52.   "Medievalism, with its saints and martyrs, its love of self-torture, its wild passions for wounding itself, its gashing with knives, and its whipping with rods— Medievalism is real Christianity, and the medieval Christ is the real Christ." Wilde, "Soul of Man under Socialism," 1196.

53.   Wilde, "Soul of Man under Socialism," 1196–97. Nicholas Berdyaev, author of *The Origins of Russian Communism*, agreed: "Russian nihilism denied God, the soul, the spirit, ideas, standards, and the highest values. And none the less, nihilism must be recognised as a religious phenomenon. . . . At the base of Russian nihilism, when grasped in its purity and depth, lies the Orthodox rejection of the world, its sense of the truth that the whole world lieth in wickedness; the acknowledgment of the sinfulness of all riches and luxury, of all creative profusion of art and thought. Like Orthodox asceticism, nihilism was an individualist movement, but it was also directed against the fullness and richness of life. . . . The intellectual asceticism of nihilism found expression in materialism; any more subtle philsophy was proclaimed a sin. . . . The attitude of the Russian nihilists to science was idolatrous. . . . There was nothing sceptical in Russian nihilism, it was a faith." Quoted in Woodcock and Avakumovic, *Peter Kropotkin*, 100.

54.   Wilde, "Soul of Man under Socialism," 1197.

55.   Wilde, "Soul of Man under Socialism," 1195.

56.   Wilde, "Soul of Man under Socialism," 1197.

57.   Quoted in Merlin Holland, *The Real Trial of Oscar Wilde: The First Uncensored Transcript of the Trial of Oscar Wilde vs. John Douglas (Marquess of Queensberry), 1895* (New York: Fourth Estate, 2003), 75.

58.   Oscar Wilde, "Notebook Kept at Oxford," in *Oscar Wilde's Oxford Notebooks: A Portrait of Mind in the Making*, ed. Philip E. Smith II and Michael S. Helfand (New York: Oxford University Press, 1989), 156.

59.   Morris, *Declaring His Genius*, 21.

60.   Ellmann, *Oscar Wilde*, 159; Jerusha McCormack, "The Wilde Irishman: Oscar as Aesthete and Anarchist," in *Wilde the Irishman*, ed. Jerusha McCormack (New Haven: Yale University Press, 1998), 84.

61.   Oscar Wilde, "The Decay of Lying," in *Collins Complete Works of Oscar Wilde*, 1082. By way of example, Wilde offers, "The Nihilist, that strange martyr who has no faith, who goes to the stake without enthusiasm, and dies for what he does not believe in, is a purely literary product. He was invented by Tourguenieff, and completed by Dostoevski." Wilde, "Decay of Lying," 1083.

62.   Ternon, "Russian Terorism," 135–37, 148–52; Butterworth, *World That Never Was*, 98; Burleigh, *Blood and Rage*, 27–29.

63.   "Unsigned Review, *The New York Times*, 21 August 1883," in *Oscar Wilde: The Critical Heritage*, ed. Karl Beckson (New York: Barnes & Noble, 1970), 56.

64.   Thomas Wright, *Oscar's Books* (London: Chatto & Windus, 2008), 292–93.

65.   Quoted in Morris, *Declaring His Genius*, 8.

66. Morris, *Declaring His Genius*, 8.

67. Emer O'Sullivan, *The Fall of the House of Wilde: Oscar Wilde and His Family* (New York: Bloomsbury Press, 2016), 44–45.

68. Quoted in O'Sullivan, *Fall of the House of Wilde*, 44.

69. Quoted in O'Sullivan, *Fall of the House of Wilde*, 51.

70. McCormack, "Wilde Irishman," 82. While Duffy was in prison, Elgee attended a ball at Dublin Castle. Jerusha McCormack suggests this episode as the source for the scene in *Vera*, wherein the protagonist appears at a nihilist meeting in a ball gown, having come straight from a party at the palace. McCormack, "Wilde Irishman," 82–83.

71. O'Sullivan, *Fall of the House of Wilde*, 52–55. Quote from 55.

72. Quoted in O'Sullivan, *Fall of the House of Wilde*, 442.

73. O'Sullivan, *Fall of the House of Wilde*, 35–37. In 1841 William Wilde conducted the first medical census of Ireland and estimated that a third of the country's children died within their first year and half within the first eight years; barely a third of the population would reach the age of thirty-eight. O'Sullivan, *Fall of the House of Wilde*, 41.

74. Quoted in O'Sullivan, *Fall of the House of Wilde*, 113.

75. Quoted in Lloyd Lewis and Henry Justin Smith, *Oscar Wilde Discovers America, 1882* (New York: Harcourt, Brace, 1936), 222.

76. Quoted in Lewis and Smith, *Oscar Wilde Discovers America*, 225–26.

77. Morris, *Declaring His Genius*, 141.

78. Lewis and Smith, *Oscar Wilde Discovers America*, 255, 269–70.

79. Oscar Wilde, "The Irish Poets of '48: A Lecture by Oscar Wilde (San Francisco, April 5, 1882)," transcript from the original draft manuscript, British Library, ADD 81636 A,B 4009A, 3.

80. Quoted in Charles Townshend, *Terrorism: A Very Short Introduction* (Oxford: Oxford University Press, 2011), 79.

81. Quoted in O'Sullivan, *Fall of the House of Wilde*, 220–21.

82. O'Sullivan, *Fall of the House of Wilde*, 221; McCormack, "Wilde Irishman," 84; Bew, *Ireland*, 363; Ellmann, *Oscar Wilde*, 196.

83. Quoted in O'Sullivan, *Fall of the House of Wilde*, 222.

84. Morris, *Declaring His Genius*, 168.

85. Quoted in Lewis and Smith, *Oscar Wilde Discovers America*, 215.

86. Wright, *Oscar's Books*, 130.

87. For an overview of the Parnell scandal as it relates to Wilde, see W. J. McCormack, "Wilde and Parnell," in McCormack, *Wilde the Irishman*. Of the scandal, Shaw commented sensibly, "The relation between Mr. Parnell and Mrs. O'Shea was a perfectly natural and right one; and the whole mischief in the matter lay in the law that tied the husband and wife together and forced Mr. Parnell to play the part of clandestine intriguer, instead of enabling them to dissolve the marriage by mutual consent, without disgrace to either party." Quoted in Beckson, *London in the 1890s*, 79.

88. Quoted in O'Sullivan, *Fall of the House of Wilde*, 144. In 1867 the Fenians proclaimed, "[All] men are born with equal rights, and in associating to protect one another and share public burdens, justice demands that such associations should rest upon a basis which maintains equality instead of destroying it. We therefore declare that, unable any longer to endure the curse of Monarchical government, we aim at founding a republic

based on universal sufferage, which shall secure to all the intrinsic value of their labour. The soil of Ireland in the possession of an oligarchy belongs to us, the Irish people, and to us it must be restored. We declare also in favour of absolute liberty of conscience, and complete separation of Church and State." Quoted in Bew, *Ireland*, 259.

89.   O'Sullivan, *Fall of the House of Wilde*, 145.

90.   O'Sullivan, *Fall of the House of Wilde*, 155.

91.   Oscar Wilde, "Mr Foude's Blue Book," in *Selected Journalism*, ed. Anya Clayworth (Oxford: Oxford University Press, 2004), 36.

92.   Wright, *Oscar's Books*, 24–25.

93.   "The Censure and *Salomé* (*The Pall Mall Budget*, June 30, 1892)," in *Oscar Wilde: Interviews and Recollections*, vol. 1, 188; Terry Eagleton, "Saint Oscar," in *The Eagleton Reader*, ed. Stephen Regan (Oxford: Blackwell, 1998), 370.

94.   Wilde, "Irish Poets of '48," 6.

95.   Wright, *Oscar's Books*, 5, 307.

96.   Oscar Wilde, "Olivia at the Lyceum," in *Collins Complete Works of Oscar Wilde*, 955.

97.   Ellmann, *Oscar Wilde*, 542–43.

98.   Wilde resented the English, not for punishing him but for refusing to face up to what they had done. Oscar Wilde, "De Profundis," in *Collins Complete Works of Oscar Wilde*, 1021.

99.   Marshall, *Demanding the Impossible*, 32. Proudhon endured a period as a French nationalist and Bakunin as a pan-Slavist. Marshall, *Demanding the Impossible*, 33–34.

100.   Oscar Wilde, "Mr Mahaffy's New Book," in *Selected Journalism*, ed. Anya Clayworth, 25.

101.   Wilde, "Mr Mahaffy's New Book," 24. In "The Rise of Historical Criticism," Wilde argued that "the only meaning of progress is a return to the Greek modes of thought. . . . Across the drear waste of a thousand years the Greek and the modern spirit join hands." Oscar Wilde, "Rise of Historical Criticism," in *Collins Complete Works of Oscar Wilde*, 1240.

102.   Wilde, "De Profundis," 1027, 1031.

103.   Oscar Wilde, "The Critic as Artist," in *Collins Complete Works of Oscar Wilde*, 1137–38.

104.   Wilde, "Critic as Artist," 1131.

105.   Oscar Wilde, "The English Renaissance of Art," in *The Uncollected Oscar Wilde*, ed. John Wyse Jackson (London: Fourth Estate, 1995), 21.

106.   Wilde, "Critic as Artist," 1152–53. "Wilde's cosmopolitan aestheticism is not then some universalized inwardness divorced from politics, but the preliminary for a global polity." Julia Prewitt Brown, *Cosmopolitan Criticism: Oscar Wilde's Philosophy of Art* (Charlottesville: University of Virginia Press, 1997), 30.

107.   Quoted in Morris, *Declaring His Genius*, 141.

108.   Quoted in Ellmann, *Oscar Wilde*, 401.

109.   Miller, "Reconsidering Wilde's *Vera*," in *Wilde Discoveries*, 79.

110.   Oscar Wilde, *The Importance of Being Earnest*, in *Collins Complete Works of Oscar Wilde*, 408.

111. Quoted in Walter Crane, *An Artist's Reminiscences* (New York: Macmillan, 1907), 273.

112. Butterworth, *World That Never Was*, 145–46.

113. Quail, *Slow-Burning Fuse*, 103–5, 112–13, 120.

114. Quail, *Slow-Burning Fuse*, 162.

115. Goodway, *Anarchist Seeds beneath the Snow*, 79.

116. Oscar Wilde, "Lord Arthur Savile's Crime," in *Collins Complete Works of Oscar Wilde*, 170.

117. Wilde, "Lord Arthur Savile's Crime," 160.

118. Wilde, "Lord Arthur Savile's Crime," 161. This sentiment is echoed in *Earnest*, when Cecily confesses, "I have never met any really wicked person before. I feel rather frightened. I am so afraid he will look just like everyone else." Wilde, *Importance of Being Earnest*, 378.

119. For a tyical example, see the cartoon from the *Los Angeles Times*, reprinted opposite page 196 in Louis Adamic, *Dynamite: The Story of Class Violence in America*, rev. ed. (Gloucester, Mass.: Peter Smith, 1963).

120. The figure of the technically obsessed and purely misanthropic bombardier reaches its fullest expression in Joseph Conrad's novel *The Secret Agent*. Joseph Conrad, *The Secret Agent: A Simple Tale*, ed. John Lyon (Oxford: University of Oxford Press, 2008).

121. Oscar Wilde, *Pen, Pencil and Poison: A Study in Green*, in *Collins Complete Works of Oscar Wilde*, 1106.

122. Oscar Wilde to Ralph Payne [Postmark Febraury 12, 1894], in *The Complete Letters of Oscar Wilde*, ed. Holland and Hart-Davis, 585.

123. Oscar Wilde, "Literary and Other Notes III," in *Selected Journalism*, ed. Clayworth, 119–20.

124. Quoted in Ellmann, *Oscar Wilde*, 341.

125. Oscar Wilde, "Mr Swinburne's Last Volume," in *Selected Journalism*, ed. Clayworth, 40.

126. Wilde, "Lord Arthur Savile's Crime," 175.

127. Wilde, "Lord Arthur Savile's Crime," 176–78.

128. Wilde, "Lord Arthur Savile's Crime," 175.

129. Wilde, "Lord Arthur Savile's Crime," 179.

130. Wilde, "Lord Arthur Savile's Crime," 178.

131. Wilde, "Lord Arthur Savile's Crime," 178.

132. For a detailed examiniation of the use of agents provocateurs during this period, see Butterworth, *World That Never Was*. From that history, Butterworth discerns a "modus operandi" common to incidents in Liège, Paris, and Walsall "and surely replicated elsewhere": "A charismatic figure . . . burning with idealism and determination, presents [himself] as an inspiration to impressionable youths who talk a good fight but lack the means. The material is provided, or else commissioned with detailed instructions for its acquisition or manufacture. Funds are supplied from a distant and affluent benefactor, ideally through an intermediary, of a generosity that dazzles any doubters. Secondary agents provocateurs, recruited locally, affirm the credulous recruits in their sense of purpose. And if the execution of attacks is part of the plan, the bombers' own preferences may be solicited but are then refined, to ensure maximum impact on public opinion." Butterworth,

World that Never Was, 343–44. To compare this pattern with more recent cases, see Kristian Williams, "Profiles of Provocateurs," in Kristian Williams and scott crow, *Witness to Betrayal: scott crow on the Exploits and Misadventures of FBI Informant Brandon Darby* ([Austin, Tex.]: Emergency Hearts Publishing, 2014).

133. For instance, in Russia: "Ultimately, the desired effect—raising the consciousness of the Russian people—was not achieved. Political killings did not kindle the spark that set Russia ablaze, and they did little to make those in power enact reforms. To the contrary, they led to increasingly harsh reprisals." Ternon, "Russian Terorism," 132. For a similar assessment of the French experience, see Sweetman, *Explosive Acts*, 378.

134. Many of the incidents and characters depicted in this canon were based on real events or real people. Rudin was modeled on Bakunin, who was in fact a friend of Turgenev. "One of the main events" in *The Possessed*, Dostoevsky explained, is "Ivanov's murder by Nechaev." James's character Hoffendahl is a stand-in for the anarchist Johann Most. The central incident in *The Secret Agent* is the explosion outside the Greenwich Observatory in 1894, and Conrad borrows his theory of the case from David Nicoll's *Greenwich Mystery* (1897). Weir, *Anarchy and Culture*, 53, 58–59, 70, and 74–76, respectively.

135. Wilde, "Soul of Man under Socialism," 1188. Alexander Berkman later argued along exactly the same lines: "As long as the world is ruled by violence, violence will accomplish results. . . . Did the Colonies win their independence by crawling on their knees before the tyrant? Were the black slaves freed by imploring the good Lord to soften the hearts of their masters? Has a single step been made on the road of progress without violence and bloodshed?" Alexander Berkman, "The Source of Violence," in *Anarchy! An Anthology of Emma Goldman's Mother Earth*, ed. Peter Glassgold (Washington, D.C.: Counterpoint, 2001), 317.

136. Howard Zinn, *A People's History of the United States, 1492–Present,* revised and updated ed. (New York: HarperPerennial, 1995), 264–66.

137. George Bernard Shaw, "My Memories of Oscar Wilde," in Frank Harris, *Oscar Wilde* (n.p.: Michigan State University Press, 1959), 334. Others had more success than Shaw. Among the names appearing on the petition were those of Eleanor Marx, Edward Carpenter, Olive Schreiner, and Annie Besant. Terence Kissack, *Free Comrades: Anarchism and Homosexuality in the United States, 1895–1917* (Oakland: AK Press, 2008), 48.

138. Quoted in Goodway, *Anarchist Seeds beneath the Snow*, 80.

139. Goodway, *Anarchist Seeds beneath the Snow*, 80.

140. Goodway, *Anarchist Seeds beneath the Snow*, 80–81.

141. Oscar Wilde to John Barlas [Postmark January 19, 1892], in *The Complete Letters of Oscar Wilde*, ed. Holland and Hart-Davis, 511.

142. Goodway, *Anarchist Seeds Beneath the Snow*, 81.

143. Quoted in Goodway, *Anarchist Seeds Beneath the Snow*, 82.

144. For details, see E. P. Thompson, *William Morris: Romantic to Revolutionary* (Oakland: PM Press, 2011) 487–97; Quail, *Slow-Burning Fuse*, 70–73.

145. Butterworth, *World That Never Was*, 242.

146. Crane, *Artist's Reminiscences*, 266–67. Emphasis in original.

147. Eugene D. LeMire, "Bloody Sunday (November 13, 1887)," in *Victorian Britain: An Encyclopedia*, ed. Sally Mitchell (New York: Garland, 1988), 84.

148. Crane, *Artist's Reminiscences*, 269–70.

149. Thompson, *William Morris*, 493–95. The Reverend Stewart Headlam, a Fabian Socialist, was also the founder of the Church and Stage Guild. He felt that the theater had a special mission in counteracting the effects of industrialization: "Our surroundings are so ugly—gloom, dirt, mud-coloured streets—our very work, which should be to us as a source of joy, is made by its monotony and its mean sub-divisions often little better than a mere grind. . . . Counteracting all this the Theatre has been at work with its heavenly mission; there the contemplation of beauty has been made possible for the people." He later bailed Wilde out of jail. Quoted in Beckson, *London in the 1890s*, 116–17.

150. Quoted in Crane, *Artist's Reminiscences*, 268.

151. Oscar Wilde to George Percy Jacomb-Hood (c. January 20, 1888), in *The Complete Letters of Oscar Wilde*, ed. Holland and Hart-Davis, 340.

152. Maya Jasanoff, *The Dawn Watch: Joseph Conrad in a Global World* (New York: Penguin Press, 2017), 251.

153. Quoted in Jasanoff, *Dawn Watch*, 252.

154. Thompson, *William Morris*, 492.

155. Sweetman, *Explosive Acts*, 317–20; Butterworth, *World That Never Was*, 300–304.

156. Butterworth, *World That Never Was*, 325.

157. Woodcock, *Anarchism*, 311–12; Sweetman, *Explosive Acts*, 320–23.

158. Sweetman, *Explosive Acts*, 230, 317.

159. Sweetman, *Explosive Acts*, 319.

160. Sweetman, *Explosive Acts*, 374–82.

161. Sweetman, *Explosive Acts*, 318.

162. Quoted in Butterworth, *World That Never Was*, 304–5.

163. Sweetman, *Explosive Acts*, 375.

164. Quoted in Oliver Hubac-Occhipinti, "Anarchist Terrorists of the Nineteenth Century," in *The History of Terrorism from Antiquity to Al Qaeda*, ed. Chalind and Blin, 113.

165. Wilde, "Soul of Man under Socialism," 1188.

166. Quoted in Sweetman, *Explosive Acts*, 373.

167. Butterworth, *World That Never Was*, 335.

168. Quoted in Townshend, *Terrorism*, 57.

169. Sweetman, *Explosive Acts*, 320.

170. Alexander Berkman, "A Few Words as to My Deed," in *Prison Blossoms: Anarchist Voices from the American Past*, by Alexander Berkman, Henry Bauer, and Carl Nold, ed. Miriam Brody and Bonnie Buettner (Cambridge, Mass.: Belknap Press, 2011), 80.

171. Butterworth, *World That Never Was*, 161.

172. Zinn, *People's History of the United States*, 266.

173. Miriam Brody, introduction to Berkman, Bauer, and Nold, *Prison Blossoms: Anarchist Voices from the American Past*, xlii.

174. Clifford Harper, *Anarchy: A Graphic Guide* (London: Camden Press, 1987), 179.

175. Alan Moore and David Lloyd, *V for Vendetta* (New York: DC Comics, 1989), 222. Emphasis in original. Concerning Wilde's influence on *V for Vendetta*, see Ellen Crowell, "Scarlet Carsons, Men in Masks: The Wildean Contexts of *V for Vendetta*," *Neo-Victorian Studies* 2, no. 1 (2008–2009): 17–45.

176. Quoted in Woodcock, *Anarchism*, 14. The psychological identification of creation and destruction also supplies the fact at the center of punk aesthetics—"a no that became a yes, then a no again, then again a yes," as Greil Marcus described the feel of the Sex Pistols' song, "Anarchy in the U.K.": "it sounded like fun, wrecking the world. It felt like freedom." Greil Marcus, *Lipstick Traces: A Secret History of the Twentieth Century* (Cambridge, Mass.: Harvard University Press, 1990), 6, 8.

177. Alexander Berkman, "Why the Blast?," in *Life of an Anarchist: The Alexander Berkman Reader*, ed. George Fellner (New York: Seven Stories, 2005), 116.

178. Wilde, "Critic as Artist," 1147. Of the classical anarchists, perhaps Proudhon comes closest to Wilde's critical approach. In his *Philosophie du Progrè*, he writes of an "incessant metamorphosis . . . the affirmation of universal movement and in consequnece the negation of all immutable forms and formulae, of all doctrines of eternity, permanence, and impeccability, of all permanent order; not excepting that of the universe, and of every subject or object, spirtual or transcendental, that does not change." Quoted in Woodcock, *Anarchism*, 30.

179. On Wilde's subversive use of paradox, and its appropriation in the pages of Emma Goldman's *Mother Earth*, see Kristian Williams, "The Anarchist Aphorist: Wilde and Gottesman, Paradox and Subversion," *Anarchist Studies* 18, no. 2 (2010), 101–8.

180. John Barlas, "Oscar Wilde," *Novel Review*, April 1892, 45–46. Barlas here defends Wilde against Wilde, contradicting these lines of Wilde's from *Vera*: "One dagger will do more than a hundred epigrams." Wilde, *Vera*, 688.

Chapter 2: The Basis for a New Civilization

1. Quoted in Sir David Hunter-Blair, "Oscar Wilde at Magdalen College Oxford," in *Oscar Wilde: Interviews and Recollections*, vol. 1, ed. E. H. Mikhail (New York: Barnes & Noble, 1979), 4–5.

2. "Oscar Wilde in Omaha [*Omaha Weekly Herald*, March 24, 1882]," in *Oscar Wilde: Interviews and Recollections*, vol. 1, 58.

3. Oscar Wilde, "The English Renaissance of Art," in *The Uncollected Oscar Wilde*, ed. John Wyse Jackson (London: Fourth Estate, 1995), 25, 28.

4. The poet Algernon Charles Swinburne declared, "Art for art's sake first of all, and afterwards we may suppose all the rest shall be added to her." Quoted in Karl Beckson, *London in the 1890s: A Cultural History* (New York: W. W. Norton, 1992), 37.

Wilde paraphrased the maxim, altering the phrasing to blasphemously introduce a biblical reference: "Love art for its own sake, and then all things that you need will be added to you." Wilde, "English Renaissance of Art," 21. (Compare: "But seek ye first the kingdom of God, and his righteousness; and all these things shall be added unto you." Matthew 6:33.)

5. Oscar Wilde, *The Picture of Dorian Gray*, in *Collins Complete Works of Oscar Wilde* (Glasgow: HarperCollins, 2003), 17.

6. See, for instance, Lloyd Lewis and Henry Justin Smith, *Oscar Wilde Discovers America [1882]* (New York: Harcourt, Brace, 1936), 5, 11, 14, 19–21, 23, 27. Wilde recalls: "The first time that the absolute stupidity of the English people was ever revealed to me was one Sunday at the University Church, when the preacher opened his sermon in

something [like] this way: 'When a young man says not in polished banter, but in sober earnestness, that he finds it difficult to live up to the level of his blue china, there has crept into these cloistered shades a form of heathenism which it is our bounden duty to fight against and crush out, if possible.' I need hardly say that we were delighted and amused at the typical English way in which our ideas were misunderstood. They took our epigrams as earnest, and our paradoxes as prose." "The Theories of a Poet," in *Oscar Wilde: Interviews and Recollections*, vol. 1, 40.

7.   Quoted in Lewis and Smith, *Oscar Wilde Discovers America*, 148.

8.   In England, too, Karl Beckson tells us, "For the industrious, pious middle classes that increasingly valued social equality, solemn responsibility, and moral energy, the pose of dandyism was patently offensive, for it implied elitist superiority, calculated irresponsibility, and cultivated languor. The image of the dandy, particularly as depicted in Wilde's social comedies, thus embodied the Decadent sensibility in its most subversive form." Beckson, *London in the 1890s*, 35.

Related fashions continued to unnerve the guardians of respectability more than half a century later. Greil Marcus reminds us: "The 'Edwardians'—the Teddy Boys, working--class London youths whose early-1950s imitation of fin-de-siècle English dandies was taken by the press as an act of violence, a disruption of class codes prefiguring a refusal of class status—arrange their bodies into nihilist manifestos." Greil Marcus, *Lipstick Traces: A Secret History of the Twentieth Century* (Cambridge, Mass.: Harvard University Press, 1990), 378.

9.   "The Puritan, like every rational type of asceticism, tried to enable a man to maintain and act upon his constant motives, especially those which it taught him itself, against the emotions. . . . [T]he most urgent task [was] the destruction of spontaneous, impulsive enjoyment, the most important means was to bring order into the conduct of its adherents." Max Weber, *The Protestant Ethic and the Spirit of Capitalism*, trans. Talcott Parsons (London: Routledge, 2005), 73. Weber's argument was extended, with special attention to the influence of Methodism, in a short section of E. P. Thompson's *The Making of the English Working Class* (New York: Random House, 1966), 355–74.

10.   Quoted in Thompson, *Making of the English Working Class*, 368, 401.

11.   Quoted in Thompson, *Making of the English Working Class*, 361–62.

12.   Weber identified the "*summum bonum* of this ethic" as "the earning of more and more money, combined with the strict avoidance of all spontaneous enjoyment of life." Weber, *Protestant Ethic and the Spirit of Capitalism*, 18.

13.   Weber, *Protestant Ethic and the Spirit of Capitalism*, 120. In his essay "Post-Christian Man," the anarchist Paul Goodman reflected on the legacy of the Protestant Ethic: "When we extend the line of development further than Weber did, to the present system of semimonopolies and state capitalism, and when we find that the Calvinist virtues of asceticism, rationality, individual self-help, etc., have been transformed precisely into their opposites—a high standard of living, various kinds of boondoggling and feather-bedding, and the morality of Organization Man and bureaucrat—nevertheless the underlying moral demands of attending to business, righteously one-upping one's fellows, and disciplining one's animal and communal self, are the same as when it was the Lord's work that was to be done." Paul Goodman, "Post-Christian Man," in *The Paul Goodman Reader*, ed. Taylor Stoehr (Oakland: PM Press, 2011), 301–2.

For a look at the current cult of work, see Derek Thompson, "Workism Is Making Americans Miserable," *Atlantic*, February 24, 2019, https://www.theatlantic.com.

14.   Quoted in George Woodcock, "The English Hymn," in *Writers and Politics* (Montreal: Black Rose Books, 1990), 221.

15.   The historian E. P. Thompson considers the result: "The Victorian bourgeoisie had constructed from bits of Adam Smith and Ricardo, Bentham and Malthus a cast-iron theoretical system, which they were now securing with the authority of the State and the Law, and sanctifying with the blessings of Religion. The laws of supply and demand were 'God's laws,' and in all the major affairs of society all other values must bend before commodity values. Capital and labour were bound together by indissoluble ties: and upon the prosperity of capital depended the prosperity of the working class. Even excessive charity might endanger the working of these 'natural' laws, by subsidizing and encouraging poverty. . . . State regulation of the hours and conditions of adult labour . . . was not only bad political economy but a monstrous interference with God's laws, which would bring down a terrible retribution. The market was the final determinant of value, and if there was insufficient demand to make fine architecture or beautifully planned towns *pay*, this was sufficient evidence that such commodities as these were insignificant in the realm of Fact." E. P. Thompson, *William Morris: Romantic to Revolutionary* (Oakland: PM Press, 2011), 9. Emphasis in original.

16.   Especially in the period of reaction following the French Revolution, institutional means of encouraging and enforcing this outlook increasingly took hold. E. P. Thompson observes: "The remedies proposed might differ; but the impulse behind Colquhoun, with his advocacy of more effective police, Hannah More, with her halfpenny tracts and Sunday Schools, the Methodists with their renewed emphasis upon order and submissiveness, Bishop Barrington's more humane Society for Bettering the Condition of the Poor, and William Wilberforce and Dr. John Bowdler, with their Society for the Suppression of Vice and the Encouragement of Religion, was much the same. The message to be given to the labouring poor was simple, and was summarised by Burke in the famine year of 1795: 'Patience, labour, sobriety, frugality, and religion should be recommended to them; all the rest is downright fraud.'" Thompson, *Making of the English Working Class*, 56.

17.   Oscar Wilde, "The Soul of Man under Socialism," in *Collins Complete Works of Oscar Wilde*, 1176. Paragraph breaks added for clarity.

18.   Richard Gallienne, "Oscar Wilde as a Symbolic Figure," in *Oscar Wilde: Interviews and Recollections*, 394.

19.   Stuart Mason [Christopher Millard], *Bibliography of Osar Wilde* (London: Bertram Rota, 1967), 96. A hymn of the period implores: "Work, for night is coming, / Work thro' the morning hours; / Work while the dew is sparkling; / Work mid springing flowers; / Work while the day grows brighter / Under the glowing Sun; / Work, for the night is coming / When man's work is done." Woodcock, "English Hymn," 226.

20.   Oscar Wilde, "Wasted Days," in *Collins Complete Works of Oscar Wilde*, 775. To wit: "Gather ye Rose-buds while ye may, / Old Time is still a flying: / And this same flower that smiles today, / To morrow will be dying." Robert Herrick, "To the Virgins, to Make Much of Time," in *The Poetical Works of Robert Herrick*, ed. F. W. Moorman (London: Oxford University Press, 1957), 84.

21.   Quoted in Frank Harris, *Oscar Wilde: His Life and Confessions*, vol. 1 (New York: Frank Harris, 1918), 166. In his studies of the East End lower classes, Charles Booth supplied some empirical evidence that both supports and complicates Wilde's aphorism. Booth noted among the "very poor" the presence of a "leisure class." Though their leisure is "bounded very closely by the pressure of want," it nevertheless becomes "habitual to the extent of second nature." He observed, "The ideal of such persons is to work when they like and play when they like. . . . There is drunkenness amongst them, especially amongst the women; but drink is not their special luxury, as with the lowest class, nor is it their passion, as with a portion of those with higher wages and irregular but severe work." Of this last group, he explained: "Some of the irregularly employed men earn very high wages, fully as high as those of the artisan class. These are men of great physical strength, working on coal or grain, or combining aptitude and practice with strength, as in handling timber. It is amongst such men, especially those carrying grain and coal, that the passion for drink is most developed." Charles Booth, "Life and Labour of the People of London (1889)," in *The Fin de Siècle: A Reader in Cultural History, c. 1880–1900*, ed. Sally Ledger and Roger Luckhurst (Oxford: Oxford University Press, 2000), 41.

22.   Wilde detected a note of hypocritical self-interest: "Each class would have preached the importance of those virtues for whose exercise there was no necessity in their own lives. The rich would have spoken on the value of thrift, and the idle grown eloquent over the dignity of labour." Wilde, *Picture of Dorian Gray*, 25.

23.   "There is only one class in the community that thinks more about money than the rich, and that is the poor. The poor can think of nothing else. That is the misery of being poor." Wilde, "Soul of Man under Socialism," 1180.

24.   Oscar Wilde, "De Profundis," in *Collins Complete Works of Oscar Wilde*, 1036.

25.   Wilde, *Picture of Dorian Gray*, 141.

26.   Quoted in Lewis and Smith, *Oscar Wilde Discovers America*, 337.

27.   Oscar Wilde, "English Renaissance of Art," 26. Another variant: "Life without industry is barren, and industry without art is barbarism." Quoted in "The Apostle of Art (*Chicago Inter-Ocean*, February 11, 1882)," in *Oscar Wilde in America: The Interviews*, ed. Matthew Hofer and Gary Scharnhorst (Urbana: University of Illinois Press, 2010), 59.

Elsewhere he reversed this formula, as he often did with his epigrams: "Life without industry is barbarism; industry without art is barren." "The Apostle of Estheticism Talks Plainly (*The Daily Record-Union* (Sacramento), March 27, 1882)," in *Oscar Wilde: Interviews and Recollections*, vol. 1, 68.

28.   Weber quotes Richard Baxter as the representative voice of English puritanism: "If God show you a way in which you may lawfully get more than in another way (without wrong to your soul or any other), if you refuse this, and choose the less gainful way, you cross one of the ends of your calling, and you refuse to be God's steward, and to accept His gifts and use them for Him when He requireth it: you may labour to be rich for God, though not for the flesh and sin." Quoted in Weber, *Protestant Ethic and the Spirit of Capitalism*, 108.

29.   Wilde, *Picture of Dorian Gray*, 46. He repeats the line in *Lady Windermere's Fan*, in *Collins Complete Works of Oscar Wilde*, 452. In his book on neoliberalism, *The Value of Nothing*, Raj Patel quotes Wilde's epigram twice in the first three pages (not counting the title). He later offers this "paraphrase": "people today know the exchange value of

everything and the use value of nothing." Raj Patel, *The Value of Nothing: How to Reshape Market Society and Redefine Democracy* (New York: Picador, 2009), 1, 3, 64.

But in this last, Patel rather misses Wilde's larger point, that utilitarian calculations of cost and benefits, like economic calculations of production and profit, fail to capture the full value of any thing, any place, or any one. Neither an impressionist painting nor a cliff by the sea nor a great personality need to be *useful* for us to love, admire, or appreciate them.

The anarchist Alexander Berkman stayed closer to Wilde's meaning when he argued that everyone should share equally in the wealth of society. "'But why not give each according to the value of his work?' you ask. Because there is no way by which value can be measured. That is the difference between value and price. Value is what a thing is worth, while price is what it can be sold or bought for in the market. What a thing is worth no one really can tell." Alexander Berkman, "The ABC of Anarchism," in *Life of an Anarchist: The Alexander Berkman Reader*, ed. Gene Fellner (New York: Seven Stories Press, 2005), 281.

30.   "Oscar Wilde to R. Clegg (April 1891?)," in *The Complete Letters of Oscar Wilde*, ed. Merlin Holland and Rupert Hart-Davis (New York: Henry Holt, 2000), 478–79.

31.   Quoted in Roy Morris Jr., *Declaring His Genius: Oscar Wilde in North America* (Cambridge, Mass.: Harvard University Press, 2013), 47.

32.   Oscar Wilde, "The Poets and the People," in *The Artist as Critic: Critical Writings of Oscar Wilde*, ed. Richard Ellmann (Chicago: University of Chicago Press, 1982), 43–45.

33.   Oscar Wilde, "The Critic as Artist," in *Collins Complete Works of Oscar Wilde*, 1142.

34.   Wilde, "Poets and the People," 45.

35.   Oscar Wilde, "Poetical Socialists," in *Selected Journalism*, ed. Anya Clayworth (Oxford: Oxford University Press, 2004), 33–34.

36.   Wilde, "Poetical Socialists," 34.

37.   Wilde, "Poetical Socialists," 35–36.

38.   Wilde, "Poetical Socialists," 34–36.

39.   For his views on "the laws of justice respecting payment of labour," see John Ruskin, "Qui Judicatis Terram (from *Unto This Last*)," in *Unto This Last and Other Writings* (London: Penguin Books, 1997), 194–201.

40.   See John Ruskin, "The Baron's Gate (from *Fora Clavigera*)," in *Unto This Last and Other Writings*, 306–7, 294. Ruskin was, in any case, no sort of anarchist, remaining vocally authoritarian and paternalistic throughout his career. Nevertheless, his work had a profound influence on others who were closer to anarchism in their views and whose work proved important to the history of the anarchist movement—not only Wilde and William Morris (both discussed in what follows), but also Tolstoy and Gandhi. Clive Wilmer, introduction to Ruskin, *Unto This Last and Other Writings*, 30, 36. On Ruskin's religious upbringing, see Emer O'Sullivan, *The Fall of the House of Wilde: Oscar Wilde and His Family* (New York: Bloomsbury Press, 2016), 180.

41.   Wilde noted both the magnitude and the limits of Ruskin's influence on the Aesthetic movement: "Master indeed of the knowledge of all noble living and of the wisdom of all spiritual things will he be to us ever, seeing that it was he who by the magic

of his presence and the music of his lips taught us at Oxford that enthusiasm for beauty which is the secret of Hellenism, and that desire for creation which is the secret of life, and filled some of us, at least, with the lofty and passionate ambition to go forth into far and fair lands with some message for the nations and some mission for the world, and yet in his art criticism, his estimate of the joyous element of art, his whole method of approaching art, we are no longer with him; for the keystone to his aesthetic system is ethical always." Oscar Wilde, "L'Envoi," in *Uncollected Oscar Wilde*, 197.

42.   "You must either make a tool of the creature or a man of him. You cannot make both." John Ruskin, "The Nature of Gothic (from *The Stones of Venice*)," in *Unto This Last and Other Writings*, 84–85.

43.   Ruskin, "Nature of Gothic," 87.

44.   Ruskin, "Nature of Gothic," 90. This unity of design and production, or mental and manual work, finds an interesting analogue in Wilde's refusal to distinguish body and soul: "Those who see any difference between soul and body have neither." Oscar Wilde, "Phrases and Philosophies for the Use of the Young," in *Collins Complete Works of Oscar Wilde*, 1244.

Galloway contrasts Ruskin's approach with the principles of scientific management formulated by Frederick Taylor (and the process of implementation known as "Taylorization"). William Galloway, "Ruskin's Road: Architecture and the Object of Work," ACSA Annual Meeting (1996), 540–41.

45.   Oscar Wilde, "Art and the Handicraftsmen," in *Uncollected Oscar Wilde*, 117–18.

46.   Peter Marshall, *Demanding the Impossible: A History of Anarchism* (Oakland: PM Press, 2010), 96–101.

47.   Wilde, "Art and the Handicraftsmen," 117–18. A slightly different version appears in Lewis and Smith, *Oscar Wilde Discovers America*, 161–62.

Accounts vary as to the quality and completeness of the road. G. T. Atkinson agrees with Wilde: "It was a very bad road." G. T. Atkinson, "Oscar Wilde at Oxford," in *Oscar Wilde: Interviews and Recollections*, vol. 1, 20. For a more fully positive assessment, see "Recollections of Ruskin," *Atlantic Monthly*, April 1900, especially 572–75.

48.   In one of his lectures, Wilde referred to Morris as "the man whose work in the handicrafts has been the real motive force of the artistic movement." Oscar Wilde, "The Irish Poets of '48: A Lecture by Oscar Wilde (San Francisco, April 5, 1882)," transcript from the original draft manuscript, British Library, ADD 81636 A,B 4009A, 2. On Morris as a likely, if indirect, inspiration for the writing of "The Soul of Man under Socialism," see Kristian Williams, "The Roots of Wilde's Socialist *Soul*: Ibsen and Shaw, or Morris and Crane," *Oscholars*, Spring 2010, http://www.oscholars.com.

49.   All these points appear in Oscar Wilde, "The Decorative Arts," in *Collins Complete Works of Oscar Wilde*, 926–37. For a comparison of Wilde's and Morris's views on art, work, and society (as well as those of Ursula Le Guin), see Laurence Davis, "Everyone an Artist: Art, Labour, Anarchy, and Utopia," in *Anarchism and Utopianism*, ed. Laurence Davis and Ruth Kinna (Manchester: Manchester University Press, 2009).

50.   Florence Boos calls him an "Aesthetic Ecocommunist"; E. P. Thompson labeled Morris's politics more simply as "Libertarian Communism." Florence S. Boos, "An Aesthetic Ecocommunist: Morris the Red and Morris the Green," in *William Morris:*

Centenary Essays—Papers from the Morris Centenary Conference organized by the William Morris Society at Exeter College Oxford, 30 June–3 July 1996, ed. Peter Faulkner and Peter Preston (Exeter: University of Exeter Press, 1999); Thompson quoted in David Goodway, "E. P. Thompson and Williams Morris," in *William Morris: Centenary Essays,* 235.

In his otherwise excellent biography of Morris, E. P. Thompson—himself ideologically suspect by mid-century Communist Party standards—is at pains to claim Morris for the Marxist tradition while also justifying his heterodox views. See, for instance, 533–34. However, when Thompson revisited the question in 1976, he found that "Morris was an original Socialist thinker whose work was complementary to Marxism," concluding that "Morris may be assimilated to Marxism only in the course of a re-ordering of Marxism itself." E. P. Thompson, "Postscript: 1976," in *William Morris,* 770, 806.

Such sectarian ambivalence is surely forgivable. On the one hand, Engels worried that Morris was "strongly under the influence of the anarchists." Quoted in Thompson, *William Morris,* 405.

On the other hand, Morris himself reflected that he had learned from "my Anarchist friends . . . , quite against their intention, that Anarchism was impossible." William Morris, "How I Became Socialist," in *On Art and Socialism: Essays and Lectures* (Paulton: John Lehmann, 1947), 276.

Nevertheless, he continued to advocate "decentralization," with society reconstituted as "not the Nation, but a Commune," or, more precisely, "a great federation of such communes." William Morris, "True and False Society," in *On Art and Socialism,* 314.

As David Goodway has pointed out, this ideal of society closely resembles that of Kropotkin. Where the two friends' thinking diverged was on the question of strategy. Kropotkin believed that the abolition of the state would precipitate the creation of a free society. Morris thought that the free society had to be created before the state could be dispensed with. David Goodway, *Anarchist Seeds beneath the Snow: Left-Libertarian Thought and British Writers from William Morris to Colin Ward* (Oakland: PM Press, 2012), 23. Ruth Kinna offers a careful examination of Kropotkin and Morris and the difference in their views, especially with regard to the role of art. Ruth Kinna, "Morris, Anti-Statism and Anarchy," in *William Morris: Centenary Essays.* On Kropotkin's likely influence on Morris, see Thompson, *William Morris,* 772.

51.   Wilde, "English Renaissance of Art," 9.

52.   Morris, "How I Became a Socialist," 225.

53.   Goodway, *Anarchist Seeds beneath the Snow,* 65.

54.   Quoted in Peter Faulkner, "William Morris and Oscar Wilde," *Journal of William Morris Studies* 14, no. 4 (Summer 2002): 30.

55.   The short collection also included W. C. Owen's "The Coming Solidarity." In his essay, Owen argues, "Looking backward we can see that the split [between anarchists and Marxists in the First International] was unavoidable; looking forward we can also see that a reunion is as certain. Of the near approach of that reunion the presence in the movement of such men as William Morris and Oscar Wilde is a very obvious sign. Both have a world-wide reputation as interpreters of that art whose breath is individualism, and whose essence is harmonious combination." W. C. Owen, "The Coming Solidarity," in *The Soul of Man under Socialism, The Socialist Ideal—Art, and The Coming Solidarity,* by Oscar Wilde, Williams Morris, and W. C. Owen (New York: Humboldt Printing, [1891]), 35.

56. Wilde, "Soul of Man under Socialism," 1184. Alexander Berkman later made much the same point: "A person can give the best of himself only when his interest is in his work, when he feels a natural attraction to it, when he likes it." Berkman, "ABC of Anarchism," 283.

57. William Morris, "The Socialist Ideal—Art," in Wilde, Morris, and Owen, *The Soul of Man under Socialism*, 36.

58. Wilde, "Soul of Man under Socialism," 1183. The complaint was commonly voiced by anarchists: Max Baginski wrote in Emma Goldman's *Mother Earth*, "People prate of 'moral satisfaction' in work well done. Are we not all familiar with the phrase, 'the dignity of labor'? The hypocrites! The man of spirit and independence can but feel humiliated by his forced labor; far from enjoying 'moral satisfaction' in his wage slavery, he can not help but be filled with hatred against conditions which degrade him to a mere tool for the accumulation of wealth—for others." Max Baginski, "Anti-Moral Reflections (from *Mother Earth*, August 1907)," in *Mother Earth Bulletin*, series 1, vol. 2, *1907–1908* (New York: Greenwood Reprint, 1968), 248.

Alexander Berkman put the point more simply: "Life in the tenements is sordid, the fate of the worker dreary. There is no 'dignity of labor.' Sweatshop bread is bitter." Alexander Berkman, *Prison Memoirs of an Anarchist* (New York: New York Review of Books, 1999), 206.

59. Donald Thomas, *The Victorian Underworld* (New York: New York University Press, 1998), 12; and Wolf Von Eckardt et al., *Oscar Wilde's London: A Scrapbook of Virtues and Vices, 1880–1900* (Garden City, N.Y.: Anchor Press, 1987), 103–4.

60. Wilde, "Soul of Man under Socialism," 1183. In "Arts and the Handicraftsman," Wilde likewise distinguished creative pleasurable work from mere drudgery, the first being the work suited to human beings and the latter better suited to machines: "Do you think . . . that we object to machinery?" he asked rhetorically. "I tell you that we reverence it; we reverence it when it does its proper work, when it relieves man from ignoble and soulless labour, not when it seeks to do that which is valuable only when wrought by the hands and hearts of men." Wilde, "Art and the Handicraftsman," 108. The idea that machines can do all unpleasant work is taken from Aristotle's *Politics*. Wilde commented in an Oxford notebook: "if hammer and shuttle cd. move themselves slavery would be unnecessary - (Aristotle) - and machinery having virtually fulfilled the condition the predicted result has followed." Oscar Wilde, "Notebook Kept at Oxford," in *Oscar Wilde's Oxford Notebooks: A Portrait of Mind in the Making*, ed. Philip E. Smith II and Michael S. Helfand (New York: Oxford University Press, 1989), 155.

61. William Morris, "The Prospects of Architecture in Civilization," in *On Art and Socialism: Essays and Lectures* (Paulton: John Lehmann, 1947), 263.

62. William Morris, "The Art of the People," in *On Art and Socialism*, 50. Again in Wilde's "English Renaissance," Morris's influence is apparent: "For what is decoration but the worker's expression of joy in his work? And not joy merely . . . but that opportunity of expressing his own individuality which, as it is the essence of all life, is the source of all art. 'I have tried,' I remember William Morris saying to me once, 'I have tried to make each of my workers an artist, and when I say an artist I mean a man.'" Wilde, "English Renaissance of Art," 26.

63. William Morris, "Art and Socialism," in *On Art and Socialism*, 111.

64.   Wilde, "Theories of a Poet," 40.

65.   "Oscar Wilde in Omaha," 58.

66.   "Oscar Wilde in Omaha," 58. It was a common complaint among workers, early in the century, that "they wish to make us tools [or 'implements' or 'machines']." Quoted in Thompson, *Making of the English Working Class*, 832.

67.   Quoted in "The Aesthetic Bard (*Philadelphia Inquirer*, January 17, 1882)," in *Oscar Wilde in America*, 32–33. Proudhon too believed that "art, that is to say, the search for the beautiful, . . . is the final stage in the evolution of the worker." Quoted in David Weir, *Anarchy and Culture: The Aesthetic Politics of Modernism* (Amherst: University of Massachusetts Press, 1997), 37.

68.   Lloyd Lewis and Henry Justin Smith's *Oscar Wilde Discovers America* provides, along with numerous details of Wilde's travels and his lectures, a good overview of the cultural and political context of his tour. For details of the economic context, including industrialization, the rise of the corporation, the prevalence of strikes, and their violent suppression, see 66–70.

69.   "Apostle of Estheticism Talks Plainly," 69–70.

70.   Richard Ellmann, *Oscar Wilde* (New York: Alfred A. Knopf, 1988), 204–5. Was it coincidence—or imitation—when, nearly two decades later, in 1897, Emma Goldman entered a mine to lecture on Shaw's plays? Richard Drinnon, *Rebel in Paradise: A Biography of Emma Goldman* (Chicago: University of Chicago Press, 1961), 155.

71.   Quoted in Lewis and Smith, *Oscar Wilde Discovers America*, 318.

72.   Oscar Wilde, "Impressions of America," in *Artist as Critic*, 10.

73.   "The Apostle of Beauty in Nova Scotia (*The Morning Herald* (Halifax), October 10, 1882)," in *Oscar Wilde in America*, 169.

74.   "Apostle of Estheticism Talks Plainly," 69–70.

75.   Lewis and Smith, *Oscar Wilde Discovers America*, 250.

76.   Quoted in "Oscar Wilde's Return (*New York World*, May 6, 1882)," in *Oscar Wilde in America*, 146.

77.   Quoted in Lewis and Smith, *Oscar Wilde Discovers America*, 245.

78.   Quoted in Morris, *Declaring His Genius*, 138; Lewis and Smith, *Oscar Wilde Discovers America*, 249.

79.   Quoted in Morris, *Declaring His Genius*, 138. A similar broadening of perspective seems to have affected Wilde's attitudes about Blacks as well. In an early letter from America, Wilde referred to his valet, a Black man (only identified in the surviving records as John), as "my slave," and compared the Black stable hand to "a little monkey." Oscar Wilde to Norman Forbes-Robertson, January 15, 1882, in *Complete Letters of Oscar Wilde*, 127.

The racial insensitivity is doubly shocking in that Wilde, an Irishman, was on this same tour regularly mocked in racist terms. That he had not grasped that all such prejudice was of a piece, equally absurd and despicable, is disappointing. However, in practice, and more crucially in public, Wilde's view of his valet, and of the race to which he belonged, seems to have altered with exposure. As they traveled through the South, the two men having spent some weeks together, a train conductor abruptly demanded that John's first-class ticket be reissued as second-class. As the Atlanta *Constitution* reported, "It was against the rules of the company to sell sleeping-car tickets to Negroes," but when "Mr. Thweatt went to the sleeping-car and stated the case to Mr. Wilde and his servant . . . [t]hey both declined to change the program they had marked out. Mr. Wilde said that he had never been interfered with before and persisted in having his darky retain his sleeping-car ticket." A tense stalemate ensued, threatening to become a scene, until a Black porter pulled John aside and (again, according to the *Constitution*) "told him the train would soon pass through Jonesboro, and if the people saw a Negro in the sleeper they would mob him." John then agreed on his own behalf to accept the second-class ticket. Quoted in Lewis and Smith, *Oscar Wilde Discovers America*, 373.

This minor episode demonstrates two points. First, Wilde, despite his earlier slurs, did not really regard John as a "slave" or a "monkey." (No one would insist that a slave or monkey travel first class.) Second, Wilde was not willing to cede to law or custom when he felt a point of honor was at stake.

80.   Quoted in "Oscar Wilde (*Denver Rocky Mountain News*, April 13, 1882)," in *Oscar Wilde in America*, 133.

81.   Oscar Wilde, "House Decoration," in *Uncollected Oscar Wilde*, 189.

82.   Wilde, "Impressions of America," 9.

83.   Wilde, "Impressions of America," 9.

84.   Quoted in "Oscar Wilde (*Denver Rocky Mountain News*, April 13, 1882)," 133.

85.   Oscar Wilde, "The House Beautiful," in *Collins Complete Works of Oscar Wilde*, 914; William Morris, "The Beauty of Life," in *On Art and Socialism*, 78. Emphasis in original. Wilde also offers this further elaboration: "Have nothing in your house that has not given pleasure to the man who made it and is not a pleasure to those who use it." Wilde, "House Beautiful," 914.

He rephrases the idea in "Art and the Handicraftsmen": "We want to see that you have nothing in your houses that has not been a joy to the man who made it, and is not a joy to those that use it." Wilde, "Art and the Handicraftsmen," 116.

Elsewhere still: "So, in years to come there will be nothing in any man's house which has not given delight to its maker and does not give delight to its user." This line immediately follows a reference to Morris as "the greatest handicraftsman we have had in England since the fourteenth century." Wilde, "English Renaissance of Art," 32.

86.   "Oscar Wilde in Montreal (*The Daily Witness*, May 15, 1882)," in *Oscar Wilde: Interviews and Recollections*, vol. 1, 83. This passion for the practical application of aesthetics to items for everyday use seems to have been an abiding one. In 1888 Wilde attended the founding of the National Association for the Advancement of Art in Relation to Industry. At the meeting, Walter Crane urged that society "must turn our artists into craftsmen and our craftsmen into artists." Walter Crane, *An Artists' Reminiscences* (New York: Macmillan, 1907), 324.

87.   Quoted in Lewis and Smith, *Oscar Wilde Discovers America*, 243. Here too Wilde echoes Morris, who declared, "The greatest foe to art is luxury, art cannot live in its atmosphere." Morris, "Beauty of Life," 77.

88.   Wilde, "Art and Handicraftsman," 112.

89.   Quoted in Lewis and Smith, *Oscar Wilde Discovers America*, 242.

90.   Quoted in Lewis and Smith, *Oscar Wilde Discovers America*, 241.

91.   Quoted in O'Sullivan, *Fall of the House of Wilde*, 231.

92.   "Wilde lacked any strong sense of ownership in his oral tales—an identifying

characteristic of oral cultures, in which the text belongs to the whole community." Deirdre Toomey, "The Story-Teller at Fault: Oscar Wilde and Irish Orality," in *Wilde the Irishman*, ed. Jerusha McCormack (New Haven: Yale University Press, 1998), 26.

93. Thomas Wright, *Oscar's Books* (London: Chatto & Windus, 2008), 185. "Appropriate what is already yours," Wilde advised Coulson Kernahan, "for to publish anything is to make it public property." Quoted in Coulson Kernahan, "Oscar Wilde," in *Oscar Wilde: Interviews and Recollections*, vol. 2, 308.

94. O'Sullivan, *Fall of the House of Wilde*, 75–77 (quote from 75). O'Sullivan comments: "From the beginning, William's cultural projects were acts of resistance. . . . The search for the true origin, as opposed to that provided by colonial history, informed his *The Beauties of the Boyne and the Blackwater*. There, and in his later *Lough Corrib*, William attempts to restore the geographical and historical identity of the land, to repeople the territory with its heroes, histories, myths, and battles. By instinct an archaeologist, William wanted to go back and back, to dig deeper and deeper, and recording the legend and lore, the expression of instinctual consciousness of the people, was a complementary aspect of this ambition." O'Sullivan, *Fall of the House of Wilde*, 289.

95. Wright, *Oscar's Books*, 18.

96. E. P. Thompson considers the preservation of such traditions as an aspect of the struggle to preserve the commons. E. P. Thompson, "Custom, Law and Common Right," in *Customs in Common* (New York: New Press, 1993), 182.

97. After his death, his widow, Lady Jane Wilde, went further in the direction of explicit politics in the two additional volumes she completed from his notes. O'Sullivan, *Fall of the House of Wilde*, 282–83. Her nationalism having grown more democratic with time, she denounced the compromise proposal for Home Rule as a "hollow fiction" that would preserve "old feudal distinctions of class and caste," and she predicted that Ireland would have to endure a period of warfare before winning its freedom: "the iconoclasts will precede the constructors." Quoted in O'Sullivan, *Fall of the House of Wilde*, 287–88.

98. Oscar Wilde, "The Selfish Giant," in *Collins Complete Works of Oscar Wilde*, 283.

99. Wilde, "Selfish Giant," 284.

100. Wilde, "Selfish Giant," 284.

101. Wilde, "Selfish Giant," 285.

102. Wilde, "Selfish Giant," 285.

103. Peter Linebaugh, "Enclosures from the Bottom Up," in *Stop, Thief! The Commons, Enclosures, and Resistance* (Oakland: PM Press, 2014), 144.

104. Linebaugh, "The City and the Commons: A Story of Our Times," in *Stop, Thief!*, 37.

105. Thompson, "Custom, Law and Common Right," 142–43.

106. Quoted in Paul Bew, *Ireland; The Politics of Enmity* (Oxford: Oxford University Press, 2007), 276. Eleanor Fitzsimons detects hints of this memory in Wilde's story "The Devoted Friend," in which a wealthy miller exploits his neighbor, taking his crops but refusing him credit, scolding him for laziness when in fact he is exhausted and starving, and insisting all the while that it is for his own good. Eleanor Fitzsimons, *Wilde's Women: How Oscar Wilde Was Shaped by the Women He Knew* (New York: Overlook Duckworth, 2016), 180.

107. *The Selfish Giant*, dir. Clio Barnard (British Film Institute/Channel 4 Television Corporation, 2013).

108. Oscar Wilde, "The Young King," in *Collins Complete Works of Oscar Wilde*, 218.

109. Wilde, "Young King," 215. This grotesque disparity, and a king's robe as a symbol of art degraded into luxury, had long been in Wilde's mind. In his "English Renaissance" lecture of 1882 he declared, "Art is no longer to be a purple robe woven by a slave and thrown over the whitened body of a leprous king to hide and to adorn the sin of his luxury." Wilde, "English Renaissance of Art," 26. He repeats the image using almost the same words in "Art and the Handicraftsman," (112).

110. Wilde, "Young King," 216.

111. Wilde, "Young King," 221. In Wilde's iconography, this image marks the young king as a kind of artist. For in "The English Renaissance in Art," Wilde declared that "the thorn-crown for the poet will blossom into roses for our pleasure." Wilde, "English Renaissance of Art," 16.

112. Wilde, "The Happy Prince," in *Collins Complete Works of Oscar Wilde*, 272.

113. Wilde, "Happy Prince," 272.

114. Fitzsimons suggests that the figure of the match-girl here "must surely represent a nod to the 1,400 women and girls who had gone on strike at the Bryant and May match factory in 1888." Fitzsimons, *Wilde's Women*, 179.

That Wilde was aware of the strike we can be certain. An item from *Fabian Society and Socialist Notes* lists Wilde along with Sydney Olivier and George Bernard Shaw in attendance at a meeting when "Walter Crane read an interesting paper on 'The Prospects of Art under Socialism,'" and "Annie Besant was invited to make a statement on the Match-Girls Strike against Bryant and May, and a collection in support of the girls was made, amounting to £7 7s. 8d." "Our Corner," *Fabian Society and Socialist Notes*, August 1888, 128. For the likely significance of this meeting for Wilde's essay "The Soul of Man under Socialism," see Williams, "Roots of Wilde's Socialist *Soul*."

115. Wilde, "Happy Prince," 275–76.

116. Wilde, "Happy Prince," 276.

117. Von Eckardt, *Oscar Wilde's London*, 116–19. In a report on "The Sanitary Circumstances of London Dressmakers," Dr. William Ord documented working conditions two decades before Wilde's time. He concluded that "the hours of work are generally too long. . . . In a considerable number of houses the arrangement appears to be as follows:—After breakfast at 8 a.m. the girls commence work at 8:30 a.m., and continue, with an interval of half an hour for dinner, and another half hour for tea, till eight or nine o'clock at night. In the season these hours are much extended. . . . In a number of houses the earliest time of quitting work during the season, is 10 or 11 o'clock, and under the pressure of court ceremonials, the work is often carried on far into the night." William Ord, "The Sanitary Circumstances of London Dressmakers," in *"Golden Times": Human Documents of the Victorian Age*, ed. E. Royston Pike (New York: Frederick A. Praeger, 1967), 171–72. Pike's collection contains a great deal of similar evidence about the lives of workers, and dressmakers in particular, in the middle Victorian period.

118. Quoted in Gavin Weightman and Steve Humphries, *The Making of Modern London: 1815–1914* (London: Sidgwick and Jackson, 1983), 63–64.

119. Wilde, "Happy Prince," 273.

120. Quoted in "Ladies Are to Blame [London Dressmakers in Evidence, Children's Employment Commission, 2nd Report]," in Pike, *Golden Times*, 179.

121. Thomas H. Bell, *Oscar Wilde without Whitewash*, bound typescript, Wilde B435M3 0814 [193-?], in Clark Library, University of California, Los Angeles, 440.

122. Nikolai Chernyshevsky, *What Is to Be Done? Tales of a New People*, trans. Laura Beraha (Moscow: Raduga Publishers, 1983), 210. Chernyshevsky's novel inspired a generation of Russian radicals, most famously Lenin's brother, who was executed after attempting to assassinate the czar. And its influence extended far beyond the Russian frontiers. *What Is to Be Done?* was translated into English by the American anarchist Benjamin Tucker and serialized in his paper *Liberty*. Goodway, *Anarchist Seeds beneath the Snow*, 89–90.

Edward Carpenter opened a cooperative café that operated according to the ideas laid out in the novel. Alex Butterworth, *The World That Never Was: A True Story of Dreamers, Schemers, Anarchists and Secret Agents* (New York: Pantheon Books, 2010), 238.

Later, Emma Goldman, Alexander Berkman, Modska Aronstam, and Helena Minkin set up a small commune based on the novel's ideas, and Goldman and Minkin then opened a dressmaker's shop as well. Berkman took a different route, accepting the role of anarchist assassin, modelling himself after the novel's ascetic revolutionary, Rakhmetov, and even taking his name as a *nom de geurre*. Paul Avrich and Karen Avrich, *Sasha and Emma: The Anarchist Odyssey of Alexander Berkman and Emma Goldman* (Cambridge, Mass.: Belknap Press, 2012), 33, 35, 41; and John William Ward, introduction to *Prison Memoirs of an Anarchist*, by Alexander Berkman, xvi.

Berkman wrote, "My own individuality is entirely in the background; aye, I am not conscious of my personality in matters pertaining to the Cause. I am simply a revolutionist, a terrorist by conviction, an instrument for furthering the cause of humanity; in short, a Rakhmetov." Berkman, *Prison Memoirs of an Anarchist*, 13.

Historian Alex Butterworth notes that Rakhmetov was "seized upon as the very model of a revolutionary. . . . That Chernyshevsky had intended the characterization as a critique of the follies of youth did nothing to deter young people from aping Rakhmetov's manner and demeanor." Butterworth, *World That Never Was*, 57.

On the influence of Chernyshevsky's book across the political spectrum—from Vladimir Lenin to Ayn Rand—see Adam Weiner, "The Most Politically Dangerous Book You've Never Heard Of," *Politico*, December 2016, https://www.politico.com/magazine/story/2016/12/russian-novel-chernyshevsky-financial-crisis-revolution-214516.

123. Oscar Wilde, "The Decay of Lying," in *Collins Complete Works of Oscar Wilde*, 1083. For a short historical examination of the real-life People's Palace, with attention to Wilde's views on it, see Simon Joyce, "Castles in the Air: The People's Palace, Cultural Reformism, and the East End Working Class," *Victorian Studies* 39, no. 4 (Summer 1996): 513–38.

124. Walter Besant, *All Sorts and Conditions of Men* (Oxford: Oxford University Press, 1997), 176. Paragraph break added for clarity.

125. Besant, *All Sorts and Conditions of Men*, 104–7 (quote from 107).

126. Besant, *All Sorts and Conditions of Men*, 259. Emphasis in original.

127. Besant, *All Sorts and Conditions of Men*, 136.

128. Oscar Wilde, *A Woman of No Importance*, in *Collins Complete Works of Oscar Wilde*, 490.

129. Wilde, "Soul of Man under Socialism," 1176. Wilde argues in the same essay that "the worst slave-owners were those who were kind to their slaves, and so prevented the horror of the system being realised by those who suffered from it." He then picks up the theme again a couple of pages later, wrongly suggesting that "slavery was put down in America, not in consequence of any action on the part of the slaves, or even any express desire on their part that they should be free," but "through the grossly illegal conduct of certain agitators in Boston." Historically that is false—see, for instance, Howard Zinn, *A People's History of the United States, 1492–Present*, revised and updated ed. (New York: HarperPerennial, 1995), 188–89—but Wilde's larger point is simply that "misery and poverty are so absolutely degrading, and exercise such a paralysing effect over the nature of men, that no class is ever really conscious of its own suffering." Wilde, "Soul of Man under Socialism," 1174, 1176–77.

Wilde's error has a pedigree. A century earlier, William Godwin, who is often cited as the first philosophical anarchist, had argued that though the "slaves in the West Indies . . . are contented with their situation [because] they are not conscious of the evils [under which they live]," that was no defense of slavery but the opposite, since it demonstrated how thoroughly degraded their condition was. Quoted in Weir, *Anarchy and Culture*, 35.

130. "Oscar Wilde to the Secretary of the Beaumont Trust (February 22, 1886)," in *Complete Letters of Oscar Wilde*, 278–79. He showed a like interest in Toynbee Hall, an institution in the Whitechapel area, associated with the "Settlement Movement" and offering educational and cultural programs to the residents in poor areas. See Paul T. Philips, "Settlement Movement," in *Victorian Britain: An Encyclopedia*, ed. Sally Mitchell (New York: Garland, 1988), 707–8.

Wilde sent the library there a copy of *The Happy Prince and Other Tales*, and with it a note expressing his "hope that it will give pleasure to some of your readers." "Oscar Wilde to the Librarian of Toynbee Hall (Postmark July 4, 1888)," in *Complete Letters of Oscar Wilde*, 354.

Later he was invited to lecture there. He declined, citing his ill health, but he promised, "Some day I will give Toynbee Hall a lecture on Irish Art if I can get someone to help me with a magic lantern—I think that pictures are really necessary to give a proper idea of what one is talking of." "Oscar Wilde to Henrietta Barnett (November 1889?)," in *Complete Letters of Oscar Wilde*, 415. So far as I know, the lecture never took place.

131. Besant would likely have found Wilde's enthusiasm puzzling, as he himself was, on the one hand, disappointed in the Palace's focus on technical instruction and, on the other, disdainful of "those poor creatures who think they lead lives devoted to art" while they "grow silly over blue china." Besant, *All Sorts and Conditions of Men*, 115.

Besant further parodied the Aesthetic movement, and Wilde in particular, in the novel *The Monks of Thelema*, presenting the young aesthetes as object lessons to caution against "the effect of too much cultivation on a weak brain." Quoted in Angela Kingston, *Oscar Wilde as a Character in Victorian Fiction* (New York: Palgrave Macmillan, 2007), 23.

132. Oscar Wilde, "The Truth of Masks," in *Collins Complete Works of Oscar Wilde*, 1169.

133. Oscar Wilde, "Pen, Pencil and Poison: A Study in Green," in *Collins Complete Works of Oscar Wilde*, 1095.

134. Quoted in Ellmann, *Oscar Wilde*, 310.

135. Wilde, "House Beautiful," 925.

136. "To discern the beauty of a thing is the finest point to which we can arrive. Even a colour-sense is more important, in the development of the individual, than a sense of right and wrong." Wilde, *Critic as Artist*, 1154.

137. Wilde, "English Renaissance of Art," 3.

138. Quoted in Morris, *Declaring His Genius*, 103.

139. Quoted in Ellmann, *Oscar Wilde*, 191.

140. Ellmann, *Oscar Wilde*, 85; Oscar Wilde, "Mr Pater's *Appreciations*," in *Uncollected Oscar Wilde*, 144. On Pater's influence on Wilde, compared to that of Ruskin, see Ellmann, *Oscar Wilde*, 47–52.

141. Walter Pater, *The Renaissance* (New York: Random House, no date), 197.

142. Wilde, "English Renaissance of Art," 26. Compare also with this, later, from *Dorian Gray*: "Yes: There was to be . . . a new Hedonism that was to recreate Life, and to save it from that harsh, uncomely Puritanism that is having, in our day, its curious revival. It was to have its service of the intellect, certainly; yet, it was never to accept any theory or system that would involve sacrifice of any mode of passionate experience. Its aim, indeed, was to be experience itself, and not the fruits of experience. . . . [It] was to teach man to concentrate himself upon the moments of a life that is itself but a moment." Wilde, *Picture of Dorian Gray*, 99–100.

143. "Theories of a Poet," in *Oscar Wilde: Interviews and Recollections*, vol. 1, 39.

144. Wilde, "Soul of Man under Socialism," 1197.

145. Emma Goldman, "The Tragedy at Buffalo (*Free Society*, October 1901)," in *Mother Earth Bulletin*, series 1, vol. 1, *1906–1907* (New York: Greenwood Reprint, 1968), 15.

146. Edward Carpenter, *My Days and Dreams, Being Autobiographical Notes* (London: George Allen & Unwin, 1916), 115. Carpenter described the society he envisaged as "embody[ing] to the fullest extent the two opposite poles of Communism and Individualism in one vital unity." Quoted in John Lauritsen and David Thorstad, *The Early Homosexual Rights Movement (1964–1935)*, revised ed. (Ojai, Calif.: Times Change Press, 1995), 95; and Goodway, *Anarchist Seeds beneath the Snow*, 60.

147. Berkman, "ABC of Anarchism," 288.

148. Berkman, "ABC of Anarchism," 288–89.

149. "To be good, according to the vulgar standard of goodness, is obviously quite easy. It merely requires a certain amount of sordid terror, a certain lack of imaginative thought, and a certain low passion for middle-class respectability." Wilde, "Critic as Artist," 1154.

150. Quoted in Ellmann, *Oscar Wilde*, 62.

151. Wilde, "Soul of Man under Socialism," 1184. Jean Grave, like Wilde, declared that "art is the supreme manifestation of individualism." Quoted in Goodway, *Anarchist Seeds beneath the Snow*, 79.

152. Wilde, "Soul of Man under Socialism," 1193.

153. Peter Kropotkin, "[Letter to Robert Ross], May 6, 1905," in *Robert Ross, Friend of Friends*, ed. Margery Ross (London: Jonathan Cape, 1952), 112.

154. Peter Kropotkin, *Mutual Aid: A Factor of Evolution* (London: William Heinemann, 1902), 295.

155. Wilde, "Soul of Man under Socialism," 1186.

156. Wilde, "Critic as Artist," 1121–22. This attitude dates back to his time at Oxford. In his commonplace book from that period, Wilde had written, "'Not to conform to what is established' is merely a synonym for progress." Oscar Wilde, "Commonplace Book," in *Oscar Wilde's Oxford Notebooks*, 108.

157. Peter [Kropotkin], "Letter to Nettlau (March 5, 1902)," *Anarchy Archives*, http://dwardmac.pitzer.edu/Anarchist_Archives/kropotkin/kropotkintonetllau3502.html.

158. George Woodcock and Ivan Avakumovic, *Peter Kropotkin: From Prince to Rebel* (Montreal: Black Rose Books, 1990), 282, 281.

159. Quoted in Marshall, *Demanding the Impossible*, 322.

160. Kropotkin, "[Letter to Robert Ross], May 6, 1905)," 112.

161. Shaw, for one, described Kropotkin as "amiable to the point of saintliness." Quoted in Woodcock and Avakumovic, *Peter Kropotkin*, 225.

162. Kropotkin then concludes: "But even these remarks will show you how highly I think of the book ["De Profundis"], as I see in it a *human document* of deep perception, a piece of inner human analysis, which reveals our nature so deeply that the book permits me to reason about its cries and moans as upon real life,—generalized by the force of genius." Kropotkin, "[Letter to Robert Ross], May 6, 1905," 113. Emphasis in original.

163. Thomas Bell, discussing anarchism with Wilde toward the end of his life, found that "the man of whom he considered himself a follower was Peter Kropotkin, and he accepted Kropotkin's views in full, 'Anarchist-Communism.'" Bell, *Oscar Wilde without Whitewash*, 93. See also 398.

164. Wilde, "Phrases and Philosophies for the Use of the Young," 1245. On education and overeducation, Wilde was remarkably egalitarian in his views, suggesting, "it is better for the country to have a good general standard of education than to have, as we have in England, a few desperately over-educated and the remainder ignorant. One of the things which delighted me most in America was that the Universities reached a class that we, in Oxford, have never been able to touch, the sons of the farmers and the people of moderate means. These are the people to whose wants the university should adapt its curriculum and expenses so that it should be able to reach them." "Oscar Wilde: The Arch-Aesthete on Aestheticism [*The Montreal Daily Star*, May 15, 1882]," in *Oscar Wilde: Interviews and Recollections*, vol. 1, 86.

165. Ellmann, *Oscar Wilde*, 120–21.

166. James Rennell Rodd, "My Quarrel with Oscar Wilde," in *Oscar Wilde: Interviews and Recollections*, vol. 1, 111–22.

167. Ellmann, *Oscar Wilde*, 412–13. The display was likely a con: "Another well-known form of begging was the 'shallow lay'—standing in the street in cold weather with scanty clothing and trying to excite the compassion of the passers-by." J. J. Tobias, *Crime and Industrial Society in the 19th Century* (London: B. T. Batsford, 1967), 75. See also Thompson, *The Making of the English Working Class*, 266.

168. Ellmann, *Oscar Wilde*, 412.

169. Quoted in George Woodcock, *The Paradox of Oscar Wilde* (New York: Mac-Millan, 1950), 211–12.

170. Quoted in Woodcock, *Paradox of Oscar Wilde*, 212.

171. Quoted in Ellmann, *Oscar Wilde*, 216.

172. Woodcock, *Paradox of Oscar Wilde*, 212–13.

173.   Ellmann, *Oscar Wilde*, 121. Wilde expected, when he was released from prison, to be "completely penniless, and absolutely homeless." But he said that this change in status did not distress him. "I would gladly and readily beg my bread from door to door. If I get nothing from the house of the rich, I would get something from the house of the poor. Those who have much are often greedy. Those who have little always share." Wilde, "De Profundis," 1019.

174.   Wilde, "Decay of Lying," 1075–76.

175.   Wilde, *Picture of Dorian Gray*, 31.

176.   Wilde, "Soul of Man under Socialism," 1175.

177.   Wilde, "Soul of Man under Socialism," 1175–76.

178.   Ellmann, *Oscar Wilde*, 284.

179.   Weightman and Humphries, *Making of Modern London*, 151; John Quail, *The Slow-Burning Fuse: The Lost History of the British Anarchists* (London: Paladin, 1978), 84–86; and Butterworth, *World That Never Was*, 248.

180.   Quoted in Thompson, *William Morris*, 531.

181.   Woodcock and Avakumovic, *Peter Kropotkin*, 232. One of the leaders of the strike was John Burns, who was later elected to Parliament and served as a cabinet minister. In that latter role, in 1912, he interceded at Kropotkin's urging to prevent the anarchist Errico Malatesta from being deported. Woodcock and Avakumovic, *Peter Kropotkin*, 264–65.

Burns had been imprisoned himself in 1887 after "Bloody Sunday," and Wilde twice suggested him as a possible author for "a prison-reform preface" to "The Ballad of Reading Gaol." "Oscar Wilde to Robert Ross (c. May 4, 1898)," in *Complete Letters of Oscar Wilde*, 1060. See also "Oscar Wilde to Leonard Smithers (c. May 4, 1898)," in *Complete Letters of Oscar Wilde*, 1059; and Thompson, *William Morris*, 530.

182.   Wilde, *Soul of Man under Socialism*, 1174.

183.   Wilde, *Soul of Man under Socialism*, 1183.

184.   Wilde, *Soul of Man under Socialism*, 1183–84.

185.   One person quick to grasp the implications was Emma Goldman. She wrote: "Oscar Wilde defines a perfect personality as 'one who develops under perfect conditions, which is not wounded, maimed, or in danger.' A perfect personality, then, is only possible in a state of society where man is free to choose the mode of work, the conditions of work, and the freedom to work. One to whom the making of a table, the building of a house, or the tilling of the soil, is what the painting is to the artist and the discovery to the scientist,—the result of inspiration, of intense longing, and deep interest in work as a creative force. That being the ideal of Anarchism, its economic arrangements must consist of voluntary productive and distributive associations, gradually developing into free communism . . . [while it] also recognizes the right of the individual, or numbers of individuals, to arrange at all times for other forms of work, in harmony with their tastes and desires." Emma Goldman, "Anarchism: What It Really Stands For," in *Anarchism and Other Essays* (New York: Dover, 1969), 55–56.

Chapter 3: Love Is Law

1.   For a short overview of the Victorian discourse concerning the New Woman, see "The New Woman" and the collected readings in that section of *The Fin de Siècle: A*

Reader in Cultural History, c. 1880–1900, ed. Sally Ledger and Roger Luckhurst (Oxford: Oxford University Press, 2000), 75–96.

2.   Quoted in Karl Beckson, *London in the 1890s: A Cultural History* (New York: W. W. Norton, 1992), 142.

3.   Quoted in Beckson, *London in the 1890s*, 141.

4.   "Oscar Wilde to Wemys Reid (April 1887)," in *The Complete Letters of Oscar Wilde*, ed. Merlin Holland and Rupert Hart-Davis (New York: Henry Holt, 2000), 297.

5.   Arthur Fish, "Memories of Oscar Wilde," in *Oscar Wilde: Interviews and Recollections*, vol. 1, ed. E. H. Mikhail (New York: Barnes & Noble, 1979), 152–53.

6.   Eleanor Fitzsimons, *Wilde's Women: How Oscar Wilde Was Shaped by the Women He Knew* (New York: Overlook Duckworth, 2016), 167.

7.   Quoted in Fitzsimons, *Wilde's Women*, 162.

8.   Fitzsimons, *Wilde's Women*, 164–65.

9.   Fitzsimons, *Wilde's Women*, 157.

10.   Quoted in Fitzsimons, *Wilde's Women*, 164.

11.   Fitzsimons, *Wilde's Women*, 165.

12.   Fitzsimons, *Wilde's Women*, 162–63, 179.

13.   Fitzsimons, *Wilde's Women*, 163; H. M. Sanwick, "A Kind Man," in *Oscar Wilde: Interviews and Recollections*, vol. 1, 141.

14.   Fitzsimons, *Wilde's Women*, 163.

15.   Fitzsimons, *Wilde's Women*, 173.

16.   In "De Profundis," Wilde writes, "Christ had no patience with the dull lifeless mechanical systems that treat people as if they were things, and so treat everybody alike: as if anybody, or anything for that matter, was like aught else in the world. . . . He would not hear of life being sacrificed to any system of thought or morals." Oscar Wilde, "De Profundis," in *Collins Complete Works of Oscar Wilde* (Glasgow: HarperCollins, 2003), 1035–36.

17.   Quoted in Ada Leverson, "The Last First Night," in *Oscar Wilde: Interviews and Recollections*, vol. 2, 269.

18.   Oscar Wilde, *Lady Windermere's Fan*, in *Collins Complete Works of Oscar Wilde*.

19.   Richard Ellmann, *Oscar Wilde* (New York: Alfred A. Knopf, 1988), 367.

20.   Quoted in Terence Kissack, *Free Comrades: Anarchism and Homosexuality in the United States, 1895–1917* (Oakland: AK Press, 2008), 47.

21.   Quoted in Emer O'Sullivan, *The Fall of the House of Wilde: Oscar Wilde and His Family* (New York: Bloomsbury Press, 2016), 350–51.

22.   Oscar Wilde, *A Woman of No Importance*, in *Collins Complete Works of Oscar Wilde*, 507.

23.   Wilde, *Woman of No Importance*, 490.

24.   Wilde, *Woman of No Importance*, 502–3.

25.   Wilde, *Woman of No Importance*, 509.

26.   Wilde, *Woman of No Importance*, 514.

27.   Quoted in Gilbert Burgess, "An Ideal Husband," in *Oscar Wilde: Interviews and Recollections*, vol. 1, 240–41.

28.   Hester Worsley initially holds this view: "If a man and a woman have sinned, let them both be branded. Set a mark, if you wish, on each, but don't punish the one and let

the other go free. Don't have one law for men and another for women." Wilde, *Woman of No Importance*, 483–84.

Some feminists, such as Christabel Pankhurst, went further, urging celibacy. Judy Greenway, "Speaking Desire: Anarchism and Free Love as Utopian Performance in Fin de Siècle Britain," in *Anarchism and Utopianism*, ed. Laurence Davis and Ruth Kinna (Manchester: Manchester University Press, 2009) 164; and Elaine Showalter, *Sexual Anarchy: Gender and Culture at the Fin de Siècle* (New York: Penguin Books, 1990), 22.

On the relationship between nineteenth-century feminists and purity crusaders, see Alan Sinfield, *The Wilde Century: Effeminacy, Oscar Wilde, and the Queer Moment* (New York: Columbia University Press, 1994), 68–69; and Showalter, *Sexual Anarchy*, 21–22. "I think that there should be no law": quoted in Burgess, "Ideal Husband," 240–41.

29.   He writes of Christ, "His morality is all sympathy, just what morality should be. If the only thing he had ever said had been, 'Her sins are forgiven her because she loved much,' it would have been worth while dying to have said it." Wilde, "De Profundis," 1035; Wilde, *Woman of No Importance*, 510.

30.   Wilde, *An Ideal Husband*, in *Collins Complete Works of Oscar Wilde*, 528.

31.   Wilde, *Ideal Husband*, 552.

32.   Goring separates public from private, logic from emotion, politics from morals, male from female—separates, and elevates the one above the other. Wilde had previously decried exactly this division. Writing in the *Woman's World*, defending the participation of women in political life, he had argued, "The cultivation of separate sorts of virtues and separate ideals of duty in man and woman has led to the whole social fabric being weaker and unhealthier than it need be." Quoted in Gary Schmidgall, *The Stranger Wilde; Interpreting Oscar* (New York: Dutton, 1994), 382–83.

Julia Prewitt Brown understands Goring as arguing that "given the institutions of government and marriage as they are, this is the most we can expect, the closest to an 'ideal' that we can hope to achieve: corrupt but not wholly bad leaders, who can sometimes be redeemed by the forgiveness of their blind, accepting wives." Julia Prewitt Brown, *Cosmopolitan Criticism: Oscar Wilde's Philosophy of Art* (Charlottesville: University of Virginia Press, 1997), 86.

33.   Wilde, *Ideal Husband*, 579.

34.   Quoted in Burgess, "Ideal Husband," 241.

35.   Wilde, *Ideal Husband*, 552–53. Paragraph breaks added for clarity.

36.   Wilde, *Ideal Husband*, 533–34.

37.   Wilde, *Ideal Husband*, 552.

38.   Wilde, *Ideal Husband*, 561, 579.

39.   In this rejection of idealism—morally, politically, and dramatically—Wilde may be following Ibsen, or Shaw's interpretation of Ibsen. See J. L. Wisenthal, ed., *Shaw and Ibsen: Bernard Shaw's The Quintessence of Ibsenism and Related Writings* (Toronto: University of Toronto Press, 1979).

40.   Quoted in Karl Beckson, "An Ideal Husband," in *The Oscar Wilde Encyclopedia* (New York: AMS Press, 1998), 151.

41.   Wilde, *Ideal Husband*, 539.

42.   Robert Chiltern's corruption in each case concerns the funding for a canal—the Suez, whose plans he sold to speculators, and the Argentine, which is a fraud reliant

on his official approval. That Wilde would choose these instances to illustrate breaches of integrity suggests too a scaling-up of his moral (or antimoral) diagnosis into a political critique of imperialism. For though Chiltern was ready to profit from the Suez project, even by illicit means, his justification is that it was *not* a mere money-making scheme but also "a very great and splendid undertaking. It gave us our direct route to India. It had imperial value. It was necessary that we should have control. This Argentine scheme is a commonplace Stock Exchange swindle." Wilde, *Ideal Husband*, 526.

In other words, Chiltern supports those projects that advance the cause of empire but not those that merely provide the opportunity for conniving people to make money. Of course, the validity of that justification would depend on the empire having a moral purpose of its own and not simply working as a system of extortion. Chiltern's elegy to pure power, delivered later in the play (as well as Wilde's own statements concerning the nature of imperialism) would seem to undercut Chiltern's rationalization. Thus, we can read his justification as an extension of his corruption.

43. Wilde, *Ideal Husband*, 537.

44. Wilde, *Ideal Husband*, 537–39.

45. Wilde, *Ideal Husband*, 543. Anticipating the lines given to Goring, Wilde had written of Chuang Tzu: "The accumulation of wealth is to him the origin of evil," and "the prizes of the world degrade a man as much as the world's punishments. The age is rotten with its worship of success." Oscar Wilde, "A Chinese Sage," in *The Artist as Critic: Critical Writings of Oscar Wilde*, ed. Richard Ellmann (Chicago: University of Chicago Press, 1982), 224–25.

Later, from prison, he was to write in "De Profundis": "A man whose desire is to be something separate from himself, to be a Member of Parliament, or a successful grocer, or a prominent solicitor, or a judge, or something equally tedious, invariably succeeds in being what he wants to be. That is his punishment. Those who want a mask have to wear it." Wilde, "De Profundis," 1037–38.

46. Wilde, *Ideal Husband*, 565. Ellipses in original.

47. Wilde, *Ideal Husband*, 536.

48. Wilde, *Ideal Husband*, 543.

49. Wilde, *Ideal Husband*, 516, 522, 582.

50. Wilde, *Woman of No Importance*, 480.

51. William Archer, "*The Importance of Being Earnest* (*World*, February 20, 1895)," in *Oscar Wilde: The Critical Heritage*, ed. Karl Beckson (New York: Barnes & Noble, 1970), 190.

52. Oscar Wilde, *The Importance of Being Earnest*, in *Collins Complete Works of Oscar Wilde*, 369–70.

53. Eric Bentley, "Wilde's Use of Ironic Counterpoint," in *Readings on* The Importance of Being Earnest, ed. Thomas Siebold (San Diego: Greenhaven Press, 2001), 163.

54. Declan Kiberd, "Oscar Wilde: The Artist as Irishman," in *Wilde the Irishman*, ed. Jerusha McCormack (New Haven: Yale University Press, 1998), 13–14. One exchange (Wilde, *Importance of Being Earnest*, 377) moves quickly from gender to economics and then back:

> Chasuble: Reading Political Economy, Cecily? It is wonderful how girls are educated nowadays. I suppose you know all about relations between Capital and Labour?
>
> Cecily: I am afraid I am not learned at all. All I know is about the relations between Capital and Idleness—and that is merely from observation. So I don't suppose it is true.
>
> Miss Prism: Cecily, that sounds like Socialism! And I suppose you know where Socialism leads to?
>
> Cecily: Oh, yes! That leads to Rational Dress, Miss Prism.

55.   I have taken this point from O'Sullivan, *Fall of the House of Wilde*, 370.

56.   Wilde, *Importance of Being Earnest*, 408. Prism's need for stable moral categories leads her to oppose repentance and redemption, without realizing that she is rejecting the very essence of Christianity. She says, "I am not in favor of these modern manias for turning bad people into good people at a moment's notice. As a man sows so let him reap." Cecily, mishearing, objects both to Prism's punitive outlook and to strict gender roles: "But men don't sew, Miss Prism. . . . And if they did, I don't see why they should be punished for it. There is a great deal too much punishment in the world." Wilde, *Importance of Being Earnest*, 376. Ellipses in original.

57.   Wilde, *Importance of Being Earnest*, 415.

58.   Ellmann, *Oscar Wilde*, 422.

59.   Quoted in Neil McKenna, *The Secret Life of Oscar Wilde* (New York: Basic Books, 2005), 308.

60.   O'Sullivan, *Fall of the House of Wilde*, 369.

61.   George Orwell, "'Lady Windermere's Fan': A Commentary by George Orwell," in *Orwell: The Lost Writings*, ed. W. J. West (New York: Arbor House, 1985), 168. For a comparison of the aesthetic, ethical, and political thought of Wilde and Orwell, see Kristian Williams, "'Not Too Good': Orwell, Wilde, and the Saints," in *Between the Bullet and the Lie: Essays on Orwell* (Chico, Calif.: AK Press, 2017).

62.   Orwell, "Lady Windermere's Fan," 170.

63.   Oscar Wilde, "Notebook Kept at Oxford," in *Oscar Wilde's Oxford Notebooks: A Portrait of Mind in the Making*, eds. Philip E. Smith II and Michael S. Helfand (New York: Oxford University Press, 1989), 168.

64.   Brown, *Cosmopolitan Criticism*, 85–86.

65.   Beckson, *London in the 1890s*, 190.

66.   Oscar Wilde, "[Poems by Henley and Sharp]," in *Artist as Critic*, 91.

67.   Wilde, *Lady Windermere's Fan*, 464; Wilde, *Woman of No Importance*, 514; Wilde, *Ideal Husband*, 582; Wilde, *Importance of Being Earnest*, 419.

68.   Seamus Heaney, "Oscar Wilde Dedication: Westminster Abbey, 14 February 1995," in McCormack, *Wilde the Irishman*, 175.

69.   Patricia J. Anderson, "*Adult, The: The Journal of Sex*," in *The 1890s: An Encyclopedia of British Literature, Art, and Culture*, ed. G. A. Cevasco (New York: Garland, 1993), 7–8.

70.   Wilde, *Woman of No Importance*, 477, 508.

71.   Wilde, *Lady Windermere's Fan*, 451.

72. Wilde, *Woman of No Importance*, 474.

73. Oscar Wilde, *The Picture of Dorian Gray*, in *Collins Complete Works of Oscar Wilde*, 46.

74. Wilde, *Importance of Being Earnest*, 363.

75. Oscar Wilde, "Lord Arthur Savile's Crime," in *Collins Complete Works of Oscar Wilde*, 163.

76. Writing in 1888, Mona Caird described the typical Victorian marriage: "The man who marries finds that his liberty is gone, and the woman exchanges one set of restrictions for another. She thinks herself neglected if the husband does not always return to her in the evenings, and the husband and society think her undutiful, frivolous, and so forth, if she does not stay at home alone, trying to sigh him back again. The luckless man finds his wife so *very dutiful* and domesticated, and so *very* much confined to her 'proper sphere,' that she is, perchance, more exemplary than entertaining. Still, she may look injured and resigned, but she must not seek society and occupation on her own account, adding to the common mental store, bringing new interest and knowledge into the joint existence, and becoming thus a contented, cultivated and agreeable being. No wonder that while all this is forbidden we have so many unhappy wives and bored husbands. The more admirable the wives, the more profoundly bored the husbands!" Mona Caird, "From 'Marriage' (1888)," in Ledger and Luckhurst, *Fin de Siècle*, 78. Emphasis in original.

77. Oscar Wilde, "Soul of Man under Socialism," in *Collins Complete Works of Oscar Wilde*, 1181.

78. Wilde, *Picture of Dorian Gray*, 64; Wilde, "Soul of Man under Socialism," 1174.

79. Wilde, "Soul of Man under Socialism," 1181.

80. Quoted in "Bakunin: Against Patriarchal Authority (1873)," in Robert Graham, ed., *Anarchism: A Documentary History of Libertarian Ideas*, vol. 1, *From Anarchy to Anarchism (300 CE to 1939)*, (Montreal: Black Rose Books, 2005), 236.

81. Quoted in Martin Henry Blatt, *Free Love and Anarchism: The Biography of Ezra Haywood* (Urbana: University of Illinois Press, 1989), 104.

82. Quoted in Blatt, *Free Love and Anarchism*, 103, 104.

83. Emma Goldman, "Marriage and Love," in *The Traffic in Women and Other Essays on Feminism* (Ojai, Calif.: Times Change Press, 1970), 37–38.

84. Goldman, "Marriage and Love," 43.

85. "Can there be anything more humiliating, more degrading than a lifelong proximity between two strangers?" Goldman, "Marriage and Love," 39.

86. Quoted in Beckson, *London in the 1890s*, 142.

87. Quoted in Ellmann, *Oscar Wilde*, 258.

88. Joyce Bentley, *The Importance of Being Constance* (New York: Beaufort Books, 1983), 74, 80; Fitzsimons, *Wilde's Women*, 151, 157, 159.

89. Quoted in Anne Clarke Amor, *Mrs. Oscar Wilde: A Woman of Some Importance* (London: Sidgwick and Jackson, 1983), 70.

90. Fitzsimons, *Wilde's Women*, 155.

91. Amor, *Mrs. Oscar Wilde*, 86.

92. Amor, *Mrs. Oscar Wilde*, 88–90, 117.

93. Vyvyan Holland, *Son of Oscar Wilde* (New York: E. P. Dutton, 1954), 41. Cyril and Vyvyan inherited their parents' rebellious nature, as they proved in a dispute over a

children's fancy-dress party. The boys wanted to go as sailors, but, as Vyvyan later recalled, "at my father's suggestion, Cyril was to be dressed as Millais's 'Bubbles,' while I was to masquerade as Little Lord Fauntleroy." A few days before the party, the Wildes were holding a reception, and Oscar asked the boys to come down in their costumes, so that his guests could see. The boys, in protest, came down to the party nude. Sailor suits were ordered the following day. Holland, *Son of Oscar Wilde*, 33.

In a later incident, both children were expelled from school after a teacher struck Vyvyan, and Cyril rushed to his defense. Together they launched a counterattack and knocked the instructor over. Bentley, *Importance of Being Constance*, 137.

94.   Wilde never saw his sons again, and after Constance's death was denied even the permission to write them. Holland, *Son of Oscar Wilde*, 177.

95.   "Those who are faithful only know the trivial side of love: it is the faithless who know love's tragedies." Wilde, *Picture of Dorian Gray*, 25.

96.   On Wilde's letters, see Kristian Williams, "'For Constance': Oscar Wilde's Letters to His Wife," *World and I*, October 2011. For his son's account, see Holland, *Son of Oscar Wilde*.

Concerning the testimony of the French boy, there is this sad story: After the publication of his memoir, Vyvyan Holland received a letter from a man who, while a boy, had known Wilde in Paris as "Monsieur Sebastian." They ate lunch in the same cafe, and one day the boy, putting on his coat, "clumsily upset something, perhaps a salt-cellar," on the gentleman's table. "He said nothing, but my mother scolded me to apologise." Wilde kindly turned to the mother, "Be patient with your little boy. One must always be patient with them. If, one day, you should find yourself separated from him—" But the child interrupted, curious: "'Have you got a little boy?' 'I've got two.' 'Why don't you bring them here with you?' [. . .] 'They don't come here with me because they are too far away.'" Monsieur Sebastian then "took my hand, drew me to him, and kissed me on both cheeks," saying a few words, quietly, in English. As the child left, he looked back, and saw that Monsieur Sebastian was crying. The next day, the gentleman was not at his usual table, and another patron asked the boy if he had understood the few English words Monsieur Sebastian had murmured. The child had not, so the stranger translated: "Oh, my poor dear boys!" he cried. Quoted in Holland, *Time Remembered after Père Lachaise* (London: Gollancz, 1966), 10–12, reprinted as "Oh, My Poor Dear Boys!" in *Oscar Wilde: Interviews and Recollections*, vol. 2, 362.

97.   "Oscar Wilde to Robert Ross (telegram) [postmark: April 12, 1898]," in *Complete Letters of Oscar Wilde*, 1054.

98.   "Oscar Wilde to Otho Holland Lloyd (telegram) [postmark: April 12, 1898]," in *Complete Letters of Oscar Wilde*, 1055.

99.   "Oscar Wilde to Carlos Blacker [April 12 or 13, 1898]," in *Complete Letters of Oscar Wilde*, 1055.

100.   Amor, *Mrs. Oscar Wilde*, 226.

101.   "Oscar Wilde to Robert Ross [c. March 1, 1899]," in *Complete Letters of Oscar Wilde*, 1128.

102.   "Oscar Wilde to George Alexander [August 1894]," in *Complete Letters of Oscar Wilde*, 599–600. Emphasis in original.

103.   "Oscar Wilde to Frank Harris, June 20, 1900," in *Complete Letters of Oscar Wilde*, 1189; Ellmann, *Oscar Wilde*, 521.

Chapter 4: A Language of Love

1. Richard Ellmann, *Oscar Wilde* (New York: Alfred A. Knopf, 1988), 275; Neil McKenna, *The Secret Life of Oscar Wilde* (New York: Basic Books, 2005), 7.

2. Nicholas Frankel, *Oscar Wilde: The Unrepentant Years* (Cambridge, Mass.: Harvard University Press, 2017), 26.

3. Quoted in McKenna, *Secret Life of Oscar Wilde*, 33. Concerning Wilde's time with Whitman, see McKenna, *Secret Life of Oscar Wilde*, 32–33; Ellmann, *Oscar Wilde*, 167–71. On Whitman's significance for gay culture, see Nicholas C. Edsall, *Toward Stonewall: Homosexuality and Society in the Modern Western World* (Charlottesville: University of Virginia Press, 2003), 65–84; Neil Miller, *Out of the Past: Gay and Lesbian History from 1869 to the Present* (New York: Alyson Books, 2006), 3–13. For Whitman's influence on anarchist sexual politics, see Terence Kissack, *Free Comrades: Anarchism and Homosexuality in the United States, 1895–1917* (Oakland: AK Press, 2008), 69–95.

4. Wilde does not seem to have ever used the word "homosexual." His preferred term was "Greek love." Quoted in McKenna, *Secret Life of Oscar Wilde*, 5.

5. Oscar Wilde, "De Profundis," in *Collins Complete Works of Oscar Wilde* (Glasgow: HarperCollins, 2003), 1042.

6. Quoted in Ellmann, *Oscar Wilde*, 324.

7. During the first trial, Queensberry's counsel read a letter from the marquess to his son, complaining repeatedly about Bosie's attempts to "defy" him. Merlin Holland, *The Real Trial of Oscar Wilde: The First Uncensored Transcript of the Trial of Oscar Wilde vs. John Douglas (Marquess of Queensberry), 1895* (New York: Fourth Estate, 2003), 216.

8. McKenna, *Secret Life of Oscar Wilde*, 281–83. Quote on 281. Queensberry had already lost one son, as he saw it, to "the Snob Queers." (Quoted in McKenna, *Secret Life of Oscar Wilde*, 319.) Bosie's older brother Francis, Viscount Drumlanrig, worked as the private secretary to Lord Rosebery, the foreign secretary and then prime minister. It was rumored—and Queensberry likely believed—that the two men were lovers. McKenna, *Secret Life of Oscar Wilde*, 248–51.

In 1894 Drumlanrig shot himself while hunting. Officially it was treated as an accident, but it was likely a suicide. McKenna, *Secret Life of Oscar Wilde*, 313–22; Linda Stratmann, *The Marquess of Queensberry: Wilde's Nemesis* (New Haven: Yale University Press, 2013), 197–98.

Queensberry's grief, along with anger and a feeling of impotence, no doubt helped motivate him in his efforts to save his younger son, though it is telling that his chosen means were domineering and abusive. McKenna, *Secret Life of Oscar Wilde*, 281–82.

The Drumlanrig incident also supplied a tactical advantage. According to several people close to the events, Queensberry had uncovered evidence compromising major figures in the Liberal Party, Rosebery included. Some speculate that he used this leverage to force the prosecution of Wilde. McKenna, *Secret Life of Oscar Wilde*, 319, 376, 402.

9. Quoted in Holland, *Real Trial of Oscar Wilde*, 119.

10. McKenna, *Secret Life of Oscar Wilde*, 288.

11. "Oscar Wilde to Lord Alfred Douglas (c. February 17, 1895)," in *The Complete Letters of Oscar Wilde*, ed. Merlin Holland and Rupert Hart-Davis (New York: Henry Holt, 2000), 632.

12. McKenna, *Secret Life of Oscar Wilde*, 333–34; Stratmann, *Marquess of Queensberry*, 209–10.

13. The exact wording is uncertain, as the note was clearly scribbled in haste and (one presumes) anger. For alternate readings, see Ellmann, *Oscar Wilde*, 438. Neil McKenna reads the card as "ponce and sodomite" and makes much of the implications for the libel case. McKenna, *Secret Life of Oscar Wilde*, 1.

14. Wilde, "De Profundis," 1000. Justice Wills likewise believed that Wilde had "no alternative but to prosecute or to be branded publicly as a man who could not deny a foul charge." Quoted in McKenna, *Secret Life of Oscar Wilde*, 337.

15. Alex Butterworth, *The World That Never Was: A True Story of Dreamers, Schemers, Anarchists and Secret Agents* (New York: Pantheon Books, 2010), 370. The accusation against Wilde might have been true, but the veracity of the witnesses was something else entirely. Many were threatened with prosecution if they refused to testify, or were bribed by detectives. One witness confided to Lord Alfred Douglas that when he told the police, "I have never had any dealings with Mr. Wilde in my life," the detective assured him, "Oh, that doesn't matter." Quoted in McKenna, *Secret Life of Oscar Wilde*, 348.

16. McKenna, *Secret Life of Oscar Wilde*, 376–78.

17. Nicholas Frankel, introduction to Oscar Wilde, *The Picture of Dorian Gray: An Annotated, Uncensored Edition*, ed. Nicholas Frankel (Cambridge, Mass.: Belknap, 2011), 17.

18. Quoted in Holland, *Real Trial of Oscar Wilde*, 110. See also Holland, *Real Trial of Oscar Wilde*, 53–55.

19. "Unsigned Notice, *Athenaeum* (June 27, 1891)," in *Oscar Wilde: The Critical Heritage*, ed. Karl Beckson (New York: Barnes & Noble, 1970), 82.

20. "Unsigned Review, *St. James's Gazette* (1890)," in *Oscar Wilde*, ed. Karl Beckson, 68–69.

21. "Unsigned Notice, *Scots Observer* (July 5, 1890)," in *Oscar Wilde*, ed. Karl Beckson, 75. It was not only the puritans who could decipher Wilde's coded references. The poet Lionel Johnson wrote, in "In Honorem Doriani Creatorisque Eius" ("In Honour of Dorian and His Creator"): "Here are apples of Sodom / Here the heart of vices / And sweet sins." Quoted in Wilde, *Dorian Gray*, ed. Frankel, 75n20.

22. McKenna, *Secret Life of Oscar Wilde*, 139–41. Quote from 39.

23. The quotes are from "Oscar Wilde to the Editor of the *St James's Gazette*, June 25, [1890]," in *Complete Letters of Oscar Wilde*, 428; "Oscar Wilde to the Editor of the *Daily Chronicle*, June 30, [1890]," in *Complete Letters of Oscar Wilde*, 435; "Oscar Wilde to the Editor of the *Scots Observer*, July 9, [1890]," in *Complete Letters of Oscar Wilde*, 439. On the moral of *Dorian Gray*, see Kristian Williams, "Dorian Gray and the Moral Imagination," *Common Review* 8, no. 3 (Winter 2010): 26–33.

24. Quoted in Holland, *Real Trial of Oscar Wilde*, 79. Wilde—and his publishers—had been careful to remove anything too definitely homoerotic from the text, including references to cruising and male prostitution. For details of this editing process, as well as the restored text, see Nicholas Frankel's lovely and erudite edition of *The Picture of Dorian Gray*.

25. "Oscar Wilde to Ada Leverson [Early December 1894]," in *Complete Letters of Oscar Wilde*, 625.

26. McKenna, *Secret Life of Oscar Wilde*, 320–21.

27. Carson asked seven times, with variations, "Did you think the story blasphemous?" Wilde did not refuse to answer but could not accept the question on its own terms: "I did not consider that story a blasphemous production.... The word blasphemous is not my word.... it is a word of yours." Quoted in Holland, *Real Trial of Oscar Wilde*, 70–71.

Wilde wrote to Ada Leverson, "The story is, to my ears, too direct: there is no nuance: it profanes a little by revelation." Still, he conceded, it "is at moments poisonous: which is something." "Wilde to Leverson [Early December 1894]," in *Complete Letters of Oscar Wilde*, 625.

28. Quoted in Holland, *Real Trial of Oscar Wilde*, 256.

29. Alfred Douglas, "Two Loves," in Caspar Wintermans, *Alfred Douglas: A Poet's Life and His Finest Work* (London: Peter Owen, 2007), 210–11. Douglas's other contribution to the *Chameleon*, touching the same theme, is almost a complement to the first. Titled "In Praise of Shame," it too tells of "strange dreams," this time featuring "live fire" taking on "many shapes." One of these burning apparitions speaks and says, "I am Shame / That walks with Love, I am most wise to turn / Cold lips and limbs to fire; therefore discern / And see my loveliness, and praise my name." This vision is followed by "A pomp of all the passions," lasting "all the night through." And in the morning, looking back on all that he has seen, the narrator concludes, "Of all sweet passions, shame is loveliest." Alfred Douglas, "In Praise of Shame," in Wintermans, *Alfred Douglas*, 221.

30. Quoted in Holland, *Real Trial of Oscar Wilde*, 257.

31. Quoted in Gary Schmidgall, *The Stranger Wilde: Interpreting Oscar* (New York: Dutton, 1994), 215.

32. Quoted in Peter Ackroyd, *Queer City: Gay London from the Romans to the Present Day* (New York: Abrams Press, 2018), 1.

33. Quoted in H. Montgomery Hyde, ed., *The Three Trials of Oscar Wilde* (New York: University Books, 1952), 236.

34. Quoted in Hyde, *Three Trials of Oscar Wilde*, 236.

35. Thomas Wright, *Oscar's Books* (London: Chatto & Windus, 2008), 90.

36. Wright, *Oscar's Books*, 92.

37. Oscar Wilde, "The Portrait of Mr. W. H.," in *Collins Complete Works of Oscar Wilde*, 325.

38. Michel Foucault, *The History of Sexuality*, vol. 2, *The Use of Pleasure*, trans. Robert Hurley (New York: Pantheon Books, 1985), 214.

39. Foucault discusses the subtleties of Greek sexual ethics at length in the second volume of his *History of Sexuality*.

40. Quoted in Foucault, *History of Sexuality*, vol. 2, 64; "Oscar Wilde to H. C. Marillier [Postmark: December 12, 1885]," in *Complete Letters of Oscar Wilde*, 272.

41. Foucault, *History of Sexuality*, vol. 2, 71.

42. "[S]elf-mastery and the mastery of others were regarded as having the same form.... Governing oneself, managing one's estate, and participating in the administration of the city were three practices of the same type." Foucault, *History of Sexuality*, vol. 2, 75–76.

43. Quoted in Frank Harris, "Oscar Wilde," in *Oscar Wilde: Interviews and Recollections*, vol. 1, ed. E. H. Mikhail (New York; Barnes & Noble, 1979), 420.

44.   Quoted in George Bernard Shaw, "My Memories of Oscar Wilde," in Frank Harris, *Oscar Wilde* (n.p.: Michigan State University Press, 1959), 338. Harris's own account is much more subdued. See Harris, *Oscar Wilde*, 117.

While Wilde was out on bail, Harris rented a coach and a yacht and urged an escape to the continent. Robert Pearsall, *Frank Harris* (New York: Twayne, 1970), 118.

Though in no respect an anarchist, Harris was friends with Emma Goldman and later wrote a fictionalized account of the Haymarket affair, *The Bomb*. In his review of the novel for *Mother Earth*, Alexander Berkman praised "its spirit of fairness and justice to an unpopular cause" and Harris's "supreme strength of defying respectable shams and cant." He then directly tied Harris's sympathetic treatment of the Haymarket martyrs to his "steadfastness in his friendship for Oscar Wilde," attributing both to "the same courage." Alexander Berkman, "The Bomb," in Peter Glassgold, ed., *Anarchy! An Anthology of Emma Goldman's Mother Earth* (Washington, D.C.: Counterpoint, 2001), 176–77.

45.   Quoted in McKenna, *Secret Life of Oscar Wilde*, 356.

46.   Quoted in Hyde, *Three Trials of Oscar Wilde*, 135.

47.   Quoted in Holland, *Real Trial of Oscar Wilde*, 164.

48.   Quoted in Holland, *Real Trial of Oscar Wilde*, 166.

49.   Quoted in Holland, *Real Trial of Oscar Wilde*, 174–75.

50.   McKenna, *Secret Life of Oscar Wilde*, 368.

51.   Wright, *Oscar's Books*, 89–90.

52.   McKenna, *Secret Life of Oscar Wilde*, 202. Regarding "it abolishes class distinctions": among men who loved men, it was not an uncommon attitude. Aristocrats often sought their pleasures among the less constrained and more spontaneous lower classes, sometimes believing that these same-sex cross-class relationships were more egalitarian than heterosexual relationships within a class. Karl Beckson, *London in the 1890s: A Cultural History* (New York: W. W. Norton, 1992), 194.

53.   Quoted in Miller, *Out of the Past*, 21.

54.   Edsall, *Toward Stonewall*, 109.

55.   Ives sent Wilde a collection of his verse, *Eros' Throne*, which Wilde thought too direct: "The ideas in the book are excellent, but the mode of presentation lacks charm." Quoted in Wright, *Oscar's Books*, 207.

56.   Quoted in McKenna, *Secret Life of Oscar Wilde*, 202.

57.   Oscar Wilde, "The Soul of Man under Socialism," in *Collins Complete Works of Oscar Wilde*, 1176, 1185–93.

58.   Quoted in Holland, *Real Trial of Oscar Wilde*, 253.

59.   Quoted in Holland, *Real Trial of Oscar Wilde*, 254.

60.   Quoted in Holland, *Real Trial of Oscar Wilde*, 273.

61.   There were, of course, some of each in Wilde's past, and when money and sex come together, especially illicit sex, it can be hard to discern precisely what is being purchased and at what cost. The lines between prostitution, blackmail, gift-giving, and other sorts of support or patronage can be very difficult to draw and may often be intentionally left vague.

62.   "Carson was turning the case into an issue of class. Part of Carson's problem was his inability to categorize Oscar's relations with men, for some were neither prostitutes nor social equals." Emer O'Sullivan, *The Fall of the House of Wilde: Oscar Wilde and His Family* (New York: Bloomsbury Press, 2016), 386.

63.   "Many of the boys were prostitutes, but Oscar treated them as individuals. He got to know them, took them out to lunch, to tea and took at least one on a shopping trip. He lavished gifts of clothes and silver cigarette cases on them, and entertained them in such restaurants as Kettner's, with champagne and other extravagances. He became known in the trade for his generosity." O'Sullivan, *Fall of the House of Wilde*, 348.

64.   Quoted in Holland, *Real Trial of Oscar Wilde*, 279.

65.   Wilde, "De Profundis," 1004–5.

66.   McKenna, *Secret Life of Oscar Wilde*, 207–8.

67.   Ellmann, *Oscar Wilde*, 459; Merlin Holland, introduction to *Real Trial of Oscar Wilde*, xxxi; Schmidgall, *Stranger Wilde*, 284.

68.   Quoted in Hyde, *Three Trials of Oscar Wilde*, 339.

69.   For an excerpt, see Wolf von Eckardt, Sander L. Gilman, and J. Edward Chamberlin, *Oscar Wilde's London: A Scrapbook of Virtues and Vices, 1880–1900* (Garden City, N.Y.: Anchor Press, 1987), 254, 258.

70.   Quoted in McKenna, *Secret Life of Oscar Wilde*, 77.

71.   On the age of consent, McKenna, *Secret Life of Oscar Wilde*, 78; on the penalty for assaulting a child, Eckardt, Gilman, and Chamberlin, *Oscar Wilde's London*, 258.

72.   On Booth's estimation: Beckson, *London in the 1890s*, 110. Taking issue with the *Pall Mall Gazette*'s treatment of the subject, William Morris wrote that the emphasis ought not be on the question of morality but on "the terrible and miserable unhappiness of the whole affair. There is much talk of immorality. Whatever is unhappy is immoral. It is unhappiness that must be rid of. We have nothing to do with mere immorality. We have to do with the causes that have *compelled* this unhappy way of living"—chief among them poverty and, ultimately, capitalism. "There is the closest of relations between the prostitution of the body in the streets and that of the body in the workshops." When the fundamental economic question is rightly resolved, the moral question will be seen to have no significance: "We desire that all should be free to earn their livelihood—with that freedom will come an end of these monstrosities, and true love between man and woman throughout society." Quoted in E. P. Thompson, *William Morris: Romantic to Revolutionary* (Oakland: PM Press, 2011), 705–6. Emphasis in original.

73.   Quoted in McKenna, *Secret Life of Oscar Wilde*, 80. Lesbianism did not command the same attention—for society or for Wilde. However, he did write of Sappho: "Never had Love such a singer. Even in the few lines that remain to us the passion seems to scorch and burn." Oscar Wilde, "English Poetesses," in *The Artist as Critic: Critical Writings of Oscar Wilde*, ed. Richard Ellmann (Chicago: University of Chicago Press, 1982), 102.

74.   Quoted in Edsall, *Toward Stonewall*, 18.

75.   John Briggs et al., *Crime and Punishment in England: An Introductory History* (New York: St. Martin's Press, 1996), 203.

76.   As Foucault put it: "Sodomy was a category of forbidden acts; their perpetrator was nothing more than the juridical subject of them. The nineteenth-century homosexual became a personage, a past, a case history, and a childhood, in addition to being a type of life, a life form, and a morphology, with an indiscreet anatomy and possibly a mysterious physiology. . . . The sodomite had been a temporary aberration, the homosexual was now a species." Michel Foucault, *The History of Sexuality*, vol. 1, *An Introduction*, trans. Robert Hurley (New York: Pantheon Books, 1978), 43.

77.   For examples throughout the history of London, see Ackroyd, *Queer City*.

78.   Edsall, *Toward Stonewall*, 87–88.

79.   Quoted in Hanne Blank, *Straight: The Surprisingly Short History of Heterosexuality* (Boston: Beacon Press, 2012), 16.

80.   Beckson, *London in the 1890s*, 186.

81.   Quoted in Edsall, *Toward Stonewall*, 87.

82.   Blank, *Straight*, 17; Jonathan Katz, *The Invention of Heterosexuality* (New York: Penguin Books, 1995), 53–54.

83.   Peter Ackroyd offers a short lexicon of some of the more common terms used throughout history. See Ackroyd, *Queer City*, 1–5.

84.   John Lauritsen and David Thorstad, *The Early Homosexual Rights Movement (1864–1935)*, revised ed. (Ojai, Calif.: Times Change Press, 1995), 7. *Dorian Gray* describes the artist Basil Hallward's love for Dorian: "The love that he bore him—for it was really love—had nothing in it that was not noble and intellectual. It was not that mere physical admiration of beauty that is born of the senses, and that dies when the senses tire. It was such love as Michael Angelo had known, and Montaigne, and Winckelmann, and Shakespeare himself." Wilde, *The Picture of Dorian Gray*, in *Collins Complete Works of Oscar Wilde*, 92.

85.   Wright, *Oscar's Books*, 67; McKenna, *Secret Life of Oscar Wilde*, 5–6.

86.   Quoted in McKenna, *Secret Life of Oscar Wilde*, 6. In the acknowledgments, Mahaffy thanks "my old pupil Mr Oscar Wilde of Magdalen College" for "improvements and corrections all through the book." Quoted in McKenna, *Secret Life of Oscar Wilde*, 6.

87.   Wright, *Oscar's Books*, 89–90. After Wilde read *Studies of the Greek Poets*, he sent Symonds a copy of *Dorian Gray*. Beckson, *London in the 1890s*, 198.

88.   Edsall, *Toward Stonewall*, 105.

89.   Quoted in Beckson, *London in the 1890s*, 199.

90.   Beckson, *London in the 1890s*, 206–7; Edsall, *Toward Stonewall*, 107–8.

91.   Edsall, *Toward Stonewall*, 108.

92.   Quoted in Jeffrey Weeks, "Havelock Ellis and the Politics of Sex Reform," in Sheila Rowbotham and Jeffrey Weeks, *Socialism and the New Life: The Personal and Sexual Politics of Edward Carpenter and Havelock Ellis* (London: Pluto Press, 1977), 152.

93.   David Weir, *Anarchy and Culture: The Aesthetic Politics of Modernism* (Amherst: University of Massachusetts Press, 1997) 189; Edsall, *Toward Stonewall*, 106.

94.   Quoted in Beckson, *London in the 1890s*, 22.

95.   Miller, *Out of the Past*, 17. Ellis decided to omit Shakespeare so as to avoid controversy. Weeks, "Havelock Ellis," 160. On the Victorian concept of degeneration and its attending anxieties, see "Degeneration" and attached readings in *The Fin de Siècle: A Reader in Cultural History, c. 1880–1900*, ed. Sally Ledger and Roger Luckhurst (Oxford: Oxford University Press, 2000), 1–24.

96.   Beckson, *London in the 1890s*, 207.

97.   Quoted in Lauritsen and Thorstad, *Early Homosexual Rights Movement*, 40–41.

98.   "Greek ideals" and "cold rectitude": George Ives, "The New Hedonism Controversy," *Humanitarian*, October 1894, 295–96. "Evolutionary anarchist": quoted in John Stokes, "Wilde at Bay: The Diary of George Ives," in *Oscar Wilde: Myths, Miracles, and Imitations* (Cambridge: Cambridge University Press, 1996), 65.

99.   Ives, "New Hedonism Controversy," 297.

100. Quoted in *Complete Letters of Oscar Wilde*, 619n2.

101. "The prurient and the impotent": "Oscar Wilde to George Ives [Postmark: October 22, 1894]," in *Complete Letters of Oscar Wilde*, 619; "bomb": quoted in Stokes, "Wilde at Bay," 74.

102. Quoted in McKenna, *Secret Life of Oscar Wilde*, 200.

103. Quoted in McKenna, *Secret Life of Oscar Wilde*, 201.

104. Wright, *Oscar's Books*, 205–6. McKenna asserts, "It is almost certain that Oscar was an early recruit to the Order of Chaeronea." McKenna, *Secret Life of Oscar Wilde*, 201. John Stokes and Gary Schmidgall disagree, finding "no evidence" (Stokes) and "no indication" (Schmidgall) that Wilde joined Ives's secret society. Stokes, "Wilde at Bay," 70; Schmidgall, *Stranger Wilde*, 299.

105. Quoted in McKenna, *Secret Life of Oscar Wilde*, 201.

106. Quoted in McKenna, *Secret Life of Oscar Wilde*, 199.

107. Quoted in Stokes, "Wilde at Bay," 70–71.

108. Quoted in Stokes, "Wilde at Bay," 73.

109. Stokes, "Wilde at Bay," 80.

110. Edsall, *Toward Stonewall*, 95; Alan Sinfield, *The Wilde Century: Effeminacy, Oscar Wilde and the Queer Moment* (New York: Columbia University Press, 1994), 110.

111. Sinfield, *Wilde Century*, 110, 115.

112. Edsall, *Toward Stonewall*, 95; Elaine Showalter, *Sexual Anarchy: Gender and Culture at the Fin de Siècle* (New York: Penguin Books, 1990), 172.

113. Sinfield, *Wilde Century*, 117.

114. Hubert Kennedy, *Anarchist of Love: The Secret Life of John Henry Mackay* (New York: Mackay Society, 1983), 5.

115. Kennedy, *Anarchist of Love*, 18. As Thomas Riley makes clear, Mackay also looked back to the Greeks: "Greek is MacKay's love for this world in which we are now living, and his refusal to adapt his life to any other. Greek is his love for external beauty.... Greek is his hedonistic delight in all sensual pleasures.... Greek was his philosophical justification of his materialism and individualism.... His hate for tradition, his belief in acting according to the laws of reason and individual desire, his advocacy of truth to the point of fanaticism, his masculinity and the masculine world he lived in ... all are characteristics of Hellenic culture. Greek was his love of sports.... Greek was his love of water.... And then there is the attraction he felt for boys, for youths from fourteen to eighteen, preferably boys from the working class. Most important of all is his Hellenic faith in the individual and the individual's sovereignty, not the great individual's but the sacred sovereignty of every man.... His Hellenic character made him an anarchist." Thomas A. Riley, *Germany's Poet-Anarchist: John Henry Mackay* (New York: Revisionist Press, 1972), 9.

116. Quoted in Kennedy, *Anarchist of Love*, 9.

117. Kissack, *Free Comrades*, 163–64.

118. Kissack, *Free Comrades*, 132–33; Tucker quoted in Kissack, *Free Comrades*, 30.

119. "The point of bunburying is its exit from categories." O'Sullivan, *Fall of the House of Wilde*, 370.

120. Sinfield makes a rather obvious point, but it bears repeating: "Men should be what-is-called-feminine and women what-is-called-masculine, and vice versa, if they want. The aim is to challenge the rules, not to increase them." Sinfield, *Wilde Century*, 47.

121. Oscar Wilde, "Commonplace Book," in *Oscar Wilde's Oxford Notebooks: A Portrait of Mind in the Making*, ed. Philip E. Smith II and Michael S. Helfand (New York: Oxford University Press, 1989), 141; translation on 194.

122. When Ernest Dowson took the exiled Wilde to a brothel, hoping to encourage "a more wholesome taste," Wilde played along but left unimpressed. "The first these ten years," he said, "and it will be the last. It was like cold mutton!" And then, raising his voice, for the benefit of all nearby, "But tell it in England, for it will surely restore my character!" Quoted in H. Montgomery Hyde, *Oscar Wilde: The Aftermath* (New York: Farrar, Strauss, 1963), 311.

123. Quoted in David Goodway, *Anarchist Seeds beneath the Snow: Left-Libertarian Thought and British Writers from Williams Morris to Colin Ward* (Oakland: PM Press, 2012), 91.

124. Blank, *Straight*, 129; Katz, *Invention of Heterosexuality*, 40–41. For a veritable catalog of Victorian social anxieties—race, class, gender, sex; nation, empire, anarchism, rebellion; degeneration, disease, insanity, immorality, crime—and much else besides, see Showalter, *Sexual Anarchy*, 4–11.

125. Sinfield, *Wilde Century*, 121.

126. Sinfield, *Wilde Century*, 118.

127. Miller, *Out of the Past*, 49.

128. It is estimated that, in the United States between 1895 and 1900, there were nine hundred sermons delivered denouncing Wilde. Miller, *Out of the Past*, 48.

129. Wilde, "Portrait of Mr. W. H.," 305, 308.

130. Wilde, "Portrait of Mr. W. H.," 319–20.

131. Wilde, "Portrait of Mr. W. H.," 305, 308.

132. Wilde, "Portrait of Mr. W. H.," 302, 310.

133. Wilde, "Portrait of Mr. W. H.," 311–12, 325–27.

134. Wilde, "Portrait of Mr. W. H.," 324.

135. Wilde, "Portrait of Mr. W. H.," 345–46.

136. Wilde, "Portrait of Mr. W. H.," 348–49.

137. Wilde, "Portrait of Mr. W. H.," 350.

138. James Campbell, "Sexual Gnosticism: The Procreative Code of 'The Portrait of Mr. W. H.,'" in *Wilde Discoveries: Traditions, Histories, Archives*, ed. Joseph Bristow (Toronto: University of Toronto Press, 2013), 175 ("homoerotic genealogy"), 174 ("secret engine").

139. Campbell, "Sexual Gnosticism," 174-75. This emphasis on intellectual rather than biological reproduction may have been borrowed from Carpenter, who believed that "homogenic love" served a "special function in the propagation of the race" by creating "those children of the mind, the philosophical conceptions and ideals which transform our lives and those of society." Quoted in Showalter, *Sexual Anarchy*, 174.

140. "I rarely think that anything I write is true," Wilde testified. "Not true in the sense of correspondence to fact; to represent wilful moods of paradox, of fun, nonsense, of anything at all—but not true in the actual sense of correspondence to actual facts of life, certainly not; I should be very sorry to think it." Quoted in Holland, *Real Trial of Oscar Wilde*, 74–75.

141. Sinfield, *Wilde Century*, 19.

142. Or rather, he is simply "I." "I am that I am," as Wilde quotes Shakespeare ("Portrait of Mr. W. H.," 320.) And, importantly, "that" here can be read as "what" but also as "because." The notion of authenticity the phrase invokes is not passive or resigned but active, self-creative.

143. Wilde, "Portrait of Mr. W. H.," 302.

144. Wilde, "Soul of Man under Socialism," 1186.

145. Wilde, *Picture of Dorian Gray*, 17; Oscar Wilde, "The Decay of Lying," in *Collins Complete Works of Oscar Wilde*, 1091–92; Oscar Wilde, "The Critic as Artist," in *Collins Complete Works of Oscar Wilde*, 1154.

146. James Campbell writes, "The story's awareness of itself as an act of fiction— and, above all, its constant offering and withdrawal of the theory as a thing in which the reader might sriously entertain belief—ensure that there will be no one great Truth about queerness, no sexological taxonomy, no perfect platonic mind sex." Campbell, "Sexual Gnosticism," 185.

147. Quoted in McKenna, *Secret Life of Oscar Wilde*, 111. Emphasis in original.

148. Alan Moore et al., "The Mirror of Love," in *Brighter than You Think: Ten Short Works by Alan Moore, with Essays by Mark Sobel* (Minneapolis: Uncivilized Books, 2016), 54-62.

149. Marc Sobel, "The Mirror of Love," in *Brighter than You Think*, 64–65. Clause 28 of the Local Government Act, introduced in December 1987, made it illegal for any government agency to "intentionally promote homosexuality" or to recognize any "pretended family relationship." Quoted in Miller, *Out of the Past*, 473.

150. Stokes, "Wilde at Bay," 78. He later wrote in his diary, addressing the bullet directly: "It is thine to save me from the force of all the state." Quoted in Schmidgall, *Stranger Wilde*, 275.

151. Quoted in Stokes, "Wilde at Bay," 78.

152. When Wilde was put in prison, Constance and the boys were forced abroad. Names were changed—*Wilde* to *Holland*, *Vyvyan* to *Vivian*. Even so, when their identity was discovered, they were turned out of hotels. Vyvyan Holland, *Son of Oscar Wilde* (New York: E. P. Dutton, 1954), 59, 62–63; Joyce Bentley, *The Importance of Being Constance* (New York: Beaufort Books, 1983), 127.

Most tragically, when Cyril learned what his father had done—which was, in a sense, the secret truth at the center of his own life as well—he grew bitter with resentment and disgust. Rebelling against everything Oscar had represented, Cyril set out (as he explained to his brother) "to wipe that stain away; to retrieve, it may be, by some action of mine, a name no longer honoured in the land. . . . The more I thought of this, the more convinced I became that first and foremost, I must be a *man*. There was to be no cry of decadent artist, of effeminate aesthete, of weak-kneed degenerate." He could imagine "nothing better than to end in honourable battle for King and County." This he did. Cyril joined the army immediately upon leaving school and died in battle during the Great War. Quoted in Sinfield, *Wilde Century*, 126. Emphasis in original.

153. Beckson, *London in the 1890s*, 222; Schmidgall, *Stranger Wilde*, 289.

154. Stephen Calloway, *Aubrey Beardsley* (New York: Harry N. Abrams, 1998), 123.

155. Beckson, *London in the 1890s*, 219; Eckardt, *Oscar Wilde's London*, 71.

156. Kissack, *Free Comrades*, 53.

157. Calloway, *Aubrey Beardsley*, 123.

158. Beckson, *London in the 1890s*, 225.

159. Edward Carpenter, *My Days and Dreams, Being Autobiographical Notes* (London: George Allen & Unwin, 1916), 196.

160. "Libel": quoted in Weeks, "Havelock Ellis," 155; "debauch": quoted in Butterworth, *World That Never Was*, 370.

161. Edsall, *Toward Stonewall*, 121.

162. Beckson, *London in the 1890s*, 230; John Quail, *The Slow-Burning Fuse* (London: Paladin, 1978), 214.

163. Judy Greenway, "Speaking Desire: Anarchism and Free Love as Utopian Performace in Fin de Siècle Britain," in *Anarchism and Utopianism*, ed. Laurence Davis and Ruth Kinna (Manchester: Manchester University Press, 2009), 159–60; Quail, *Slow-Burning Fuse*, 215.

164. Quoted in Beckson, *London in the 1890s*, 230.

165. Edsall, *Toward Stonewall*, 121; Beckson, *London in the 1890s*, 230; Greenway, "Speaking Desire," 161; Weeks, "Havelock Ellis," 155; Sweeney quoted in Edsall, *Toward Stonewall*, 121.

166. Quoted in Jerusha Hull McCormack, *The Man Who Was Dorian Gray* (New York: St. Martin's Press, 2000), 232.

167. Seamus Heaney, "Oscar Wilde Dedication: Westminster Abbey, 14 February 1995," in *Wilde the Irishman*, ed. Jerusha McCormack (New Haven: Yale University Press, 1998), 175.

168. Quoted in Weeks, "Havelock Ellis," 155. The historian Nicholas Edsall argues that the very taboo helped create a sense of identity: "The more clearly the line was drawn, the more emphatically the homosexual or any other subculture was labeled as different and distinct, the more likely it was that such a subculture would develop a group consciousness, a sense of its own separateness and identity . . . [and then] a sense of solidarity within the subculture, of grievance against the society that stigmatized it, and finally . . . the desire to redefine and assert itself in its own terms." Edsall, *Toward Stonewall*, 69.

169. Quoted in Schmidgall, *Stranger Wilde*, 322.

170. Moore et al., "Mirror of Love," 59.

171. Eduard Bernstein, "On the Ocassion of a Sensational Trial," *Die Neue Zeit*, April 1895, trans. Angela Clifford, https://marxists.org/. Emphasis in original.

172. Eduard Bernstein, "The Judgment of Abnormal Sexual Intercourse," *Die Neue Zeit*, May 1895, trans. Angela Clifford, https://marxists.org/.

173. Quoted in Gregory Woods, *Homintern: How Gay Culture Liberated the Modern World* (New Haven: Yale University Press, 2016), 141.

174. Edsall, *Toward Stonewall*, 92, quote on 94.

175. Lauritsen and Thorstad, *Early Homosexual Rights Movement*, 63.

176. Woods, *Homintern*, 142; Edsall, *Toward Stonewall*, 91.

177. The petition cited expert opinion on the subject, the tolerant laws of other countries, the great men of both past and present who shared these inclinations, and the tendency of prohibition to create prostitution and facilitate blackmail. Woods, *Homintern*, 142; Edsall, *Toward Stonewall*, 91.

178. Greenway, "Speaking Desire," 159.

179. Ellmann, *Oscar Wilde*, 482. For a survey of other defenses of Wilde, see Schmidgall, *Stranger Wilde*, 283–94.

180. Reg Carr, *Anarchism in France: The Case of Octave Mirbeau* (Manchester: Manchester University Press, 1977), 94, 97n32.

181. Quoted in Ellmann, *Oscar Wilde*, 483.

182. Quoted in H. Montgomery Hyde, "Prefatory Note [to "Some Unpublished Recollections by Stuart Merrill"]," *Adam: International Review*, 1954, 7.

183. Hyde, "Prefatory Note," 6–7; Goodway, *Anarchist Seeds beneath the Snow*, 84.

184. Stokes, "Wilde at Bay," 79.

185. Kissack, *Free Comrades*, 54–56; Hal D. Sears, *The Sex Radicals: Free Love in High Victorian America* (Laurence: Regents Press of Kansas, 1977), 226–27; Greenway, "Speaking Desire," 160.

186. Peter Marshall, *Demanding the Impossible: A History of Anarchism* (Oakland: PM Press, 2010), 491.

187. Quoted in Schmidgall, *Stranger Wilde*, 287.

188. Quoted in Schmidgall, *Stranger Wilde*, 288.

189. Quoted in Greenway, "Speaking Desire," 155.

190. Kissack, *Free Comrades*, 186.

191. Kissack, *Free Comrades*, 10, 44.

192. Alexander Berkman, *Prison Memoirs of an Anarchist* (New York: New York Review of Books, 1999), 169–72.

193. Berkman, *Prison Memoirs*, 439.

194. Berkman, *Prison Memoirs*, 324–25. Likewise, just after the publication of "De Profundis," the anarchist Gustav Landauer wrote to Auguste Haushner expressing his admiration for Wilde as one who "has given us a great deal of beauty" but also confessing an ambivalent and uncertain attitude about Wilde's crimes. He writes: "That young people enjoy each other's nakedness and enter tender relationships I can only find beautiful. That women might be excluded from this, I find ugly . . . unnatural . . . repulsive." But, he warns, "we need to be careful in our judgment. . . . To use terms like 'perverted' seems entirely inappropriate. . . . It's wrong to call these artists 'sick.'" To illustrate his point, he recounts a conversation with Lord Alfred Douglas. Landauer asked "whether he didn't fear posterity's judgment," to which Douglas replied, most reasonably, "What is posterity? My posterity is my son." This attitude, Landauer remarks, "does not sound perverted in any way." In its sanity, with just a touch of defiant courage, it may even be thought admirable. Landauer concludes, "Maybe you now understand why I try to abstain from moralising when speaking about these things." Quoted in James Horrox, "The Artist as Critic: Gustav Landauer on Wilde," *Wildean: Journal of the Oscar Wilde Society*, January 2015, 64–65.

195. Wilde, "De Profundis," 981.

196. Wilde, "De Profundis," 1026.

197. Wilde, "De Profundis," 984.

198. Wilde, "De Profundis," 985.

199. Wilde, "De Profundis," 1018.

200. Wilde, "De Profundis," 985.

201. Wilde, "De Profundis," 1018.

202. Wilde, "De Profundis," 1018, 1026.

203. Wilde, "De Profundis," 1041.

204. Thomas H. Bell, *Oscar Wilde without Whitewash*, bound typescript, Wilde B435M3 0814 [193-?], in Clark Library, University of California, Los Angeles, 110–11. Emphasis in original.

Chapter 5: Refuse to Be Broken by Force

1.   "Oscar Wilde to Helena Sickert, April 25, 1892," in *The Complete Letters of Oscar Wilde*, ed. Merlin Holland and Rupert Hart-Davis (New York: Henry Holt, 2000), 166.

2.   Thomas Wright, *Oscar's Books* (London: Chatto & Windus, 2008), 233; Philip Priestley, *Victorian Prison Lives: English Prison Biography, 1830–1914* (London: Methuen, 1985), 14–16.

3.   Richard Ellmann, among others, suggests that Wilde was returned to Holloway for a few days before being moved to Pentonville. Richard Ellmann, *Oscar Wilde* (New York: Alfred A. Knopf, 1988), 479–80. Even contemporary sources disagree as to whether Wilde went back to Holloway. I have here followed H. Montgomery Hyde, based on his review of the official records. H. Montgomery Hyde, *Oscar Wilde: The Aftermath* (New York: Farrar, Strauss, 1963), 12.

4.   For details of the admission process, see Hyde, *Oscar Wilde: The Aftermath*, 4; Wright, *Oscar's Books*, 240; Priestley, *Victorian Prison Lives*, 18–23.

5.   Quoted in Frank Harris, *Oscar Wilde* (n.p.: Michigan State University Press, 1959), 194.

6.   The guard sympathized but followed his instructions: "It cut me to the heart to have to be the person to cause him his crowning shame. Warders have feelings, although their duty will not always allow them to show it.'" Anonymous, "In the Depths," in *Oscar Wilde: Interviews and Recollections*, vol. 2, ed. E. H. Mikhail (New York: Barnes & Noble Books, 1979), 328–29.

7.   Erving Goffman, "On the Characteristics of Total Institutions," in *Asylums: Essays on the Social Situation of Mental Patients and Other Inmates* (Garden City, N.Y.: Anchor Books, 1961), 14.

The prison officials were aware of this effect. As Captain Donald Shaw reported, the mandatory bath "admirably fulfils its twofold function; it insures a thorough wash, and it removes the last trace of one's former self." Quoted in Priestley, *Victorian Prison Lives*, 19.

The effect this had on Wilde in particular may be indicated by the urgency with which he sought to reverse the process upon release. He wrote to More Adey about the preparations necessary for his return, and included an amazingly long and detailed list of items to be procured ahead of time, including "a blue-serge suit from Doré and an ulster," "*and boots*," "a brown hat, and a grey hat," "*eighteen* collars made after the pattern you have," "two dozen white handkerchiefs, and a dozen with coloured borders. Also some neckties: some dark blue with white spots and diapers, and some of whatever is being worn for summer wear. I also want eight pair of socks, coloured summer things," "two or three sets of plain mother-of-pearl . . . studs." "Also, some nice French soap, Houbigant's if you can get it. . . . Also, some scent; Canterbury Wood Violet I would like, and some 'Eau de Lubin' for the toilet, a large bottle. Also some of Pritchard's tooth-powder, and a medium toothbrush," "hair-tonic," "night-shirts . . . with a turn-down collar, and a breast-pocket for a handkerchief: coloured border to collar and cuffs." He explained: "I want, for psychological reasons, to feel entirely physically cleansed of the stain and soil of prison life, so these things are all—trivial as they may sound—really of great importance." Oscar Wilde to More Adey, May 6, 1897," in *Complete Letters of Oscar Wilde*, 808–9. Emphasis in original.

8.   Quoted in Hyde, *Oscar Wilde: The Aftermath*, 2.

9.   The following schedule is from Wright, *Oscar's Books*, 241–42.

10.   "Oscar Wilde to More Adey, September 25, 1896," in *Complete Letters of Oscar Wilde*, 664.

11.   Quoted in Hyde, *Oscar Wilde: The Aftermath*, 7.

12.   [Thomas Martin], "The Poet in Prison," in Robert Harborough Sherard, *The Life of Oscar Wilde* (New York: Dodd, Mead, 1928), 391.

13.   Quoted in [Martin], "Poet in Prison," 391–92.

14.   Oscar Wilde, "Two Letters to the *Daily Chronicle* [May 28, 1897]," in *Collins Complete Works of Oscar Wilde* (Glasgow: HarperCollins, 2003), 1062.

15.   Wilde, "Two Letters [May 28, 1897]," 1062.

16.   Oscar Wilde, "Two Letters to the *Daily Chronicle* [March 24, 1898]," in *Collins Complete Works of Oscar Wilde*, 1068.

17.   Oscar Wilde, "De Profundis," in *Collins Complete Works of Oscar Wilde*, 1009–10. Kropotkin similarly observed: "[T]he regular life of the prison acts depressingly on men by its monotony and its want of impressions. . . . [It] results in an atrophy of the best qualities of men and a development of the worst of them." He adds, a little later, "In a prisoner's greyish life, which flows without passions and emotions, . . . [the] brain has no longer the energy for sustained attention; thought is less rapid, or, rather, less persistent: it loses depth." Peter Kropotkin, *In Russian and French Prisons* (New York: Schocken Books, 1971), 283, 320–21.

18.   Oscar Wilde, "The Ballad of Reading Gaol," in *Collins Complete Works of Oscar Wilde*, 888, 894, 888.

19.   Quoted in Priestley, *Victorian Prison Lives*, 137.

20.   Hyde, *Oscar Wilde: The Aftermath*, 26.

21.   Priestley, *Victorian Prison Lives*, 121–23.

22.   Donald Thomas, *The Victorian Underworld* (New York: New York University Press, 1998), 270; Priestley, *Victorian Prison Lives*, 127.

23.   Thomas, *Victorian Underworld*, 269.

24.   Quoted in Priestley, *Victorian Prison Lives*, 195.

25.   On the influence of utilitarianism, see John Briggs et al., *Crime and Punishment in England: An Introductory History* (New York: St. Martin's Press, 1996), 158–60. On that of Quakers and other religious groups, see Briggs et al., *Crime and Punishment in England*, 160–62; Randall McGowen, "The Well-Ordered Prison: England, 1780–1865," in *The Oxford History of the Prison: The Practice of Punishment in Western Society*, ed. Norval Morris and David J. Rothman (New York: Oxford University Press, 1998), 86–88.

26.   For more on the Protestant Ethic, see chapter 2.

27.   Both quoted in Priestley, *Victorian Prison Lives*, 102. For more on vice as the perceived cause of crime, see Briggs et al., *Crime and Punishment in England*, 126–27.

28.   Kropotkin, *In Russian and French Prisons*, 333–34.

29.   Alexander Berkman, "Prisons and Crime: Punishment—Its Nature and Effects," in *Prison Blossoms: Anarchist Voices from the American Past*, by Alexander Berkman, Henry Bauer, and Carl Nold, ed. Miriam Brody and Bonnie Buettner (Cambridge, Mass.: Belknap Press, 2011), 159.

30.   Percival W. H. Almy, "New Views of Mr. Oscar Wilde," in *Oscar Wilde: Interviews and Recollections*, vol. 1, ed. E. H. Mikhail, 232–33.

31.   Oscar Wilde, "The Soul of Man under Socialism," in *Collins Complete Works of Oscar Wilde*, 1182.

32.   Oscar Wilde, "A Chinese Sage," in *The Artist as Critic: Critical Writings of Oscar Wilde*, ed. Richard Ellmann (Chicago: University of Chicago Press, 1982), 224. The bamboo cage shows up again in Wilde's second letter to the *Daily Chronicle*, suggesting that Chuang Tzu was still on his mind: "With regard to the punishment of insomnia, it only exists in Chinese and in English prisons. In China it is inflicted by placing the prisoner in a small bamboo cage; in England by means of the plank bed." Wilde, "Two Letters [March 24, 1898]," 1068.

33.   Wilde, "Soul of Man under Socialism," 1182. It is not only anarchists who have suggested a causal relationship between punishment and crime. Cesare Beccaria also argued, "The severity of punishment itself emboldens men to commit the very wrongs it is supposed to prevent." Quoted in David J. Rothman, "Perfecting the Prison: United States, 1789–1865," in Morris and Rothman, *Oxford History of the Prison*, 102.

34.   Peter Kropotkin, "Prisons and their Moral Influence on Prisoners," in *The Essential Kropotkin*, ed. Emile Capouya and Keitha Tompkins (New York: Liveright, 1975), 55.

35.   Quoted in Paul Eltzbacher, *The Great Anarchists: Ideas and Teachings of Seven Major Thinkers*, trans. Steven T. Byington (Mineola, N.Y.: Dover, 2004), 245–46.

36.   Wilde, "Soul of Man under Socialism," 1181–82. Compare Wilde's argument with this line from George Woodcock's *Anarchy or Chaos*: "In a society where there is no inequality of property, and where every man's needs are satisfied, there will be no incentive to crime, except among the pathological, who are not subjects for prison or law courts." George Woodcock, *Anarchy or Chaos* (Willamantic, Conn.: Lysander Spooner, 1992), 23.

37.   Wilde, "Soul of Man under Socialism," 1181–82. Writing from an American prison a few years later, the anarchist Carl Nold reached precisely the same conclusion: "Remove poverty and ignorance; remove class-distinctions and senseless laws as well as corrupt politicians; remove private property. Give the people economical independence and political freedom in the fullest sense of the word. . . . Take away all the conditions creating and fostering crime, and thus the evil will be abolished, for without the incentive, without the necessity of stealing, robbery, etc., no sane man will turn criminal. In a society based upon the economical independence of every member, all problems of crime, criminals, and prisons will be solved by and through this very condition. . . . There, crime will be a rare exception and not the rule, as it is today. Probably instances of crime will be regarded in the light of a disease and the subject entrusted to the care—not of a jailer—but of the physician." Carl Nold, "Prisons and Crime: Crime and its Sources," in Berkman, Bauer, and Nold, *Prison Blossoms*, 190–91.

38.   Wilde later wrote in the third person of things he experienced in the first: "The result of the food . . . is disease in the form of incessant diarrhoea. . . . The wretched prisoner is then left a prey to the most weakening, depressing, and humiliating malady that can be conceived: and if, as often happens, he fails from physical weakness to complete his required revolutions at the crank or the mill, he is reported for idleness, and punished with the greatest severity and brutality." Wilde, "Two Letters [March 24, 1898]," 1067.

39.   Ellmann, *Oscar Wilde*, 495.

40.   Quoted in Frank Harris, *Oscar Wilde*, 196.

41.   Wilde, "Two Letters [March 24, 1898]," 1067.

42.   Quoted in Hyde, *Oscar Wilde: The Aftermath*, 34.

43.   Quoted in Hyde, *Oscar Wilde: The Aftermath*, 26.

44.   Hyde, *Oscar Wilde: The Aftermath*, 34n1; Richard Burdon Haldane, "Oscar Wilde in Prison" in *Oscar Wilde: Interviews and Recollections*, vol. 2, ed. E.H. Mikhail, 324; Oscar Wilde, *Complete Letters of Oscar Wilde*, 1022n5.

45.   Quoted in Hyde, *Oscar Wilde: The Aftermath*, 36–37. Emphasis in original.

46.   Peter Southerton, *Reading Gaol by Reading Town* (Stroud, UK: Berkshire Books, 1993), 33.

47.   [Martin], "Poet in Prison," 398.

48.   "Oscar Wilde to Robert Ross, October 8, 1897," in *The Complete Letters of Oscar Wilde*, 956–7.

49.   Hyde, *Oscar Wilde: The Aftermath*, 139.

50.   Wilde, "The Ballad of Reading Gaol," 894.

51.   Southerton, *Reading Gaol by Reading Town*, 44; Priestley, *Victorian Prison Lives*, 21.

52.   [Martin], "Poet in Prison," 389.

53.   Anonymous, "In the Depths," 328.

54.   Quoted in Neil McKenna, *Secret Life of Oscar Wilde*, 420.

55.   Quoted in Frank Harris, *Oscar Wilde*, 193.

56.   Haldane, "Oscar Wilde in Prison," 323.

57.   Haldane also offered some sincere, if sanctimonious, words of encouragement. He told Wilde that he "had not fully used his great literary gift, and the reason was that he had lived a life of pleasure and had not made any great subject his own. Now misfortune might prove a blessing for his career, for he had got a great subject." Wilde, Haldane says, then "burst into tears, and promised to make the attempt." Haldane later received, anonymously, a copy of "The Ballad of Reading Gaol." "It was the redemption of his promise to me." Haldane, "Oscar Wilde in Prison," 323–24.

58.   Wright, *Oscar's Books*, 243.

59.   Hyde, *Oscar Wilde: The Aftermath*, 42n4.

60.   Wilde, "Two Letters [May 28, 1897]," 1066.

61.   Anonymous, "In the Depths," 328–29.

62.   Both quoted in Wright, *Oscar's Books*, 271.

63.   Anonymous, "In the Depths," 328.

64.   Quoted in Hyde, *Oscar Wilde: The Aftermath*, 75.

65.   Quoted in Hyde, *Oscar Wilde: The Aftermath*, 77–78.

66. The second petition appears as "Oscar Wilde to the Home Secretary, November 10, 1896," in *Complete Letters of Oscar Wilde*, 667–68. The following quotations are drawn from those pages.

67. Alexander Berkman argued along similar lines: "Deprived of his liberty, his rights, and the enjoyment of life, all his natural impulses, good and bad alike, suppressed, subjugated to indignities, and disciplined by harsh and often inhumanely severe methods and generally maltreated and abused by official brutes whom he despises and hates, the young prisoner . . . is brutalised by the treatment he receives and the revolting sights he is often forced to witness in prison . . . until the perhaps undefined inclination to do wrong is turned into a strong desire, which gradually becomes a fixed determination. . . . [S]ociety had made him an outcast, and he regards it as his natural enemy; nobody had shown him any mercy, and he resolves to be as bad as he was made out to be." Berkman, "Prisons and Crime," 159–60.

68. The petition was rejected almost at once. Again the Home Office concluded, "The prisoner's fear of mental breakdown or decay of his literary capability is expressed in too lucid orderly and polished a style to cause apprehension on that point." Quoted in Hyde, *Oscar Wilde: The Aftermath*, 84.

69. Quoted in Seymour Hicks, "Unbreakable Spirit," in *Oscar Wilde: Interviews and Recollections*, vol. 2, ed. E.H. Mikhail, 286.

70. Sometimes Wilde was not as anonymous as he might have liked: Henri Bauër was told by the minister of fine arts in France that the police were watching Wilde, looking for an excuse to arrest him. Robert Harborough Sherard, *The Life of Oscar Wilde* (New York: Dodd, Mead, 1928), 419.

71. "Their cheerfulness under terrible circumstances, their sympathy for each other, their humility, their gentleness, their pleasant smiles of greeting when they meet each other, their complete acquiescence in their punishments, are all quite wonderful, and I myself learned many sound lessons from them." Wilde, "Two Letters [May 28, 1897]," 1063.

72. Quoted in Ellmann, *Oscar Wilde*, 497. See also Hyde, *Oscar Wilde: The Aftermath*, 20. Reflecting on this story, Albert Camus wrote: "Am I wrong in thinking that, at that moment, Wilde was conscious of a happiness of a kind he had never hitherto so much as imagined? All at once, he was no longer alone. . . . He realised that his brothers were not people who lived at the Ritz but men like the one who tramped ahead of him during that same exercise, muttering incoherently, or that other who was to inspire "The Ballad of Reading Gaol." Albert Camus, "The Artist in Prison," *Encounter*, March 1954, 27.

73. Later, in the *Chronicle*, Wilde wrote, "Prisoners are, as a class, extremely kind and sympathetic to each other. Suffering and the community of suffering makes people kind, and day after day as I tramped the yard I used to feel with pleasure and comfort what Carlyle calls somewhere 'the silent rhythmic charm of human companionship.'" Wilde, "Two Letters [May 28, 1897]," 1063.

74. Hyde, *Oscar Wilde: The Aftermath*, 153. Wilde wrote to Reginald Turner in anticipation of Arthur Cruttenden's visit: "You see what a good chap he is: he was one of my great friends at Reading. . . . Now I have asked him to come and stay a week here with me, so that he may have a holiday after eighteen months' hard labour. . . . You don't know, Reggie, what a pleasure it is to me to think I shall have the chance of being kind to a chap

who has been in trouble with me. I look forward to it with tears of joy and gratitude." "Oscar Wilde to Reginald Turner, June 7, 1897," in *Complete Letters of Oscar Wilde*, 887–88.

75.   See, for example, "Oscar Wilde to an Unidentified Correspondent, circa May 28, 1897," in *Complete Letters of Oscar Wilde*, 861–62; "Oscar Wilde to Frank Harris, June 13, 1897," in *Complete Letters of Oscar Wilde*, 897.

76.   "Oscar Wilde to Reginald Turner, June 7, 1897," 887.

77.   "Oscar Wilde to Major J. O. Nelson, May 28, 1897," in *Complete Letters of Oscar Wilde*, 863.

78.   Wilde, "De Profundis," 1020.

79.   See, for example, "Oscar Wilde to William Rothenstein, February 1898," in *Complete Letters of Oscar Wilde*, 1024.

80.   Wilde, "Two Letters [May 28, 1897]," 1064.

81.   *Oscar Wilde Prison Letters and Other Documents*, bound manuscript, Clark Library, University of California, Los Angeles, 21d; reprinted as "Oscar Wilde to Thomas Martin, circa April 1897," in *Complete Letters of Oscar Wilde*, 798.

82.   Wilde had begun a poem (now lost) called "The Ballad of the Fisher-Boy." It was to be "a joy-song," and, had he completed it, it would have served as a counterpoint to "Reading Gaol," "sing[ing] of liberty instead of prison, joy instead of sorrow, a kiss instead of an execution." Quoted in McKenna, *Secret Life of Oscar Wilde*, 459.

As it was, however, Wilde knew that "Reading Gaol" would be his "*chant de cygne*" and said, "I am sorry to leave with a cry of pain . . . but Life, that I have loved so much— too much—has torn me like a tiger. . . . [I am now] the ruin and wreck of what once was wonderful and brilliant, and terribly improbable." "Oscar Wilde to Carlos Blacker, March 9, 1898," in *Complete Letters of Oscar Wilde*, 1035.

83.   The crime itself—poaching rabbits—is interesting and symbolic. First, it speaks to Wilde's point that "starvation . . . is the parent of modern crime." Wilde, "Soul of Man under Socialism," 1182.

And we would do well to remember that prior to the enclosures—when the gentry privatized land by force—the forests, and the game to be found there, were part of the commons, freely available to all. A traditional poem, reportedly of Irish origin, laments: "The law locks up the man or woman / Who steals the goose from off the common / But lets the greater villain loose / Who steals the common from the goose." Quoted in Peter Linebaugh, "Stop, Thief! A Primer on the Commons and Commoning," in *Stop, Thief! The Commons, Enclosures, and Resistance* (Oakland: PM Press, 2014), 20.

84.   Wilde, "Two Letters [May 28, 1897]," 1060.

85.   On two occasions, May 25 and May 27, Michael Davitt (who had himself been jailed himself for Fenian activities) questioned the home secretary, Sir Matthew White Ridley, about the cause for Martin's dismissal. Ridley refused to cite specific reasons but insisted that they were not those reported. Stuart Mason [Christopher Millard], *Bibliography of Oscar Wilde* (London: Bertram Rota, 1967), 51.

Wilde wrote to Davitt afterward to encourage him to keep "*in some way* stirring in the matter. No one knows better than yourself how terrible life in an English prison is and what cruelties result from the stupidity of officialism, and the immobile ignorance of centralisation." "Oscar Wilde to Michael Davitt, May or June 1897," in *Complete Letters of Oscar Wilde*, 870. Emphasis in original. Wilde later suggested that Davitt write a preface to "The Ballad of Reading Gaol." "Oscar Wilde to Leonard Smithers, May 2, 1898," in *Complete Letters of Oscar Wilde*, 1058.

86.   Wilde, "Two Letters [May 28, 1897]," 1060.

87.   Wilde, "Two Letters [May 28, 1897]," 1061.

88.   Wilde, "Two Letters [May 28, 1897]," 1061.

89.   Wilde, "Two Letters [May 28, 1897]," 1064.

90.   Wilde, "Two Letters [May 28, 1897]," 1065.

91.   Wilde, "Two Letters [May 28, 1897]," 1066.

92.   Wilde, "Two Letters [May 28, 1897]," 1060–61.

93.   It was not until "De Profundis" appeared—posthumously—that Wilde's more directly autobiographical account of prison became known.

94.   Wilde, "De Profundis, 1027." Emphasis in original.

95.   Wilde, "Two Letters [May 28, 1897]," 1063.

96.   *Oscar Wilde Prison Letters and Other Documents*, Clark Library, 20a. Emphasis in original. This note and those following are also reprinted as "Oscar Wilde to Thomas Martin, circa April 1897," in *Complete Letters of Oscar Wilde*, 798; "Oscar Wilde to Thomas Martin, May 17, 1897," in *Complete Letters of Oscar Wilde*, 831. There is something special, though, in seeing the originals, those tiny scraps of paper covered over with marks from a dull pencil. The documents themselves seem to hold traces of the circumstances in which they were produced. Evidence, in this case, is not purely textual.

97.   *Oscar Wilde Prison Letters and Other Documents*, Clark Library, 21c.

98.   *Oscar Wilde Prison Letters and Other Documents*, Clark Library, 20b. Emphasis in original.

99.   Wilde, "Two Letters [May 28, 1897]," 1063.

100.   Captain Joshua Jebb, who designed Pentonville and served as the first administrator there, used the metaphor of contagion to justify the Separate System: "in depriving a prisoner of the contaminating influences arising from being associated with his fellow prisoners, all the good influences which can be brought to bear upon his character are substituted for them." Quoted in Priestley, *Victorian Prison Lives*, 36.

101.   Wilde, "Two Letters [May 28, 1897]," 1063.

102.   Mason, *Bibliography of Oscar Wilde*, 50; Nicholas Frankel, *Oscar Wilde: The Unrepentant Years* (Cambridge, Mass.: Harvard University Press, 2017), 99.

103.   Quoted in Mason, *Bibliography of Oscar Wilde*, 51–52.

104.   Wilde, "Two Letters [May 28, 1897]," 1060. Bakunin said much the same thing: "We are in fact enemies of all authority, for we realize that power and authority corrupt those who exercise them as much as those who are compelled to submit to them." Mikhail Bakunin, *The Political Philosophy of Bakunin: Scientific Anarchism*, ed. G. P. Maximoff (New York: Free Press, 1953), 249.

Later Berkman likewise wrote: "For a punishment is . . . always harmful to both sides, the punished and the punisher; harmful even more spiritually than physically, and there is no greater harm than that, for it hardens and corrupts you." Alexander Berkman, "The ABC of Anarchism," in *Life of an Anarchist: The Alexander Berkman Reader*, ed. Gene Fellner (New York: Seven Stories Press, 2005), 323.

105.   Wilde, "Ballad of Reading Gaol," 896.

106.   Wilde, "Ballad of Reading Gaol," 897.

107. The poem goes on: "Each narrow cell in which we dwell / Is a foul and dark latrine, / And the fetid breath of living Death / Chokes up each grated screen." Wilde, "Ballad of Reading Gaol," 897.

108. In the poem, neither Wooldridge nor Wilde are named directly. The poem is dedicated to "CTW," and the poet is identified only by his cell number, C.3.3.

109. Mason, *Bibliography of Oscar Wilde*, 426; Southerton, *Reading Gaol by Reading Town*, 75. Given the nature of Wooldridge's crime, it is worth recalling something that Wilde wrote in "The Soul of Man under Socialism": "Jealousy, which is an extraordinary source of crime in modern life, is an emotion closely bound up with our conceptions of property, and under Socialism and Individualism will die out. It is remarkable that in communistic tribes jealousy is entirely unknown." Wilde, "Soul of Man under Socialism," 1183.

110. Anonymous, "In the Depths," 331.

111. Southerton, *Reading Gaol by Reading Town*, 76.

112. "Oscar Wilde to Robert Ross, October 8, 1897," in *Complete Letters of Oscar Wilde*, 956.

113. "Oscar Wilde to Robert Ross, October 19, 1897," in *Complete Letters of Oscar Wilde*, 964.

114. Oscar Wilde, "The Decay of Lying," in *Collins Complete Works of Oscar Wilde*, 1077.

115. "Oscar Wilde to Laurence Housman, August 22, 1897," in *Complete Letters of Oscar Wilde*, 928.

116. "Oscar Wilde to W. R. Paton, August 1897," in *Complete Letters of Oscar Wilde*, 922.

117. Ian Small writes that Wilde "drew inspiration from the example of contemporaries such as Rudyard Kipling, who had demonstrated the appropriateness of popular vernacular forms for addressing contemporary political and social issues." Ian Small, introduction to *The Complete Works of Oscar Wilde*, vol. 1, *Poems and Poems in Prose*, ed. Bobby Fong and Karl Beckson (Oxford: Oxford University Press, 2000), xxxvi.

118. "Oscar Wilde to Edward Strangman, July 20, 1897," in *Complete Letters of Oscar Wilde*, 916; "Oscar Wilde to Robert Ross, October 19, 1897," 964. Writing to his publisher, Leonard Smithers, he explained his reasoning in somewhat different terms: "My idea is *Reynolds*. It has, for some odd reason, always been nice to me, and used to publish my poems when I was in prison, and write nicely about me. Also, it circulates widely amongst the criminal classes, to which I now belong, so I shall be read by my peers—a new experience for me." "Oscar Wilde to Leonard Smithers, October 19, 1897," in *Complete Letters of Oscar Wilde*, 966.

119. "Oscar Wilde to Leonard Smithers, February 18, 1898," in *Complete Letters of Oscar Wilde*, 1019. See also "Oscar Wilde to More Adey, February 21, 1898," in *Complete Letters of Oscar Wilde*, 1023.

120. Mason, *Bibliography of Oscar Wilde*, 417, 420, 422, 423.

121. Sherard, *Life of Oscar Wilde*, 461–63; Hyde, *Oscar Wilde: The Aftermath*, 183. Later, Bulgarian, Czech, Danish, Dutch, Finnish, Hebrew, Hungarian, Japanese, Polish, Portuguese, Serbo-Croat, Swedish, and White Russian translations would be added to this list.

122. C.3.3. (Oscar Wilde), with woodcuts by Frans Masereel, "The Ballad of Reading Gaol" (repr., London: Journeyman Press, 1978).

123. Benj. R. Tucker, "The Ballad of Reading Gaol," *Liberty*, March 1899, reprinted in *Liberty, Volumes 13–14, 1897–1905* (Westport, Conn.: Greenwood Reprint, 1970), 5. Tucker's paper, *Liberty*, later devoted more than six columns of text to reprinting excerpts of the poem's reviews. "The Critics on Oscar Wilde's Poem," *Liberty*, May 1899, reprinted in *Liberty, Volumes 13–14, 1897–1905*, 4–5, 8.

124. Edward Carpenter, *Prisons, Police, and Punishment: An Inquiry into the Causes and Treatment of Crime and Criminals* (London: Arthur C. Fifield, 1905), 8, 128–30; Carpenter again quotes from "Reading Gaol," without attribution, on 41.

125. Alexander Berkman, *Prison Memoirs of an Anarchist* (New York: Mother Earth, 1912), unpaged epigraph, as well as 342 and 389.

126. Terence Kissack, *Free Comrades: Anarchism and Homosexuality in the United States, 1895–1917* (Oakland: AK Press, 2008), 67.

127. Quoted in Kissack, *Free Comrades*, 119.

128. Kissack, *Free Comrades*, 66.

129. Quoted in Kissack, *Free Comrades*, 97.

130. Emma Goldman, "Prisons: A Social Crime and Failure," in *Anarchism and Other Essays* (New York: Dover, 1969), 111, 126.

131. *Forces of Law and Order (Selected Articles from the Anarchist Journal "Freedom")* (London: Freedom Press, 1963), unpaged epigraph. The original is from Wilde, "Soul of Man under Socialism," 1178.
Somewhat reversing this pattern, H. Montgomery Hyde dedicated his account of Wilde's prison life "To the memory of those who have toiled in the cause of penal reform." Hyde, *Oscar Wilde: The Aftermath*, v.

132. Wilde, "Two Letters [March 24, 1898]," 1066–67. The quotes in the following paragraph are likewise from these pages. Wilde's knowledge of the issues went beyond his "long personal experience." At the time of his death, among his few possessions were numerous books, pamphlets, and articles on prison reform. Wright, *Oscar's Books*, 297; Sherard, *Life of Oscar Wilde*, 411.

133. Quoted in Hyde, *Oscar Wilde: The Aftermath*, 2.

134. Wilde, "Two Letters [March 24, 1898]," 1067–68.

135. "Oscar Wilde to the Home Secretary, July 2, 1896," in *The Complete Letters of Oscar Wilde*, 658.

136. Wilde, "Two Letters [March 24, 1898]," 1068–69. Edward Carpenter points out that, at the time of Wilde's incarceration, *every* prisoner spent the first nine months in solitary—nine months, because that was thought to be the longest the *average* person could endure. Carpenter, *Prisons, Police, and Punishment*, 118–19.

137. Wilde, "Two Letters [March 24, 1898]," 1068–70.

138. Frankel, *Oscar Wilde*, 200.

139. Christopher Millard, "Oscar Wilde's Letters on Prison Reform," *Athenaeum*, May 3, 1908, 638.

140. Briggs et al., *Crime and Punishment in England*, 237; Southerton, *Reading Gaol by Reading Town*, 5; Priestley, *Victorian Prison Lives*, 123. Briggs et al. specifically note the influence of "The Ballad of Reading Gaol" in shifting popular opinion about prison

conditions (238). In 1899 the British government further ceased housing juvenile prisoners with adults, and the remainder of Wilde's proposed reforms were implemented in the first decades of the twentieth century. Frankel, *Oscar Wilde*, 321n35, 201.

141. "Oscar Wilde to Georgina Weldon, May 31, 1898," in *Complete Letters of Oscar Wilde*, 1080.

142. Southerton, *Reading Gaol by Reading Town*, 101.

143. Angela Y. Davis, *Are Prisons Obsolete?* (New York: Seven Stories Press, 2003), 40–43.

144. "Prison 'reform' is virtually contemporary with the prison itself; it constitutes, as it were, its programme. From the outset, the prison was caught up in a series of accompanying mechanisms, whose purpose was apparently to correct it, but which seem to form part of its very functioning, so closely have they been bound up with its existence throughout its long history." Michel Foucault, *Discipline and Punish: The Birth of the Prison*, trans. Alan Sheridan (New York: Vintage Books, 1977), 234.

145. Wilde, "Soul of Man under Socialism," 1194. Similar dilemmas continue to haunt today's prison abolition movement. See, for example, Davis, *Are Prisons Obsolete?*, 20.

146. Wilde, "Soul of Man under Socialism," 1180.

147. Oscar Wilde, "Phrases and Philosophies for the Use of the Young," in *Collins Complete Works of Oscar Wilde*, 1244.

148. Oscar Wilde, *The Picture of Dorian Gray*, in *Collins Complete Works of Oscar Wilde*, 134.

149. Wilde, "Ballad of Reading Gaol," 898.

150. Wilde, "Two Letters [May 28, 1897]," 1064. Emphasis added.

151. Wilde, "Two Letters [March 24, 1898]," 1070.

152. Kropotkin also struggled with the possibilities of reform: "If I were asked, what could be reformed in this and like prisons, *provided they remain prisons*, I could really only suggest improvements in detail, which certainly would not substantially ameliorate them." But, like Wilde, Kropotkin then went on to itemize a few simple changes, like higher pay for prison labour, an end to mandatory silence, and the allowance of tobacco. He concluded: "The more one reflects about the partial improvements which might be made; the more one considers them under their real, practical aspect, the more one is convinced that the few which can be made will be of no moment, while serious improvements are impossible under the present system. Some thoroughly new departure is unavoidable. The system is wrong from the very foundation." Kropotkin, *In Russian and French Prisons*, 301, 303–4. Emphasis in original.

153. In his "Ballad of Reading Gaol" it was another matter. Wilde's publishers worried about charges of libel, especially concerning the doctor, the chaplain, and the governor. Wilde insisted that, in each case, "the description is generic." Then he added, "The only people I have libeled in the poem are the Reading warders. They were—most of them—as good as possible to me. But to poetry all must be sacrificed, even warders." "Oscar Wilde to Leonard Smithers, November 19, 1897," in *Complete Letters of Oscar Wilde*, 987.

154. Wilde, "Two Letters [May 28, 1897]," 1066.

155. Wilde, "Ballad of Reading Gaol," 888.

156. Wilde, "De Profundis," 1025, 1040.

157. Wilde, "De Profundis," 1026, 1025.

158. Wilde, "Ballad of Reading Gaol," 898.

159. Kevin Van Meter drew my attention to this aspect of the poem, in conversation, May 20, 2009. The murderer is specifically identified with the narrator: "Like two doomed ships that pass in storm / We had crossed each other's way: / . . . Two outcast men we were." Wilde, "Ballad of Reading Gaol," 887. Ellmann makes this point at greater length. Ellmann, *Oscar Wilde*, 532.

After his death, Wilde was personally identified with Wooldridge. The epitaph on the poet's tomb is a quote from "The Ballad of Reading Gaol": "And alien tears will fill for him / Pity's long-broken urn, / For his mourners will be outcast men, / And outcasts always mourn." Quoted in Ellmann, *Oscar Wilde*, 588–89.

160. Wilde, "Ballad of Reading Gaol," 893, 889, 896.

161. Wilde, *Picture of Dorian Gray*, 39.

162. Wilde, "Ballad of Reading Gaol," 889, 884.

163. Wilde, "Ballad of Reading Gaol," 889.

164. Wilde, "De Profundis," 1057.

165. Wilde, "Ballad of Reading Gaol," 896.

166. As Wilde wrote in "Soul of Man": "As one reads history, . . . one is absolutely sickened, not by the crimes that the wicked have committed, but by the punishments that the good have inflicted." Wilde, "Soul of Man under Socialism," 1182.

Chapter 6: The Eternal Rebel

1. André Gide, *Oscar Wilde: A Study*, ed. Stuart Mason (Oxford: Holywell Press, 1905), 82.

2. Oscar Wilde, *The Importance of Being Earnest*, in *Collins Complete Works of Oscar Wilde* (Glasgow: HarperCollins, 2003), 362.

3. For the medical argument linking Wilde's treatment in prison with his eventual death, see Nicholas Frankel, *Oscar Wilde: The Unrepentant Years* (Cambridge, Mass.: Harvard University Press, 2017), 277–82.

4. Frankel, *Oscar Wilde*, 12.

5. Quoted in Frankel, *Oscar Wilde*, 297.

6. Quoted in Gary Schmidgall, *The Stranger Wilde: Interpreting Oscar* (New York: Dutton, 1994), 404–5.

7. Frankel makes the same point: "Imprisonment and exile, paradoxically, had liberated him to pursue an uninhibited life, and the pleasure he received in consequence could be enjoyed more fully, as a total experience of heart, mind, soul, and body, with conversation as its medium, and laughter its index. . . . Wilde had been cut free from the cords of the self-righteous and the wicked. . . . Ambling along the boulevard or seated in some café terrace, he pursued his own course with bemusement, irony, and self-conviction, unbowed and impervious to the harsh judgments of smaller natures." Frankel, *Oscar Wilde*, 303.

8. Wilde wrote, "The world is angry because their punishment has had no effect. They wished to be able to say 'We have done a capital thing for Oscar Wilde: by putting him in prison we have put a stop to his friendship with Alfred Douglas and all that that implies.' But now they find that they have not had that effect, that they merely treated me barbarously, but did not influence me, they simply ruined me, so they are furious." "Oscar

Wilde to Robert Ross, November 25, 1897," in *The Complete Letters of Oscar Wilde*, ed. Merlin Holland and Rupert Hart-Davis (New York: Henry Holt, 2000), 993.

9.   Quoted in W. H. Auden, "An Improbable Life," in Richard Ellmann, ed., *Oscar Wilde: A Collection of Critical Essays* (Englewood Cliffs, N.J.: Prentice-Hall, 1969), 129.

10.   Quoted in Richard Ellmann, *Oscar Wilde* (New York: Alfred A. Knopf, 1988), 570.

11.   Oscar Wilde, "De Profundis," in *Collins Complete Works of Oscar Wilde*, 1026.

12.   Gustav Landauer, in his review of "De Profundis," suggests that this drive to embrace and encompass everything, without limit or exception, was the unifying element in Wilde's character: "The sexuality of a longing human being, the imagination of an artist, and the creative and transformative love are all forms of a spirit that wants to conquer and own everything eternally alien to him." No wonder, then, that he thought of Wilde as "the English Nietzsche." Quoted in James Horrox, "The Artist as Critic: Gustav Landauer on Wilde," *Wildean: Journal of the Oscar Wilde Society*, January 2015, 59, 64.

13.   Wilde, "De Profundis," 1020.

14.   Wilde, "De Profundis," 1041.

15.   Quoted in André Gide, "Oscar Wilde: In Memoriam," in *Oscar Wilde: Interviews and Recollections*, vol. 2, ed. E. H. Mikhail (New York: Barnes & Noble, 1979), 293. The story appears in a different version as Oscar Wilde, "The Doer of Good," in *Collins Complete Works of Oscar Wilde*, 900–901. Another account of Wilde's oral version appears in Gedeon Spilett, "An Interview with Oscar Wilde," in *Oscar Wilde: Interviews and Recollections*, vol. 2, 357.

16.   Quoted in Anna, Comtesse de Bremont, "I Have Lived," in *Oscar Wilde: Interviews and Recollections*, vol. 2, 450.

17.   Quoted in H. Montgomery Hyde, *Oscar Wilde: The Aftermath* (New York: Farrar, Strauss, 1963), 192.

18.   Quoted in Ellen Crowell, "Scarlet Carsons, Men in Masks: The Wildean Contexts of *V for Vendetta*," *Neo-Victorian Studies*, 2, no. 1 (2009): 22.

19.   Coulson Kernahan, "Oscar Wilde," in *Oscar Wilde: Interviews and Recollections*, vol. 2, 298.

20.   Quoted in Kernahan "Oscar Wilde," 298.

21.   Emer O'Sullivan, *The Fall of the House of Wilde: Oscar Wilde and His Family* (New York: Bloomsbury Press, 2016), 442.

22.   After minor public outcry, the company reversed itself, calling its initial decision a "mistake" while continuing to promise its customers "freedom from porn." Quoted in Catherine Smith, "Apple Censors—Then Approves—Gay Kiss in Oscar Wilde Comic," *Huffington Post*, June 14, 2010.

23.   David Sweetman, *Explosive Acts: Toulouse-Lautrec, Oscar Wilde, Félix Fénéon and the Art and Anarchy of the Fin de Siècle* (New York: Simon & Schuster, 1999), 390; Philip Hoare, *Oscar Wilde's Last Stand: Decadence, Conspiracy, and the Most Outrageous Trial of the Century* (New York: Arcade Publishing, 1998), 73. The discussion is this section is chiefly drawn from Hoare's exhaustive account.

24.   Hoare, *Oscar Wilde's Last Stand*, 61.

25.   Elaine Showalter, *Sexual Anarchy: Gender and Culture at the Fin de Siècle* (New York: Penguin Books, 1990), 159–60.

26. Sweetman, *Explosive Acts*, 416–17.

27. "Oscar Wilde to Robert Ross, March 10, 1896," in *Complete Letters of Oscar Wilde*, 652–53. He was later to reflect, "The production of *Salomé* was the thing that turned the scale in my favour, as far as my treatment in prison by the Government was concerned." "Oscar Wilde to Lord Alfred Douglas, [June 2?, 1897]," in *Complete Letters of Oscar Wilde*, 872.

In another letter he wrote of finally meeting Lugné-Poe: "I was quite charmed with him: I had no idea he was so young and so handsome. . . . What I want him to say [in his article] is how grateful I was and am to France for their recognition of me as an artist in the day of my humiliation, and how my better treatment in an English prison was due to the French men of letters." "Oscar Wilde to More Adey, [Postmark: May 25, 1897]," in *Complete Letters of Oscar Wilde*, 847.

28. Quoted in Douglas Murray, *Bosie: A Biography of Lord Alfred Douglas* (New York: Hyperion, 2000), 217.

29. Gregory Woods, *Homintern: How Gay Culture Liberated the Modern World* (New Haven: Yale University Press, 2016), 45.

30. Quoted in Hoare, *Oscar Wilde's Last Stand*, 152.

31. Hoare, *Oscar Wilde's Last Stand*, 180, 218–21.

32. Quoted in Hoare, *Oscar Wilde's Last Stand*, 186.

33. Hoare, *Oscar Wilde's Last Stand*, 188–89, 210–13. Lord Alfred Douglas, for his part, became the editor of *Plain English*, a paper that, while also taking stands against birth control and Irish independence, was primarily interested in propagating anti-Semitic conspiracy theories. One such story, which accused Winston Churchill and a group of Jewish businessmen of murdering Lord Kitchener, landed Douglas in prison for libel. Murray, *Bosie*, 227, 223–24, 242–43.

34. "While in London one hides everything," he told *L'Echo* in an interview. "In Paris one reveals everything." Quoted in Sweetman, *Explosive Acts*, 212.

35. Jacob Epstein, *Epstein: An Autobiography* (London: Vista Books, 1963), 51–53. Epstein was cagey about his political commitments, writing in his autobiography: "In connection with political meetings and what could now be called 'left wing' sympathies and friends, I was an observer only, and never a participant, as my loyalties were all for the practice of art, and I have always grudged the time that is given to anything but that." Epstein, *Epstein*, 9.

36. Mark Antliff, "Contagious Joy: Anarchism, Censorship, and the Reception of Jacob Epstein's *Tomb of Oscar Wilde*, c. 1913," *Journal of Modern Periodical Studies* 4, no. 2 (2013): 195–225, "flying demon angel": 200.

37. Quoted in Epstein, *Epstein*, 254. Compare to Wilde's views of the freedom art requires: Oscar Wilde, "The Soul of Man under Socialism," in *Collins Complete Works of Oscar Wilde*, 1184–92.

38. Ellen Crowell, "Oscar Wilde's Tomb: *Silence* and the Aesthetics of Queer Memorial," *BRANCH: Britain, Representation and Nineteenth-Century History*, extension of *Romanticism and Victorianism on the Net*, http://www.branchcollective.org/?ps_articles=ellen-crowell-oscar-wildes-tomb-silence-and-the-aesthetics-of-queer-memorial.

39. Ellen Crowell remarks that the demon-angel sculpture "has always . . . stood in as proxy for Wilde's physical body." Describing it as "a figure of erotic dignity," she

continues: "The 'Wilde' being adored in Père Lachaise is a Wilde defiantly bold yet invested with fragility, imperious in his ability to resist any attempts to defile or contain him, yet powerfully seductive in his ability to solicit physical acts of both affection and outrage." Crowell, "Oscar Wilde's Tomb."

40.   Crowell, "Oscar Wilde's Tomb."

41.   Edward Carpenter, "Defense of Criminals, a Criticism of Morality," in *Civilisation: Its Cause and Cure, and Other Essays* (New York: Charles Scribner's Sons, 1921), 125.

42.   Hakim Bey, *Oscar Wilde* [mixed media], 2010, in Hans Ulrich Obrist, "In Conversation with Hakim Bey," *e-flux*, no. 21, December 2010 https://www.e-flux.com/journal/21/67669/in-conversation-with-hakim-bey. In an appendix to *T.A.Z.*, titled "Applied Hedonics," Bey lists Wilde, along with Fourier, Rabelais, Vaneigem, and Goldman in his "gallery of forebears, heroes who carried on the struggle against bad consciousness but still knew how to party, . . . great minds not just for Truth, but for the *truth of pleasure*." Hakim Bey, *T.A.Z.: The Temporary Autonomous Zone: Ontological Anarchy, Poetic Terrorism*, 2nd ed. (Brooklyn: Autonomedia, 2003), 144.

43.   Clifford Harper, *Designs for Anarchist Postage Stamps* (London: Rebel Press, 1997), pages not numbered.

44.   Bash Back Pittsburgh, https://myspace.com/bashbackpgh/mixes/profilemix-120670/photo/6730296.

45.   On Jean Grave, see Sweetman, *Explosive Acts*, 121. Concerning Herbert Read: in "My Anarchism" Read cites Edward Carpenter, rather than Wilde, as the inspiration for his "conversion," though he lists Wilde among the "many writers who have expressed an anarchist philosophy." Herbert Read, "My Anarchism," in *The Cult of Sincerity* (New York: Horizon Press, 1968), 76–77.

Nevertheless, Woodcock observes, "Read wrote almost all his works on anarchism from the viewpoint of the artist or the poet, and, conversely, . . . his anarchist views often found their way into works that were not political in their general orientation. In this he resembled and may have been more influenced than he admitted by Oscar Wilde, whose *Soul of Man Under Socialism* anticipated *Poetry and Anarchism* in presenting a libertarian society as the best environment for the nurture of the arts." George Woodcock, *Herbert Read: The Stream and the Source* (London: Faber and Faber, 1972), 255–56.

In fact, in Read's essay "The Freedom of the Artist" we encounter the line "there is not one type of art to which all types of men should conform, but as many types of art as there are types of men." Herbert Read, "The Freedom of the Artist," in *The Politics of the Unpolitical* (London: Routledge, 1945), 116.

This is surely an adaptation of Wilde's remark, "There is no one type for man. There are as many perfections as there are imperfect men." Wilde, "Soul of Man under Socialism," 1181.

On Goodman: Paul Goodman wrote favorably of Wilde as a political thinker, a philosopher, and as "the chief English general man of letters of his age." Paul Goodman, "Tardy and Partial Recognition," *Kenyon Review*, 10, no. 2 (Spring 1948): 340.

On McLaren: Alan Moore and Malcolm McLaren once briefly considered making a movie that "took as its unlikely starting point the poet Oscar Wilde's surprisingly successful tour of Wild West mining camps and from there bloomed into a tale of a female performer much more in the mode of a late 19th century Madonna prototype than of the divine Oscar, visiting the girl- and entertainment-starved encampments of the Gold Rush." Alan Moore, introduction to *Fashion Beast*, by Alan Moore et al. (Rantoul, Ill.: Avatar Press, 2013), no page number. Regarding Malcolm McLaren's politics, see Greil Marcus, *Lipstick Traces: A Secret History of the Twentieth Century* (Cambridge, Mass.: Harvard University Press, 1990), 28–30.

Finally: Wilde is twice quoted in CrimethInc. Writers' Bloc, *Contradictionary: A Bestiary of Words in Revolt* (Salem, Ore.: CrimethInc. Far East, 2013), 76, 166.

46.   Sweetman, *Explosive Acts*, 426, 468.

47.   "Salomé (Let's Twist Again)" and "Waiting, Shouting," in Chumbawamba, *Swingin' with Raymond* [notes] (London: One Little Indian, 1995)

48.   Terence Kissack, *Free Comrades: Anarchism and Homosexuality in the United States, 1895–1917* (Oakland: AK Press, 2008), 64–65.

49.   Kissack, *Free Comrades*, 65–66.

50.   John Cowper Powys, "Oscar Wilde," in *Suspended Judgments: Essays on Books and Sensations* (New York: G. Arnold Shaw, 1916), 410.

51.   David Goodway, *Anarchist Seeds beneath the Snow: Left-Libertarian Thought and British Writers from William Morris to Colin Ward* (Oakland: PM Press, 2012), 216.

52.   "Prince Peter Kropotkin, [Letter to Robbie Ross], April 12, 1905," in *Robert Ross, Friend of Friends*, ed. Margery Ross (London: Jonathan Cape, 1952), 112.

53.   Horrox, "Artist as Critic," 56.

54.   Quoted in Horrox, "Artist as Critic," 68.

55.   Quoted in Horrox, "Artist as Critic," 69.

56.   Quoted in John Zerzan, "Why Hope?," in *Why Hope? The Stand against Civilization* (Port Townsend, Wash.: Feral House, 2015), 135. The quote also appears on the cover of Zerzan's book. Kropotkin likewise believed, "It is hope, not despair, which makes successful revolutions." Quoted in Paul Goodman, "Kropotkin at This Moment," *Anarchy* 98 (April 1969): 127.

This sentiment was present in Wilde's thought from at least his time at Oxford. In his commonplace book, he wrote: "We turn our eyes not to the deeper depths from which we may have sprung, but to the higher heights to which we can rise." Oscar Wilde, "Commonplace Book," in *Oscar Wilde's Oxford Notebooks: A Portrait of Mind in the Making*, ed. Philip E. Smith II and Michael S. Helfand (New York: Oxford University Press, 1989), 125.

57.   Wilde, "De Profundis," 1057.

58.   Alan Moore, *Jerusalem: A Novel* (New York: Liveright Publishing, 2016), 972. Moore's mouthpiece, Henry George, is a former slave, bringing additional poignancy to the notion of navigating by the stars and identifying it with the search for freedom. Henry considers the folk tales, hymns, myths, and pulp heroes that can serve as this guiding ideal, only to conclude that "a man should be his own ideal and champion, however long it takes him to arrive there" (974).

59.   Quoted in Uri Gordon, "Utopia in Contemporary Anarchism," in Laurence Davis and Ruth Kinna, ed., *Anarchism and Utopianism* (Manchester: Manchester University Press, 2009), 260.

60.   Wilde, "Soul of Man under Socialism," 1184.

61.   Quoted in Michelle Cowen Verter, "Censored Selections: Persons Die, but Noble Ideas are Eternal," *Anarchy: A Journal of Desire Armed*, Fall–Winter 2006, 34.

62.   William Godwin, *The Anarchist Writings of William Godwin*, ed. Peter Marshall (London: Freedom Press, 1986), 61–62. Rudolf Rocker seemed to marry Godwin's perspective with that of Gustav Landauer, while denying that the resulting perfectionism is utopian: "Anarchism is no patent solution for all human problems, no Utopia of a perfect social order . . . , since in principle it rejects all absolute schemes and concepts. It does not believe in any absolute truth, or in definite final goals for human development, but in an unlimited perfectibility of social arrangements and human living conditions, which are always striving after higher *forms* of expression, and to which for this reason one can assign no definite terminus nor set any fixed goals." Quoted in Gordon, "Utopia in Contemporary Anarchism," 266. Emphasis in original.

63.   Oscar Wilde, "The Critic as Artist," in *Collins Complete Works of Oscar Wilde*, 1121.

64.   Wilde, "Soul of Man under Socialism," 1178.

65.   "Art should never try to be popular. The public should try to make itself artistic." Wilde, "Soul of Man under Socialism," 1184.

66.   "Individualism does not come to man with any sickly cant about duty. . . . In fact, it does not come to a man with any claims upon him at all. It comes naturally and inevitably out of man. . . . And so Individualism exercises no compulsion over man. On the contrary, it says to man that he should suffer no compulsion to be exercised over him." Wilde, "Soul of Man under Socialism," 1194.

Bakunin said something similar: "Liberty . . . recognizes no other restrictions than those which are traced for us by the laws of our own nature. . . . [T]hese laws are not imposed on us by some outside legislator, beside us or above us; they are immanent in us, inherent, constituting the many bases of our being, material as well as intellectual and moral; instead, therefore, of finding them a limit, we must consider them as the real conditions and effective reason for our liberty." Quoted in Peter Marshall, *Demanding the Impossible: A History of Anarchism* (Oakland: PM Press, 2010), 39.

67.   Wilde, "Soul of Man under Socialism," 1181.

68.   See, for example: Wilde, "Soul of Man under Socialism," 1178–80. Again he sounds like Godwin: "Society is an ideal existence, and not, on its own account, entitled to the smallest regard. The wealth, prosperity and glory of the whole are unintelligible chimeras. Set no value on anything but in proportion as you are convinced of its tendency to make individual men happy and virtuous. . . . [Be] not deceived by the specious idea of affording services to a body of men, for which no individual man is the better. Society was instituted, not for the sake of glory, not to furnish splendid materials for the page of history, but for the benefit of its members." Godwin, *Anarchist Writings*, 107.

69.   Wilde, "Soul of Man under Socialism," 1177–78.

70.   "When each member of the community has sufficient for his wants, and is not interfered with by his neighbour, it will not be an object of any interest to him to interfere with any one else." Wilde, "Soul of Man under Socialism," 1182–83.

71.   "Under Individualism people will be quite natural and absolutely unselfish. . . . When man has realised Individualism, he will also realise sympathy and exercise it freely and spontaneously." Wilde, "Soul of Man under Socialism," 1195.

72.   Wilde, "Soul of Man under Socialism," 1178. Later he writes, in the character of Jesus: "Personal property hinders Individualism at every step. . . . It hinders you realising your perfection. It is a drag upon you. It is a burden. Your personality does not need it. It is within you, and not outside of you, that you will find what you really are, and what you really want." Wilde, "Soul of Man under Socialism," 1180.

73.   Wilde, "Soul of Man under Socialism," 1174–75.

Index

Also by Kristian Williams

Whither Anarchism?
(AK Press, 2018)

Between the Bullet and the Lie: Essays on Orwell
(AK Press, 2017)

Our Enemies in Blue: Police and Power in America, 3rd ed.
(AK Press, 2015)

Fire the Cops: Essays, Lectures, and Journalism
(Kersplebedeb, 2014)

Hurt: Notes on Torture in a Modern Democracy
(Microcosm, 2012)

American Methods: Torture and the Logic of Domination
(South End Press, 2006)

AK Press is small, in terms of staff and resources, but we also manage to be one of the world's most productive anarchist publishing houses. We publish close to twenty books every year, and distribute thousands of other titles published by like-minded independent presses and projects from around the globe. We're entirely worker-run and democratically managed. We operate without a corporate structure—no boss, no managers, no bullshit.

The Friends of AK program is a way you can directly contribute to the continued existence of AK Press, and ensure that we're able to keep publishing books like this one! Friends pay $25 a month directly into our publishing account ($30 for Canada, $35 for international), and receive a copy of every book AK Press publishes for the duration of their membership! Friends also receive a discount on anything they order from our website or buy at a table: 50% on AK titles, and 20% on everything else. We have a Friends of AK ebook program as well: $15 a month gets you an electronic copy of every book we publish for the duration of your membership. You can even sponsor a very discounted membership for someone in prison.

Email FRIENDSOFAK@AKPRESS.ORG for more info, or visit the Friends of AK Press website: HTTPS://WWW.AKPRESS.ORG/FRIENDS.HTML.

There are always great book projects in the works—so sign up now to become a Friend of AK Press, and let the presses roll!